# DARFUR AND THE CRIME OF GENOCIDE

In 2004, the State Department gathered more than a thousand interviews from refugees in Chad that substantiated Colin Powell's UN and congressional testimonies about the Darfur genocide. The survey cost nearly a million dollars to conduct, and yet it languished in the archives as the killing continued, claiming hundreds of thousands of murder and rape victims and restricting several million survivors to camps. This book for the first time fully examines that survey and its heartbreaking accounts. It documents the Sudanese government's enlistment of Arab Janjaweed militias in destroying Black African communities. The central questions are these: Why is the United States so ambivalent about genocide? Why do so many scholars deemphasize racial aspects of genocide? How can the science of criminology advance understanding and protection against genocide? This book gives a vivid firsthand account and voice to the survivors of genocide in Darfur.

John Hagan is John D. MacArthur Professor of Sociology and Law at Northwestern University and Co-Director of the Center on Law and Globalization at the American Bar Foundation. He served as president of the American Society of Criminology and received its Edwin Sutherland and Michael J. Hindelang awards. He received the C. Wright Mills Award for *Mean Streets: Youth Crime and Homelessness* (with Bill McCarthy; Cambridge University Press, 1997) and a Guggenheim Fellowship and the Albert J. Reiss Award for *Northern Passage: American Vietnam War Resisters in Canada* (2001). He is author most recently of *Justice in the Balkans* (2003) and co-author of several articles on the Darfur genocide published in the *American Sociological Review*, *Criminology*, *Annual Review of Sociology*, and *Science*.

Wenona Rymond-Richmond is an Assistant Professor of Sociology at the University of Massachusetts Amherst. She was a research assistant at the American Bar Foundation and a pre-doctoral Fellow with the National Consortium on Violence Research. Publications include "Transforming Communities: Formal and Informal Mechanisms of Social Control" in *The Many Colors of Crime* (editors Ruth Peterson, Lauren Krivo, and John Hagan), and co-authored articles about the Darfur genocide published in *Criminology*, *American Sociological Review*, and *Ohio State Journal of Criminal Law*.

# CAMBRIDGE STUDIES IN LAW AND SOCIETY

*Cambridge Studies in Law and Society* aims to publish the best scholarly work on legal discourse and practice in its social and institutional contexts, combining theoretical insights and empirical research.

The fields that it covers are studies of law in action; the sociology of law; the anthropology of law; cultural studies of law, including the role of legal discourses in social formations; law and economics; law and politics; and studies of governance. The books consider all forms of legal discourse across societies, rather than being limited to lawyers' discourses alone.

The series editors come from a range of disciplines: academic law, socio-legal studies, and sociology and anthropology. All have been actively involved in teaching and writing about law in context.

*Series Editors*

Chris Arup
*Victoria University, Melbourne*
Martin Chanock
*La Trobe University, Melbourne*
Sally Engle Merry
*Wellesley College, Massachusetts*
Pat O'Malley
*University of Sydney, Australia*
Susan Silbey
*Massachusetts Institute of Technology*

*Books in the Series*

*Continued after Index*

# Darfur and the Crime of Genocide

**John Hagan**

Northwestern University

**Wenona Rymond-Richmond**

University of Massachusetts Amherst

**CAMBRIDGE**
UNIVERSITY PRESS

CAMBRIDGE UNIVERSITY PRESS
Cambridge, New York, Melbourne, Madrid, Cape Town, Singapore, São Paulo, Delhi

Cambridge University Press
32 Avenue of the Americas, New York, NY 10013-2473, USA

www.cambridge.org
Information on this title: www.cambridge.org/9780521731355

First published 2009

Printed in the United States of America

*A catalog record for this publication is available from the British Library.*

*Library of Congress Cataloging in Publication Data*

Hagan, John, 1946–
Darfur and the crime of genocide / John Hagan, Wenona Rymond-Richmond.
    p.   cm. – (Cambridge studies in law and society)
Includes bibliographical references and index.
ISBN 978-0-521-51567-2 (hardback)
1. Genocide.   2. Crimes against humanity.   3. Human rights.   I. Rymond-Richmond,
Wenona, 1972–   II. Title.   III. Series.
K5302.H34   2009
345′.0251–dc22      2008017809

ISBN   978-0-521-51567-2 hardback
ISBN   978-0-521-73135-5 paperback

# Contents

# Glossary

AAAS – American Academy for the Advancement of Science

ABA-CEELI – American Bar Association Central and East European Law Initiative

ADS – Atrocities Documentation Survey of Darfur refugees in Chad in summer 2004

Al Geneina (Al Junaynah) – Capital of West Darfur and organizational center for government counterinsurgency efforts

Al Qaeda – International alliance of Islamic militant organizations founded in 1988 by Osama Bin Laden and other "Afghan Arabs" after the Soviet war in Afghanistan

Amnesty International – Pioneering international nongovernmental organization focused on human rights abuses and compliance with international standards

Antonov – Russian-made and -supplied airplane used to bomb Darfur villages

Baggara tribes – Powerful Arab tribes armed and supported by Sudanese government in attacks on Black African villages in Darfur

Beida – Settlement forming part of triangle with Terbeba and Arara in West Darfur near Al Geneina that forms the westernmost point of border with Chad

Bendesi (Bindisi) – Town subjected to repeated violent attacks in the southwestern part of West Darfur

Bophuthatswana – One of four so-called independent homelands granted independence by South Africa in 1977

Bureau of Democracy, Human Rights, and Labor – Part of the U.S. State Department that promotes democracy, human rights, and labor rights internationally

Bureau of Intelligence and Research – Part of the U.S. State Department that collects and analyzes foreign intelligence data

CIJ – Coalition for International Justice, an international nonprofit organization that conducted advocacy campaigns targeting decision makers in Washington, DC

CDC – Centers for Disease Control, which serves as the premier U.S. public health agency

Centre for Research on the Epidemiology of Disasters – Public and population health research organization at the University of Louvain in Brussels, Belgium

Chad – Landlocked country in central Africa that borders Darfur on its eastern border and received more than 200,000 refugees during the Darfur conflict

C/L International – Washington-based lobbying firm

CMR – Crude mortality rate, often expressed as deaths per 10,000 population per day

CPA – Comprehensive Peace Agreement for southern Sudan signed in 2004

Darfur – Western region of Sudan, bordering Chad, Central African Republic, and Libya

Darfur Investigation Team – Unit within the Office of the Prosecutor at the International Criminal Court in The Hague

Democratic Republic of the Congo – The third-ranking nation by land mass on the African continent, bordering Sudan and suffering high mortality levels

DLF – Darfur Liberation Front, which preceded the Sudanese Liberation Army

El Fasher – Location of Sudan government air base attacked by rebels in April 2003, marking an early success in the insurgency

European Union – Political and economic community composed of twenty-seven European member states

Foro Burunga – Town in southwestern area of West Darfur viciously and
repeatedly attacked

Fur tribe – Largest of Black African tribes in Darfur

GAO – U.S. Government Accountability Office, which assesses government programs and agencies

Genocide – Intended destruction in whole or part of a racial, religious,
ethnic, or national group

Genocide Convention (Convention on the Prevention and Punishment
of the Crime of Genocide) – Resolution that defines genocide in legal
terms and that was adopted by the UN General Assembly in December 1948

GoS – Government of Sudan, with capital in Khartoum

Guedera – Military camp near Al Geneina

Habilah – Village in West Darfur

Helsinki Watch – American human rights NGO that evolved into
Human Rights Watch in 1988

High Commission on Human Rights (UNHCHR) – Principal UN office
mandated to promote and protect human rights

High Commission on Refugees (UNHCR) – Principal UN office mandated to lead international action to protect refugees and resolve
refugee issues

Human Rights Watch – U.S.-based international nongovernmental organization that conducts research and advocacy on human rights

Hutu – Large ethnic group living in Burundi and Rwanda; extrem-
ist Hutu militia groups were responsible for the 1994 genocide in
Rwanda

ICTR – International Criminal Tribunal for Rwanda

IDP – Internally displaced persons

International Criminal Court (ICC) – Independent, permanent court
that prosecutes individuals accused of the most serious violations of
international criminal law

ICTY – International Criminal Tribunal for the former Yugoslavia

International Crisis Group – Independent nongovernmental organization committed to resolving and preventing deadly international conflicts

Janjaweed (Jingaweit, Jingaweet, Janjawiid) – Armed Arab militia groups who usually travel on horses and camels; literally translates as "a man (devil) on horseback"

Jebal – Black African tribal group in Darfur

JEM – Justice and Equality Movement, rebel group in Darfur

Karnoi (Kornoi) – Settlement in North Darfur

Kebkabiya (Kabkabiyah) – Town in North Darfur

Khartoum – Capital of Sudan

Kojo – Town south of Masteri in West Darfur

*Lost Boys of Sudan* – Documentary film produced by Megan Mylan and John Shenk

Masalit tribe (Masaleit) – Black African tribe in West Darfur

Masteri – Town in West Darfur near the Chad border

Misteriha (Mistariha) – Base of Janjaweed commander, Musa Hilal, in North Darfur, near Kebkabiya

Monroe Doctrine – U.S. doctrine proclaiming in 1823 that European countries would no longer intervene in affairs in the Americas

MSF – Médecins Sans Frontières, international medical and humanitarian aid organization

Mujahideen – Muslim religious fighters

Mukhabarat – Sudan government's security service

Mukjar – Town in southwestern part of West Darfur near the Jebel Marra Mountains

My Lai massacre – Mass killing of unarmed citizens by U.S. Army soldiers in 1968 during the Vietnam War

NATO – North Atlantic Treaty Organization

NMRD (National Movement for Reform and Development) – Relatively recently formed Darfur rebel group

Nuba – Pejorative term used in Sudan to refer to Black African persons and/or slaves

Nuremberg Trial – Trials of the most prominent political, military, and economic leaders of Nazi Germany

OSCE – Organization for Security and Co-operation in Europe

PHR – Physicians for Human Rights, American-based nongovernmental human rights organization

Save Darfur – An alliance of more than 100 faith-based, humanitarian, and human rights organizations concerned with the genocide in Darfur

SLA/SPLA (Sudan People's Liberation Army) – Large rebel group in Darfur

Srebrenica – A town in eastern Bosnia and site of the Srebrenica massacre, where 8,000 men and boys were killed in July 1995

Sudanese Ministry of Health – Government of Sudan's federal health ministry

Terbeba – Town just east of Masteri on the border with Chad

Tora Bora – Racialized term taken from Osama Bin Laden's retreat to the mountains in Afghanistan and used by Sudan and Janjaweed to refer to rebels in West Darfur

Tutsi – Large ethnic group massacred by Hutus in Rwanda genocide

UN Commission of Inquiry on Darfur – Official inquiry of UN Security Council to determine whether genocide and other war crimes occurred in Darfur

UN High Commissioner for Refugees – UN agency headed by Louise Arbour

US AID – U.S. Agency for International Development, which funded Atrocities Documentation Survey

WFP – World Food Program

*What Is the What* – Dave Eggers's novel based on the lost boys of Sudan

WHO (World Health Organization) – Leading UN health agency based in Geneva

WHO/SMH Survey – World Health Organization/Sudanese Ministry of Health summer 2004 health and mortality survey conducted in camps across three states of Darfur

Zaghawa tribe – Large tribal group concentrated in North Darfur

Zaka – Social norm that fostered reintegration of children in displaced families

Zourga (Zurug) – Derogatory term for Blacks used in Sudan

# List of Characters

Madeleine Albright – Former U.S. Secretary of State

Kofi Annan – Former Secretary-General of the United Nations

Louise Arbour – Former UN High Commissioner on Human Rights and former Chief Prosecutor of the Hague Tribunal for the former Yugoslavia

Hannah Arendt – German American Jewish political theorist who coined the phrase "banality of evil"

Patrick Ball – Social scientist formerly with American Association for the Advancement of Science and currently with Human Rights Program at Benetech

Omar al-Bashir – President of Sudan who seized power in 1989

Atta El-Battahani – Authority on Sudan at the University of Khartoum

Hilary Benn – British Secretary of State for International Development

Bruno Bettelheim – Holocaust survivor who wrote about his own concentration camp experiences

John Bolton – Former American UN Ambassador and critic of international courts

Jan Coebergh – British physician and early analyst of Darfur mortality

Albert Cohen – Early student of Edwin Sutherland, known for his work on delinquent gangs

Hamid Dawai – Arab militia leader near Al Geneina and emir of Arab tribe

Sam Dealey – Author of *New York Times* op-ed questioning Darfur mortality estimates

Carla del Ponte – Chief UN War Crimes Prosecutor at The Hague Tribunal for the former Yugoslavia

Jan Egeland – UN emergency relief coordinator and source of Darfur mortality estimate

Dave Eggers – Author of *What Is the What*, story about the Lost Boys of Sudan

Stefanie Frease – Human rights investigator who played a prominent role in the Srebrenica Trial and led the Atrocities Documentation Survey Team in Chad

General Gadal (Janobo Gadal) – GoS military leader

Kitty Genovese – Young woman murdered in Queens, New York, who became known as victim of the "bystander effect"

Boutros Boutros-Ghali – Former Secretary-General of UN during the Rwandan genocide

Eleanor Glueck – Collaborated with her husband, Sheldon Glueck, in studying the adolescent and later lives of delinquents

Sheldon Glueck – Harvard criminologist and law professor who played a prominent role in lead-up to the Nuremberg Trials and in American delinquency research

Mark Goldberg – Senior correspondent for the *American Prospect* and writer in residence at the UN Foundation

Major General Salah Abdallah Gosh – Chief of Sudan's intelligence/security service

Günter Grass – Prize-winning German author and playwright who wrote about the Holocaust

David Halberstam – American Pulitzer–Prize–winning author and journalist known for his writings on American culture and politics

Ahmad Harun (Ahmad Muhammad Harun) – Sudan's Minister of State for Humanitarian Affairs and one of two persons currently wanted by the ICC for war crimes and crimes against humanity in Sudan

Gunnar Heinsohn – German demographer who writes about mass violence

Musa Hilal – Sudanese Arab Janjaweed militia leader associated with attacks in North Darfur

Sheikh Hilal – Father of Musa Hilal and famous tribal sheik

David Hoile – Director of European-Sudanese Public Affairs Council

Jonathan Howard – Research analyst at the U.S. State Department who played a prominent role in the design and direction of the Atrocities Documentation Survey

Abduraheem Mohammed Hussein – Former Minister of the Interior and representative of the president for Darfur; current Minister of Defense/Sudan.

Mustafa Osman Ismail – Former Foreign Minister of Sudan

Superior Court Justice Robert Jackson – Head of the American prosecution team at the Nuremberg trial

Mukesh Kapila – Former UN Resident and Humanitarian Coordinator for the Sudan

Alfred Kinsey – Founder of the Institute for Research in Sex, Gender and Reproduction at Indiana University who pioneered large-scale survey research on human sexuality

Henry Kissinger – German-born U.S. Secretary of State in the Nixon Administration

Nicholas Kristof – *New York Times* columnist who writes extensively on Darfur

Ali Kushayb (Ali Muhammad Abd-al-Rahman, Ali Kosheib) – Arab Janjaweed militia leader charged by the ICC and known as an "Emir of Mujahideen" or a "leader of religious fighters"

Osama Bin Laden – Militant Islamist reported to be architect of 9/11 and the founder and current leader of the terrorist organization called al Qaeda

Raphael Lemkin – Lawyer/Holocaust survivor who coined the concept of genocide

Sadiq al-Mahadi – Prime Minister of Sudan in 1980s

Michael Marrus – Prominent Nuremberg scholar

Ross Matsueda – Professor of sociology at the University of Washington

Slobodan Milosevic – First sitting head of state charged with crimes against humanity and later genocide, who died before the conclusion of his trial in 2006

Henry Morgenthau – Jewish Treasury Secretary in Roosevelt's administration who argued for deindustrialization of Germany following World War II

Megan Mylan – Produced documentary, *Lost Boys of Sudan*, with Jon Shenk

David Nabarro – British former Executive Director of WHO and spokesman about Darfur mortality

Andrew Natsios – U.S. Special Envoy to Sudan

Aryeh Neier – Human rights activist and former president of Human Rights Watch and current president of Open Society Institute

Peter Novick – Author of *The Holocaust in American Life*

Luis Moreno Ocampo – Chief Prosecutor of the International Criminal Court

Alberto Palloni – President, Population Association of America

Jan Pfundheller – Member of the ADS investigation team and war crimes investigator known for expertise on rape and sexual assault in international conflicts

Mark Phelan – U.S. State Department Public Health specialist

Colin Powell – Former U.S. Secretary of State in the Bush administration who designated Darfur as genocide

Samantha Power – Author of *"A Problem from Hell": America and the Age of Genocide*, which received the 2003 Pulitzer Prize

John Prendergast – American human rights activist

Gerard Pruiner – Author of *Darfur: The Ambiguous Genocide*

Muammar Qaddafi – President of Libya

Ali Abd-Al-Rahman (Ali Kushayb) – Arab militia leader, see Ali Kushayb

Eric Reeves – American activist and scholar on Darfur genocide at Smith College

Condoleezza Rice – U.S. Secretary of State in the Bush administration

John Shenk – Co-producer of documentary, *Lost Boys in Sudan*, with Megan Mylan

Abdullah Mustafa Abu Shineibat – Arab Janjaweed militia leader

Al Hadi Ahmed Shineibat – Brother of Arab militia leader with same last name

David Springer – State Department, geo-spatial analyst

Donald Steinberg – Senior State Department official

Ibrahim Suleiman – Former governor of North Darfur

Edwin Sutherland – Prominent American criminologist, known for his study of white-collar crime and his broader differential association theory of crime

Ali Uthman Muhammad Taha – First vice president of Sudan

Alex de Waal – Prominent researcher and author of books about famine and war crimes in Darfur

Jody Williams – Chair, "Mission on the Situation of Human Rights in Darfur," and Nobel Peace Prize winner who spearheaded an international treaty on land mines

Robert Zoellick – Former U.S. Deputy Secretary of State to Condoleezza Rice, current president of the World Bank

# Prologue: On Our Watch

In the best of circumstances, it is a challenge to travel hundreds of miles across the barren desert of Chad to the Darfur region of Sudan. Stefanie Frease knew this when she told State Department representatives in the summer of 2004 that, with little more than a month of advance warning, she could oversee a survey of a thousand war-ravaged refugees from Darfur. The refugees had escaped to UN camps across the border in neighboring Chad. More than 200,000 Darfurian refugees huddled there under straggly trees and plastic tarps as they struggled to survive the loss of family members and most of their meager possessions.

Frease was only in her middle thirties, but she was already a veteran human rights investigator, having uncovered the evidence that convicted a Serbian general of genocide at Srebrenica. Yet, Africa was a whole new story. Within a month she supervised the collection of several hundred interviews that formed the basis for Secretary of State Powell's testimony before the UN Security Council. Within two months, her team supplied Powell with a sample of more than one thousand interviews from what criminologists call a victimization survey. Powell summarized the findings for the powerful Senate Foreign Relations Committee in the following testimony:

> In July, we launched a limited investigation by sending a team to visit the refugee camps in Chad to talk to refugees and displaced personnel. The team worked closely with the American Bar Association and

the Coalition for International Justice, and were able to interview 1,136 of the 2.2 million people the U.N. estimates have been affected by this horrible situation, this horrible violence.

Those interviews indicated: first, a consistent and widespread pattern of atrocities: killings, rapes, burning of villages committed by Jingaweit and government forces against non-Arab villagers; second, three-fourths of those interviewed reported that the Sudanese military forces were involved in the attacks; third, villagers often experienced multiple attacks over a prolonged period before they were destroyed by burning, shelling or bombing, making it impossible for the villagers to return to their villages. This was a coordinated effort, not just random violence.

When we reviewed the evidence compiled by our team, and then put it beside other information available to the State Department and widely known throughout the international community, widely reported upon by the media and others, we concluded, I concluded, that genocide has been committed in Darfur and that the Government of Sudan and the Jingaweit bear responsibility – and that genocide may still be occurring. . . .

Mr. Chairman, as I have said, the evidence leads us to the conclusion, the United States to the conclusion, that genocide has occurred and may still be occurring in Darfur. We believe the evidence corroborates the specific intent of the perpetrators to destroy "a group in whole or in part," the words of the [Genocide] Convention. This intent may be inferred from their deliberate conduct. We believe other elements of the convention have been met as well. . . .

Mr. Chairman, some seem to have been waiting for this determination of genocide to take action. In fact, however, no new action is dictated by this determination. We have been doing everything we can to get the Sudanese Government to act responsibly. So let us not be too preoccupied with this designation. . . .

I expect – I more than expect, I know, that the government of Khartoum in Khartoum will reject our conclusion of genocide anyway. Moreover, at this point, genocide is our judgment and not the judgment of the international community. . . .

Specifically, Mr. Chairman, the most practical contribution we can make to the security of Darfur in the short term is to do

everything we can to increase the number of African Union monitors. That will require the cooperation of the Government of
Sudan.

Secretary Colin Powell
Testimony before the Senate Foreign Relations Committee
Washington, D.C.
September 9, 2004

Sending African Union "monitors" was a disturbingly modest response
to genocide. The very term "monitor" contradicted President Bush's
often-quoted campaign pledge not to allow genocide to occur on his
"watch." Several thousand African Union monitors spent several years
watching what the Bush administration intermittently called a genocide.
Nearly three years after the survey-based determination of genocide, in
May 2007, President Bush said from the "Diplomatic Reception Room"
of the White House, "I promise this to the people of Darfur: The United
States will not avert our eyes from a crisis that challenges the conscience
of the world." The three-year interlude made this a non sequitur of massive proportions.

The topic of genocide is consistently controversial. An introduction
to this fact was an "above the fold" *New York Times* op-ed by a journalist, Sam Dealey, linking our work on Darfur mortality (discussed in
Chapter 4) to full-page advertisements by the advocacy group *Save Darfur*. Dealey cited the British Advertising Standards Association as saying
*Save Darfur* "breached standards of truthfulness" in citing our estimate
of the death toll in Darfur.

Although a Sudanese-supported business group filed such a claim
with the British association, this regulatory group actually rejected its
claim and found instead that *Save Darfur* should simply in the future
acknowledge a diversity of opinions about the number of dead in Darfur. This is how a *Guardian* columnist described David Hoile, the head
of the business group that filed the claim of "untruthfulness":

David Hoile, [is] a right-wing polemicist best remembered in the pages of the *Guardian* for wearing a "Hang Mandela" sticker on his tie when he was a young Tory. Dr. Hoile had angrily demanded a correction when the *Guardian Diary* claimed in 2001 that he had worn a T-shirt emblazoned with the offensive slogan. When a picture of the sticker surfaced a few weeks later, he claimed to have no recollection of it, but stressed that the picture did not show a T-shirt. Such are Khartoum's current friends in Britain.

Ten days after the offending op-ed was published, the *New York Times* admitted and corrected its false claim. Still, the article and adjudication by the British Standards Association correctly pointed to a disparity in views about Darfur. The State Department's survey contained valuable information about many of the issues and questions raised by the Darfur conflict.

Yet, this remarkable 2004 survey, which cost the U.S. government nearly one million dollars to complete, languished largely unused in the archives of the State Department. This was a humanitarian and criminological disgrace. We acquired the survey and began to write this book. This book addresses the following kinds of questions: Why is the United States so ambivalent in its response to genocide? Why is criminology – the science of crime – so slow to study the "crime of crimes"? Why does the U.S. government flip-flop in its characterization of the violence in Darfur as genocide? Why are many scholars so reluctant to emphasize the racial nature of the genocide in Darfur? Why is race so central to the explanation of the genocidal scale of the death and rape in Darfur? Why is genocidal violence such a long-lasting threat to human security both within and beyond Darfur? Most of all we ask, What can the science of criminology contribute to the understanding of genocide as a basis for responding more responsibly to this "crime of crimes"?

As this book went to press, five and a half years after the violence in Darfur escalated, Prosecutor Luis Moreno Ocampo asked the International Criminal Court's judges to issue an arrest warrant charging Sudanese President Omar al-Bashir with genocide, crimes against humanity, and war crimes.[1] We explain in Chapter 2 that there was strong opposition to a genocide charge both at the UN and from within the Prosecutor's own office. Yet the Prosecutor eventually became convinced by the kind of evidence presented in this book that al-Bashir had mobilized the entire apparatus of the Sudanese state with the intention of genocidal group destruction. This mobilization included joining the Government of Sudan's military forces with local Arab and Janjaweed militias in highly organized attacks on villages. Ocampo reported that 35,000 African villagers were killed outright in Darfur, and that 100,000 died overall. We show in Chapter 4 that this number of deaths is implausibly small and that the death toll is actually far higher.

The Prosecutor further identified the dead as mostly from three ethnic groups – the Fur, Masalit, and Zaghawa – whom al-Bashir collectively and derogatorily called "Zourga" and whose history he wanted to end. The Prosecutor has set the stage for a strong legal case that identifies the role of ethnic targeting for purposes of genocide. However, at this writing, the Prosecutor has not yet elaborated the socially constructed nature of the term "Zourga" as a racial slur or epithet about Black Africans. Nor has he fully exposed the explicitness or extensiveness of the government's use of *race* to organize the targeting of killings, rapes, displacement, and destruction of these groups.

Further, the Prosecutor has not yet adequately differentiated the overlapping meanings of ethnicity and race in Darfur. Among the differences, there are several that are salient for purposes pursued here. Ethnic group identities tend to be plural, whereas racial identity tends to be binary, and ethnic identities tend to be developed by the groups themselves, whereas racial group identity is often imposed by others. Thus it is one thing for groups in Darfur to have identified themselves as the Fur, Masalit, and Zaghawa, and it is quite another for President al-Bashir to have called them collectively "Zourga." Consolidating the identity of

---

[1] International Criminal Court, Office of the Prosecutor, Prosecution's Application for Warrant of Arrest under Article 58 Against Omar Hassan Ahmad Al Bashir, July 14, 2008, The Hague, Netherlands.

several ethnic groups as "Zourga," or as Black in a contemptuous and derogatory way, was a crude step toward identifying and stigmatizing an enlarged and combined grouping as suitable for genocidal victimization.

Identities can be especially confusing in Darfur, where groups often overlap in their skin tones and can also shift in their feelings of being Arab and non-Arab, African and Black African. It was through the simplifying imposition of a binary racial identification that some African groups were designated as Black. It was when the imposed meaning of race by others became more starkly binary and stigmatic, separating "us" from "them," that genocide could begin. When President al-Bashir collectively identified the selected groups as "Zourga," he opened a door to stigmatization and violence.

The challenge is to explain and demonstrate how the genocide in Darfur was made to happen along these racial lines, even though differences in skin tone between attacking and victim groups were often subtle or even nonexistent. Beginning in Chapter 1, we learn how racial identification in Darfur has self– and other–imposed meanings. It is important for the reader to think about this mixture of meanings. We report the salient role of race from the refugee interviews. We emphasize in the last half of the book how the Sudanese government maliciously linked differences between Arabic-speaking nomadic herders and non-Arab African farmers with perceived or observed racial attributes to organize and mobilize the Janjaweed and militia attacks on villages in Darfur.

As important as the Prosecutor's latest charges are as intermediate steps in a legal process leading to conviction and punishment for the perpetrators of horrific crimes, the development of the criminology of genocide and the pursuit of justice in Darfur remain conspicuously overdue. The work has barely begun. The prospect for restoration of group life remains remote for the Fur, Masalit, and Zaghawa victims of the Darfur genocide. It is with this in mind that the voices recorded and analyzed herein from the U.S. State Department interviews with refugees in Chad are offered as an historically unprecedented and uniquely rich source of neglected evidence for an urgently needed advancement of both science and justice goals in Darfur.

# DARFUR AND THE CRIME OF GENOCIDE

# Settlement Cluster Map of Darfur, Sudan

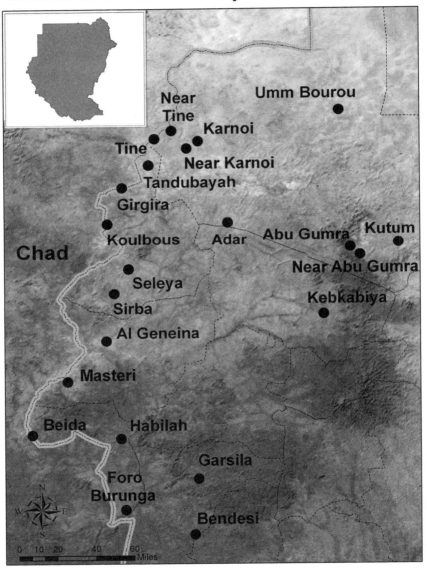

# 1 Darfur Crime Scenes

## The Mass Graves of Darfur

"I was hiding and saw this," Mohamed explained.[1] "I saw them take fifty-two men from my village, including my cousin, and they took them to the edge of the mountain, made them go on their knees, put the gun in their mouths, and shot each one of them." He heard the attackers say that "we came here because we want to kill all the Black people."

Mohamad is a member of the African Zaghawa tribe who lived in a small village near Karnoi in North Darfur. The Sudanese government feared the Zaghawa were leading a rebellion and targeted them early in 2003. Mohamed buried the last bodies and set out on a dangerous journey to a refugee camp in the neighboring Chad, where he became one among more than 200,000 Darfurian refugees. He was also one of those interviewed in the U.S. Department of State Atrocities Documentation Survey.

After patiently providing a detailed description of the attack and the attackers, and the names of slaughtered family members and villagers, Mohamed concluded in despair, "I just want to say the United Nations has come too late; there are too many people who have already died." Four years later, the United Nations had still not arrived in sufficient force and numbers, and the toll of the dead continued to mount. More than five years later, the chief prosecutor of the International Criminal

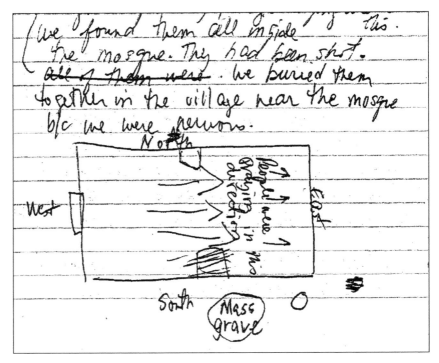

FIGURE 1.1. Rendering of Mass Grave Based on Interviews.

Court was still obliged to report to the UN Security Council that, "the entire Darfur region is a crime scene."[2]

We assess the reliability and representativeness of the ADS survey reports in the Appendix to this book. Often, we rely on overlapping eyewitness accounts to assess their validity. Unfortunately, the massiveness of the atrocities allows many opportunities for cross-checks. Some refugees drew maps of mass graves they left behind. Esikiel, a member of a Fur tribe, drew the accompanying map of where he buried the bodies of fellow villagers in a mass grave after an attack (see Figure 1.1). This burial and his description of the events displayed a reverence for the deceased and provided a poignant record of their deaths. Eskiel risked his own life by taking time to bury the bodies and make the witness statement.

As in the Holocaust and other genocides, some of the grave sites in Darfur are massive and grotesque. Fatima, a female Zaghawa refugee, remembered, "Along the road there were many people dead, and there were also big graves with many people in them, because you could see hands and legs and other parts sticking out of the dirt on top." This victim survived vicious rapes and now vicariously experienced these further acts of atrocity. She pleaded with the interviewer to "please let the Sudanese government know what we are telling you because they are saying that they don't know anything and that nothing happened to us."

Colin Powell's testimony to Congress contained only a superficial summary of the Atrocities Documentation Survey (ADS) in an eight-page report. The ADS cost nearly one million dollars and included more than one thousand interviews conducted in Chad with refugees from Darfur. We report the details of the ADS in the following chapters. Here, we introduce in their own voices the stories of Mohamad and Esikiel and Fatima, as well as the many other refugees who shared their experiences of loss and survival during the genocide in Darfur.

The refugee interviews are a genocidal trove of evidence. They include a large amount of eyewitness evidence – including descriptions of weapons, locations of mass graves, names of dead and raped victims, names and descriptions of Arab Janjaweed militia leaders, and accounts of the government direction, supervision, and participation in attacks on Black African groups. The annotated drawing in Figure 1.2 of planes and vehicles used in the attacks shows the precision and detail of these eyewitness accounts. Survivors provided these details at the risk of revealing their identities and possibly losing their lives.

Such evidence is central to the legal charge of genocide and should not languish in U.S. State Department files. "They killed all our men," a female victim explained. "I want those responsible prosecuted." Both the qualitative and quantitative evidence are essential to providing a criminological description and explanation of genocide and holding the architects of genocide accountable. This evidence describes, in sequence, some of the salient empirical elements in the genocidal victimization of Black African groups in Darfur.

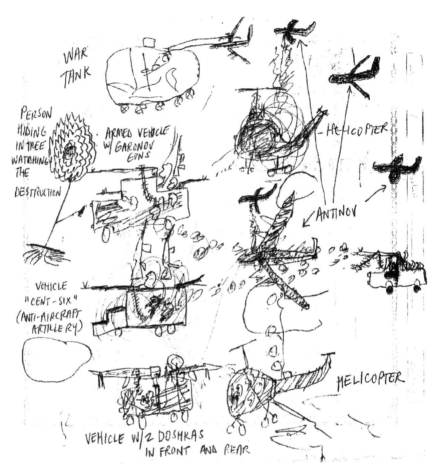

FIGURE 1.2. Drawings of Weapons Based on Interviews.

## The Genocidal Pattern

Determining who dies and how many die is inevitably central to the history of a genocide, but there is much more to be documented. A pattern of elements characterized the repeated attacks by the Sudanese government and the Arab Janjaweed militia on African groups in Darfur. These elements are central to the theoretical model developed and tested in this book. In this section, we use excerpts from the ADS interviews to introduce and illustrate key elements of the genocidal pattern of events in Darfur.

The first element is the background of tension between Arab and Black groups in Darfur. The Sudanese state, especially in recent years, has implemented Arab-Islamic supremacist and demonizing policies that pit Arabs and Blacks against one another in an "us" and "them" kind of conflict. This conflict is played out against a growing competition for land and resources between settled Black African farmers and predominantly nomadic Arab herders. The property, possessions, livestock, and the cultivated land itself are incentives for the crimes that are often at the core of genocides in Africa and elsewhere. In this chapter, we present Black African perceptions of the Arab-dominated Sudanese government's role in the genocide in Darfur. Later chapters provide quantified evidence that substantiates these perceptions.

One refugee succinctly suggested, "There were some problems between Arabs and the Black tribes....The Arabs want to replace all of the Black farmers....The government supports the Arabs." Other refugees drew a broader connection, however, between the more recent attacks in Darfur and the earlier and longer twenty-year conflict in southern Sudan: "We heard about problems between Arabs and Black tribes in South Darfur. Now there is an agreement between Arab tribes and the government to displace Black tribes. After that, they will let their animals live in our homelands."

Another refugee went further back in history, noting that "since independence [in the 1950s], the government of Sudan hasn't given anything to the people of Darfur – the people were asking for education and other things, and the government didn't want us to ask for these things, so they are killing us." Another observed, "Africans from the area told the Sudanese government, we want our rights (development, education). So the Sudanese government decided to kill everyone to get rid of the headache." A third simply said, "We don't have schools, hospitals or other things. The government said we don't deserve things."

The interviews highlighted the cultural aspect of the "us" versus "them" conflict – even though both groups are Muslim. "I think this happened to Darfur because we are all Black Africans or [because of] African culture. They killed people inside the Mosque and even destroyed the Mosque." Another refugee remembered, "When the new Islamic government came to power in Sudan in the early 1990s, they prepared Arab tribes to kill African tribes in western Sudan. All the Arab countries gave Sudan money, weapons, and support to kill African tribes – the government of Sudan wants to kill Darfurians and replace them with Arabs." This refugee noted that the government targeted the Zaghawa, Masalit, and Fur tribes.

The second element in the genocidal pattern is the arming of the Arab Janjaweed militias. Arms have poured into Darfur since at least the famine of the mid-1980s, and the Sudanese government began distributing weapons to Arab groups in Darfur in the 1990s. "For approximately 13 years," one of the respondents in the ADS reported, "the government has had a policy of arming Arabs and giving them horses to attack the villages of Darfur."

Another reasoned, "I know it's the government because otherwise how would they [the Arab attacking groups] have the Antonovs [planes], the helicopters, and the troops." This logic led many to conclude that "the government does not want Blacks to live in Darfur because they give Arabs weapons to attack us." Even more specifically, a refugee remarked, "It is a farmer versus nomad issue.... The Sudanese government has armed the Janjaweed and told them to get rid of all the Black people in Darfur." A local leader reported, "The Janjaweed said that the President of Sudan offered them weapons and ordered them to go and attack and '*yemseho*' (clean) Darfur of the dirty slaves in order to establish the beginning of the Arab union." An interviewer summarized the view of one refugee that "the government gives them the weapons and it's all political."

The third element is the Sudanese government bombing of African villages. Russian-built Antonov aircraft and helicopters bomb and strafe the villages. Sometimes, these attacks terrify the African villagers into submission before ground attacks begin; at other times, the bombings coincide with ground attacks lasting days, weeks, and even months. "All I knew," a refugee explained, "was that the Antonovs were bombing.... It was like a bad dream." These attacks were often indiscriminate: "I don't know, but they wanted to kill me and anyone in Tine.... I saw daily, up to four times a day, the Antonov bombers." The result was the large-scale loss of life. One respondent reported that "118 people were killed in his village;... his brother went deaf from the explosion." Another refugee blamed President Omar al-Bashir personally, saying, "I left because of Omar. I saw airplanes. They poured fire on us. He brought fire from the sky and we ran away."

The ground attacks are the fourth element in the pattern of the genocidal violence in Darfur. The Sudanese government soldiers often join Janjaweed charges into the villages on horses and camels. They storm the villages in armed land cruisers, pickup trucks, tanks, and cars. Sometimes, refugees report government and Janjaweed forces attacking separately, but they more often describe joint ground attacks, as in this account:

> The Arabs chased us. The horse riders and camel riders and military cars came and frightened the people, shouting here and there. The aircraft came and bombed our village and the people ran away from fear. They bombed even the men and the children while they were running away.

The bombing and ground assaults often are coordinated, and when the air and ground attacks coincide, they are more racially charged and violent. We demonstrate this pattern quantitatively in later chapters.

One refugee noted, "When the Arabs come, aircraft also come." Another observed, "The forces...went through the village shooting people, looting, and burning houses." The nature of this coordination is shown in the following description:

> First vehicles attacked the village. After one hour, planes came and bombed; after this military came on camels and horses and began shooting at random. They cut open the stomachs of pregnant women

and split the throats of male fetuses. Bombs from airplanes killed a lot of animals and people. The military took women away. The village was burned and destroyed. They shot at everyone: man, woman, or child.

Some eyewitness descriptions provide even more explicit details about the military hardware used in the attacks, as in the following example:

The village was attacked by the Antonovs, Migs, six helicopters (some black/dark blue, one white, one military green). Helicopters came with vehicles to bomb and shoot guns from the sides. Vehicles and Janjaweed surrounded the village in green and grey vehicles. Small trucks came with the Doskas (guns on top)...30 men in each. Green uniforms. Leader had red stars on shoulders. Took 15 men away. Five girls taken. Village burned. Burned Mosque with minaret on top.

Following this attack, and many others, village members reported killings and injuries as they fled to the Chad refugee camps, as in the following account:

Three boys were caught and slaughtered. Their throats were cut, a foot was cut open from the big toe to the ankle, hands were cut off, brains removed, sexual organs cut off. Boys were five, six, and seven.... The seven-year-old's stomach was slit open and his clothes were torn off. A man who tried to return to the village was caught and killed. His skin was removed. Found his body.... Man traveling with him was killed. Shot in head and side.

The interviews include exact names and ages of victims and vivid descriptions of the attacks. We substitute pseudonyms for victims' names and suppress some factual details to protect identities.

The violence is obviously important in its own right, but it is equally important to note the explicitly racial form of these rampages that target members of Black tribes. This is the fifth element in the genocidal patterning of events in Darfur. These sprees of violence are racially animated. In the heat of the attacks, perpetrators often shout racial epithets that are both dehumanizing and degrading. We include only a few examples of the racial epithets heard in the attacks:

- They called her Nuba (a derogatory terms for Blacks) dog, son of dogs, and we came here to kill you and your kids.
- You donkey, you slave, we must get rid of you.
- We kill our cows when they have Black calves – we will kill you too.
- All the people in the village are slaves, you make this area dirty, we are here to clean the area.
- Black prostitute, whore, you are dirty – Black.

We analyze the dehumanizing roles of these racial curses and slurs as important motivating and intentional elements of the genocide in this and in following chapters.

The ADS documents sexual violence as well as other kinds of victimization, and this is a sixth crucial element in the scenarios of genocide in Darfur. Jan Pfundheller, drawing from her experience at the International Criminal Tribunal for the former Yugoslavia, led this part of the fieldwork. She tells the story of gaining the confidence of a sheikh in one of the refugee camps who arranged for her to meet with a group of women rape victims. She planned a time and location that allowed for some privacy, near a wadi (i.e., a river bed) and close to the refugee camp. Over a small rise, the women could be seen walking toward the meeting place in their colorful clothing in a long, almost procession-like fashion. She reports, "They came and they came." There were almost 300; more than seventy women sat in an inner circle, indicating their willingness to speak. All reported sexual assaults.

Sexually victimized women in Arab cultures rarely marry, and if they are already married, they are at high risk of losing their husbands after they are attacked. Pfundheller approached the interviews with special care, knowing that rape was a source of stigma and dishonor in Muslim society. Yet, these women spoke forcefully of their experiences – often graphically and in disturbing detail. Pfundheller told the women that an important U.S. government leader, Colin Powell, had visited Sudan and wanted to know more about what had happened to them. Pfundheller said, "I can only promise you that what happened to you will be told to my government, and then perhaps to the world."

These women told horrifying stories. Some were abducted, raped, and told they were now the wives of Arabs and would bear Arab babies. Some attackers spoke of distinguishing Arabs from Black Africans by skin tone (i.e., Arabs are often said to have a redder skin color), telling the women that subtle differences in skin tone would signify the identity of the children resulting from these coerced pregnancies. One woman in the ADS interviews reported hearing, "We will kill all men and rape the women. We want to change the color. Every woman will deliver red. Arabs are the husbands of those women."

Aisha, another of the young women interviewed, offered this horrifying account:

> A soldier took my baby son and said, "I will kill him." I told the soldier, "You killed my husband; don't kill my boy." One other said, "Don't kill the baby." . . . I was knocked down, and the first soldier had sex with me from the front. They were saying the government from Khartoum sent [them]. . . . Ten soldiers raped me and left me. I was bleeding and could not walk. They did this to me for nearly three hours. . . . A man fleeing from another village found me and took me and my children to Masteri.

We describe later the conditions in the town of Masteri from where this woman fled before crossing the border to Chad.

Attackers killed the women they raped in Rwanda, whereas in Darfur, they often returned raped women to their villages or camps. This practice intensified the terror and dishonor of the sexual violation, as these raped women became living symbols of stigma and subordination. Jan Pfundheller emphasized that "as a tool of terror, killing your men and raping your women seemed effective. If you have women without men to make a family, it changes the face of their society." Men in our interviews were victimized sexually as well. Brent Pfundheller,

Jan's husband, interviewed Black African men who recounted being sexually assaulted with sticks and rifles. Recalling her work in the former Yugoslavia, Jan concluded, "What happened in Kosovo was evil. This is more vast and equally evil."

Although extensive attention has been paid to the killing and some attention to rapes in Darfur, there is less attention to the seventh element of the conflict: the confiscation of property – including animals, grains, seeds, farm equipment, household items, and money. These possessions are required to sustain and reproduce a way of life for individuals and groups; indeed, they are necessary for physical survival. A common charge is that "they [i.e., Arab attackers] want to kill everyone who is Black and want to take our cattle and money and our land." Many African refugees blamed the government: "I don't know exactly, but for a long time the military would come to take our cattle. They have done this for a long time. They want our land and our cattle."

The refugees charge that the government enabled if not directly engaged in this looting: "Because there is a war. First we were battling between us and the Arabs; later the government engaged and helped the Arabs, because the Arabs were running and stealing the Masalit livestock." Many described an attack on the town of Terbeba: "What happened in Terbeba is a terrible thing. They came, killed many people, looted the houses, stores, burned houses with property inside, and left our people with nothing." In Terbeba attackers took not only lives but also a way of life.

The eighth element, displacement, is perhaps the most obvious, but also potentially the most consequential. Survival of the Black African tribes in Darfur depends on their ability to pursue their livelihoods in their settlements. Between two and three million Black Africans have been displaced from their lands into "internal displacement camps" in Sudan. These camps contain in concentrated and confined areas the overwhelming majority of the African Black population of Darfur.

The Sudanese Ministry of Health has put in place a government minister, Ahmad Harun, who was charged by the International Criminal

Court (ICC) for crimes against humanity, to oversee these camps. The ICC charged Harun with organizing the government and Arab Jan-jaweed militia attacks that sent the persons to these camps in the first place. During the period of the most intense attacks, Harun was an official in the much-feared Ministry of Security. Now as a Minister of Humanitarian Affairs, he oversees persons whose displacement he directed. This shift of Harun into a position of responsibility for the internal displacement camps coincided with increased harassment of humanitarian aid workers and problems in getting food, medicine, and other forms of assistance to the displaced African villagers.

More than 200,000 of the displaced persons fled across the border to the United Nations camps in Chad. The complaints of the refugees are almost restrained given these circumstances. One observed, "The government has been saying for three years that they want to throw all the Black people off the land." Another remarked, "I believe it was because of colour, they want to genocide the Blacks, they want us to never be able to go back again."

In the final chapter, we review quantitative evidence of the resettlement by Arab groups on land previously held by Black African tribes. This is the ninth and final element in the Darfur genocide. Many respondents reported their understanding of their situation. This understanding is rooted in a history they have lived and continue to recognize in their language: "Darfur – the name means 'home of the Fur.' They want to destroy the people, take the land, and kill the people." More specifically, "it is Omar Bashir's policy to eliminate the Black race." The interviewer noted, "He knows this in part because an Arab settlement is a five-hour walk away, and the Guimer tribe [there] were not hurt at all. They were not targeted." The shared perception in the Black African tribes is that the government wants to remake Darfur in an Arab image: "The government wants to change 'Darfur' to 'Tajamo Arabi.' All African tribes have left to go to another African country because the Arabs want land. The rumor for 20 years is now a fact." Other refugees explained that "their aim is to get rid of the Blacks and I heard that they [the Arabs] went back and live in our villages" and that "they want to take [land] from the Blacks to give to the nomads who have no land."

The interviews included specific accounts of how this resettlement was planned and then took place: "The government made a grazing corridor for them, but the solution was unfair. Some people on the seized land decided to fight. The government responded by arming the Arabs to keep us down." Rumors play a role in shaping their understanding of recent events: "They want to clean us out to take our land for their cattle" because, a refugee reported, "they have heard a route from Libya to their areas will be created." There is a wide suspicion that the Arab Janjaweed militia are not just from Darfur or even the larger Sudan: "They want to kill all African tribes and give the land to Arabs because they didn't have any. Most Janjaweed are not from Sudan; they are from Chad and Central Africa. They are nomads who want to find a place to live." The widespread conclusion of Black Africans in Darfur is that "the government wants to kill everyone. They have destroyed our houses and now they will build Arab houses."

## Legal Elements of Genocide

It is important to consider how these elements of genocidal violence in Darfur – the background tensions between Arab and Black Africans, arming of the Janjaweed, racial targeting, government bombing, government involvement in ground attacks and killing, sexual violence, confiscation of property, displacement, and Arab resettlement – relate to the acts that are defined by international law as genocide. According to Article II of the Genocide Convention, genocide means any of the following five acts committed with intent to destroy, in whole or in part, a national, ethnic, racial, or religious group:

1. killing members of the group
2. causing serious bodily or mental harm to members of the group

3. deliberately inflicting on the group conditions of life calculated to bring about its physical destruction in whole or in part
4. imposing measures intended to prevent births within the group
5. forcibly transferring children of the group to another group

The nine elements we described above in Darfur are variants on these five legal elements. Any one of the five specified elements can legally constitute genocide. The third act – with its reference to "conditions of life" – is perhaps the most all-encompassing and meaningful one in understanding how genocidal violence denies sustainable group life to entire communities.

Thus, international criminal law includes within genocide the intentional creation of physical conditions leading to the destruction of the group life of protected groups in individual communities, as well as in multiple communities and whole nations. For example, the International Criminal Tribunal for the former Yugoslavia found that a genocide occurred in the former Yugoslavian town of Srebrenica in the mid-1990s. This judgment cited evidence of the selective killing of young adult ("fighting age") men and the forced displacement of women and children, which made it "impossible for the Bosnian Muslim people of Srebrenica to survive."[3] Forced displacement and killing ended an era of group life for Bosnian Muslims in this community.

We show in Chapter 8 that a parallel pattern of killing fighting-aged men and displacement of others occurred across settlement clusters in Darfur. The final part of this chapter focuses on the destruction of Black African group life in the cluster of settlements around the town of Masteri in West Darfur. Masteri exemplifies crime scenes repeated to varying degrees across numerous settings in Darfur.

## Destroying Group Life in Masteri

Most of the evidence in this book comes from the ADS interviews with refugees who fled from twenty-two settlement clusters in Darfur, all of

which are discussed in later chapters. Table A.1 in the Appendix contains information that is useful in introducing the pattern of events in
the cluster of settlements around the single town of Masteri. The area of
Masteri is distinguished in several highly unenviable ways.

*An Overview:* The cluster of settlements that includes Masteri ranks
third in Table A.1 in reports of racial epithets during attacks, second in
personal rapes, and first in reports of rapes and sexual assaults either of
themselves or of others. Masteri also ranks third in an overall score of
victimization severity discussed in Chapter 7 that takes into account not
only rape but also a variety of other forms of violence and property loss.
It is therefore unsurprising that the Masteri area provides vivid examples of all the elements of genocide that we describe and explain in this
book.

Masteri is located in the Dar Masalit region of Darfur, the home-
land or home territory of the Masalit tribe. It is located just south and
slightly west of Al Geneina, the capital of the state of West Darfur. A
struggle for scarce resources led ultimately to deadly attacks in this area
in the late 1990s.[4] Arab herders clashed with the local Masalit farmers
over the grazing of animals. The Arab attackers destroyed hundreds of
Masalit villages and killed thousands of Masalit farmers; many thousands
of Masalit survivors fled to Chad. A government-led reconciliation conference failed to calm the conflict permanently, and violence resumed
with increased intensity in 2003. At that time, government forces joined
with Arab Janjaweed militia in attacking the Masalit villages.

The ADS data contain seventy-nine interviews with survivors of
attacks on the cluster of villages in the Masteri area; fifty-one of the
refugees fled from this area to camps in Chad during a wave of attacks in
January and February 2004. These refugees were divided about equally
by gender, 95 percent were Masalit, and the median age was 32 years.

The first months of 2004 marked the peak of a second government
offensive in Darfur. The victims heard commands shouted in Arabic.
Even though village women attended school less often and understood
Arabic less than men, nearly half the women (46.8%) and more than half

the men (55.1%) reported they heard racial epithets during the attacks. Nearly two-thirds (65.8%) reported that the Janjaweed and government forces attacked together.

Only 1 to 2 percent reported that rebels defended their villages, and few reported rebels were in the area. A refugee explained, "My village was not defended. And how could we defend – there was no equality of power – there were no rebels nearby." Some of the villages organized self-defense units, but most indicated little or no armed presence at all. The rebels in Darfur usually camped in nearby hills, away from the villages, often hiding under outcroppings of rocks and in ravines. Human Rights Watch confirmed attacks from mid-2003 against villages, rather than against rebel positions.[5] The tendency of the rebels to hide in the hills is a source of references during attacks to "Tora Bora." The analogy is to Osama Bin Laden and Al Qaeda hiding in the mountainous borderland area of Afghanistan and Pakistan.

More than 10 percent (12.7%) indicated that attacking forces spared Arab villages in the surrounding area. Nearly half of the refugees (45.6%) reported rapes during attacks on their villages, and more than three-quarters (78.%) reported at least one villager killed. Almost 10 percent (8.9%) indicated personally being raped, and nearly 14 percent (13.9%) indicated the killing of a member of their immediate nuclear family. More than two-thirds (67.1%) reported that a member of their extended family was killed or raped, with 187 family members killed or raped overall. This is an average of more than two persons killed or raped per extended family.

*Joint Government-Janjaweed Violent Attacks:* The narrative accounts by the refugees of the attacks in the cluster of settlements around Masteri provide insight into the organization of scorched-earth tactics in Darfur. We describe here a set of attacks in early 2004 that illustrate the ways in which the Sudanese government and Janjaweed militias formed what in international criminal prosecutions is called a joint criminal enterprise. Later sections focus more specifically on the shouting of racial epithets along with rapes and on the extent of the looting of possessions and livestock.

Thus, our focus is first on how government and militia forces joined together in highly organized genocidal attacks. Hamid Dawai, a leading Janjaweed leader, coordinated attacks with government forces in the Masteri area. Dawai was called "the emir of the emirate of Dar Masalit" on local state-run radio.[6] Eyewitness accounts of Dawai's leadership role in the chain of command are presented in Chapter 6.

The death toll was large in Masteri and other settlements in this cluster, with the largest number killed in Terbeba, just east of Masteri, on the border with Chad. Tensions escalated in the months preceding the largest attack on February 15, 2004. On that day, Halima recalled that two government planes bombed and several hundred men on horses surrounded the village. Government cars and pickup trucks with mounted guns joined the attack after the Janjaweed horsemen swept into the village.[7]

Halima was sleeping with her husband, Mustafa, and her child, Fatima, when militia men entered their home in the early morning and killed Mustafa. She grabbed her daughter and ran, but the Janjaweed followed and beat her with a whip. She said, "They wanted to kill my child, but I was able to get away." They were shouting, "Kill the Nuba, Kill the Nuba!" In addition to Mustafa, they killed four other members of her family. They completely burned the village, and Halima estimated they killed 130 villagers. She recalled that they threw into the fire women who ran slowly or people who refused to leave. She saw eight bodies as she ran. She saw more on the far side of the village. They killed mostly men, but also women and children.

Another woman reported seeing forty-five men and one woman killed as they ran from the burning village. The estimates of death in Terbeba range up to 400.[8] A midwife who delivered many babies in Terbeba reported that soldiers tore the pages from a registration book in which she had recorded more than 250 births, thus eliminating all signs of Masalit presence. "What happened in Terbeba is a terrible thing," a survivor concluded: "They came, they killed many people, looted houses, shops, burned houses – with properties inside – and they left our people with nothing."

Kojo, just south of Masteri, was bombed or attacked on the ground every three or four days, from the middle of January through the middle of February. "I think the government and the Janjaweed have the same aim," observed a refugee from Kojo. "They work together." They killed about forty-five men in these attacks. They abducted several women in each of the attacks and returned them several days later. They raped the women and poisoned the town wells.

Planes circled but did not bomb Kojo the day before an attack on February 15, 2004. A refugee reported that an Arab man who brought his camels to the village gardens threatened the day before the attack that "I can feed my camels here and I will shoot you if you resist." The refugee continued, "The government wants to take over the land, and so they sent the Arabs to do this." This victim reported that he saw many people shot and killed. He saw the soldiers run over and crush small children with their horses. He reported seeing about thirty dead people as he ran. Six girls told him they were raped. Attackers abducted boys to care for Janjaweed camels and dragged others to their death by the neck behind horses. Janjaweed and government troops destroyed five flour mills and poisoned the village wells. They did not attack surrounding Arab villages.

On the same day in the middle of February, about 600 soldiers attacked another settlement west of Masteri. A refugee from this town recalled that soldiers and Janjaweed set huts on fire, looted, and randomly shot automatic weapons from attacking trucks. The attackers called to each other to loot and burn the huts and "don't leave anything." They poisoned the wells with DDT and took all the food and livestock they could, while burning the rest. This refugee reported the rapes of seven girls between 8 and 9 years of age. Attackers threw nine women into burning huts and buried some alive. Altogether, another refugee estimated that 300 were killed and 200 injured in a town of 1,500. A few scattered huts remained after three hours of steady attack, yet when villagers returned a week later they found that "the attackers had returned and destroyed even these."

Attackers destroyed another settlement north of Masteri. The assault was highly organized. The army participated with the Janjaweed in the killing, burning, and looting. They attacked the village together from three directions – north, south, and east – and they stole as many as 1,000 cattle. Government helicopters landed three times with ammunition blazing while Janjaweed attacked on horse and camel. Several refugees indicated that the attackers yelled, "Masalit! Nuba! Kill them all!" They again poisoned the wells. Janjaweed stopped ten persons on the road and executed one after the other with guns. Groups of men raped six women repeatedly and then returned them to the village. They tied their hands behind their backs and pulled their legs apart.

One man described being shot eight times while running from the village with his five children and his wife. His wife took the children and left him behind, but fleeing villagers rescued him later. This refugee recalled that he saw "Arabs cross his path as he was running," but that "they [the attackers] did not touch the Arabs."

Attackers poisoned the well of a nearby settlement; three villagers drank the water and died before they could be warned. They shot ten persons who ran away and then tied, blindfolded, and shot thirty others. The refugee interviewed about this attack saw ten women tied together and beaten with sticks. He heard attackers tell five infant children to "go, go to your mother," and then they shot them.

Attackers struck Masteri itself in early January, but did not harm Arab civil servants who lived in a separate part of the village. Nearby Arab villagers had abandoned their settlements in the months before the attacks. A refugee recalled, "There were Arabs living outside our village before. They all moved to Beida about six months before the attacks." The attacks targeted Black Africans. A woman refugee saw eighteen men and six women dead in her quarter of town. The attackers took the livestock away, took control of the wells, and prevented the villagers from getting access to any water. Refugees reported contamination of the wells in all the settlements in and around Masteri.

The evidence of coordination and a joint army-Jangaweed initiative in the Masteri area in January and February 2004 includes the following: the coordination of the attacks by time and place, the close working relationship of the government and Janjaweed forces, their arrival and departure together, and the recurring features of the attacks – including killing of fighting-aged men and the poisoning of the wells. The attacks around Masteri systematically cleared the Black African settlements and left mostly Arab groups as the remaining presence. Planes not only bombed these settlements beforehand; they circled the settlements for days after to make sure the villagers left and did not return. When Human Rights Watch returned to the Masteri area after the attacks, "the only civilian life encountered was a terrified group of some fifteen people – men and women, and pitifully thin – who were attempting to reach their former village to dig up buried food stores."[9]

*Racial Epithets and Rapes:* Attackers shouted racial epithets during gang rapes in Masteri and the surrounding cluster of settlements. We begin with several reports of rapes where the racial motivation is less certain. Then we consider cases where the role of race is explicit. When all the cases are closely considered, the clear implication is that race plays a central role.

A 14-year-old girl described how she was raped with seven other girls her age. The rapes followed destruction of their village by five planes in a joint attack by government soldiers and Janjaweed militia. The girls had escaped the initial attack and fled to Chad, where they stayed for five days before returning to check on the tomatoes and mangos they raised in their valley. The girls could not understand what the attackers said in Arabic, so they did not know if the attack was racial.

> When we were checking the fields, more than ten soldiers who were on horses and camels came and told us that if we ran they would shoot us. They were wearing green khaki uniforms. The soldiers took [us]...back into a forest near the village. They took six and one escaped. They took my clothes off and the others as well. The rest

of the girls were my age or a little older. They threw me on the ground – naked – one was holding my hands and the other soldier raped me. He took off his pants before he raped me. They were saying something, but it was all in Arabic. After the first finished, he held my hands and the other soldier raped me. I wasn't physically injured and when they finished they left me. The four other women were each raped by two soldiers and after they left we all returned to Chad. One of the other women had also been beaten and her left arm was broken. She had tried to fight the soldiers.

Another refugee reported the abduction and gang rapes of fifteen girls between the ages of 12 and 17. The rapes continued two days, after which they were returned. They required a month-long hospitalization after the rapes.

Ten soldiers in a truck raped a woman to the north of Masteri. This series of rapes followed the initial attack that killed her husband and others. This victim reported rapes of adult men as well:

I was running... carrying my baby [boy] and my 3-year-old daughter. Two pickups, Toyotas, followed me with soldiers.... They ripped off all [my] clothes. There were ten soldiers there, but ten soldiers raped.... They were wearing green Khaki Sudanese uniforms. They told [us]... that President Omar Al Bashir sent us to do this, to kill and rape and drive you from this land. My baby was lying near me and my daughter was crying and trying to come to me, and they kicked her away. I was knocked down and the first soldier had sex with me.... Ten soldiers raped me and left me. I was bleeding and could not walk. They did this to me for nearly three hours. I was lying there while my village burned.... There were eight women total that were raped from our village. Four others were taken and have not been seen again. Four men were raped in the village by the soldiers.... These men were then shot and killed. I watched this after my rape.

This victim concluded her account by adding that the soldiers urinated on the Koran in the Iman's house, burned the Mosque, and burned the

Holy Book in the grass. The rapes appeared race related, but no specific racial epithets were explicitly reported in the interview.

A middle-aged woman from a settlement south of Masteri described a rape by government soldiers and Janjaweed militia. She said soldiers abducted two young women, ages 19 and 20, and took them to their military camp in Masteri. The soldiers were shouting, "Nuba, slave, Nuba, slave." They held the women for a week and raped them repeatedly. They both required hospital treatment. Janjaweed gang-raped four other women – ages 15, 17, 32, and 24 – at a military base east of Masteri.

Another attack east of Masteri began with the Arab soldiers shouting, "Masalit, Nuba, Masalit, Nuba." A 20-year-old woman reported on thirteen girls who were taken during the attack from the village to a military camp. Soldiers held them for four days and raped them repeatedly. Arab soldiers shouted, "Nuba, Nuba" and "Zourga, Zourga" (i.e., a derogatory term for Blacks) during a bombing attack west of Masteri. The soldiers took five girls between 12 and 15 years of age away with them for five days. They raped them all.

In her narrative account of a young woman respondent from just north of Masteri, an interviewer wrote that both she and her interpreter "strongly believe that she was raped – [there was] very strong indication from her body language, change in voice, downcast eyes, and the way she discussed the other women's rapes." The attack she described involved government planes, pickup trucks, and Janjaweed men on horseback. The soldiers entered her hut, grabbed her, and beat her with a stick on the head. They stripped her of her sari. She explained that "they want to eliminate the Blacks and take our land." Altogether, she reported rapes of ten women and three girls – four never returned, whereas the soldiers brought the others back. She saw and heard these rapes. The interviewer described her as traumatized.

In other cases, the interviewers recorded accounts of male and female rapes with a detail and thoroughness that left no doubts about their viciousness. The attackers forced helpless family members to watch, as described in this account:

> I saw ladies in the village (as I lay wounded) being raped right in front of everyone, even their fathers and their children. By the Janjaweed. They would catch them and do this terrible thing. I saw several with my own eyes. We could do nothing, nothing. We had no way to fight. Five young girls were taken and are still missing.

The public display of these rapes is consistent with a race-linked intent to create terror and facilitate the goal of group displacement.

A 35-year-old woman from a small settlement just north of Masteri described the rapes of sixteen women and the castration and killing of five men. She gave very specific details for the rapes of two women, three girls, and herself. The scale and detail of this description left little doubt that the motivation and intent was to terrify and expel the Black African victims as a group from the area.

> First Woman: Raped vaginally – breasts slashed, deep cut on thigh – shoved a stick in her vagina.
>
> Second Woman: Very pregnant at the time. Four government soldiers held her hands and feet. Took turns – vaginal rape. Shoved stick far inside her, baby dead. Slashed her breasts.
>
> First Girl: Age 14. Four government soldiers. Vaginal and anal rape. Shoved stick in her vagina.
>
> Second and Third Girls: Ages 15 and 18. Both died after gang rape – bleeding badly from breast cuts and vagina.
>
> Herself: Horsemen had me. Four held me down. Raping me one after another. They took my clothing. Vaginal rape – oral rape. Full green uniforms, stripes on sleeves. Only took down their pants. They were laughing and shouting at all of us – "If you like this – stay in Sudan – if you don't – go to Chad."

This victim stoically completed her description by saying, "I found water. I washed myself. I made my way back into the village. Many dead bodies. Everything on fire."

*Looting and Livestock:* Livestock accounts for the majority of agricultural production and is an important part of the overall economy of

Sudan. Even poor Masalit farmers owned as many as ten goats, five to ten sheep, seven cattle, and one camel. A better-off Masalit farmer typically owned 200 each of goats, sheep, and cattle, as well as five horses, one or more donkeys, and camels. Fully grown camels are worth more than US $1,000 – as much as most Sudanese workers earn in a year. Because sheep, cattle, and goats are worth less, they can often be sold and traded more readily. Such "assets on the hoof" are prized and fought over.[10]

Ownership of camels, sheep, goats, and cattle thus serves as an important marker of wealth, power, and prestige. The livestock are integral to trading relationships within and between African and Arab groups. Black African farmers as well as nomadic Arab herders move up and down the social ladders of their communities through animal ownership.[11]

So it was that Hadia, a Masalit agricultural and commercial entrepreneur, lost both his material livelihood and social position in a community during the mid-February 2004 government offensive in the Masteri area. Hadia was among the most well-off in his community. He owned many huts and buildings as well as a small shop. He also kept a herd of cattle and goats close by.

Sudanese government soldiers and Janjaweed militia attacked Hadia's village at sunrise on February 15. He decided to make a run for it. Hadia was shot in the leg while running from the village. However, the wound was minor, and he returned to the village near sundown, after the soldiers left. He gave a complete accounting of his lost fortune. "When I returned to the village later that evening," he said, "I found that my herd of 1,900 cattle had been stolen. I also lost 170 goats and two horses. My shop was looted and I lost about 500,000,000 Sudanese pounds' worth of stock and 290,000,000 Sudanese pounds in cash." He nonetheless acknowledged that at least he and his son had survived.

One refugee reported that, when his settlement north of Masteri was attacked, the soldiers looked first for the umda (i.e., tribal leader), who left before they arrived. They searched his home, took everything out, and then burned the house. Four captured men disappeared permanently. He indicated that "there were over 1,000 houses burned. There were no defenders, nor were there rebels in the village. All the [surrounding] villages were burned. We could see many more villages burning after our attack. We lost twenty-five cows, eight goats, and all our household goods were either stolen or burned."

Attacking Janjaweed called nearby villagers "Noab" (plural of Nuba) and insisted that "Sudan is Arab." A former construction worker in Libya reported that "everything is lost but my clothes. I worked in Libya for years and had many nice things, but now I have only the clothes I wear." He lost fifty cows, two horses, and one camel. He said the village was totally destroyed by the time the attack ended.

The accounts fit into a recurring pattern for most if not all of the settlements clustered in and around Masteri. The attackers took livestock, food, and furniture from the houses and huts and then burned the homes. Refugees also saw the villages around them going up in flames as they fled to the border of Chad.

The accounts of looting and livestock loss are repetitive and could seem tedious if they did not so clearly document the "livelihoods under siege" of the affected victims.[12] Almost all Darfurians own some livestock, and almost all of the refugees report the loss of these animals as well as all of their possessions. We closely examined reports of lost livestock for the seventy-nine households from Masteri represented in the ADS data. The numbers of lost animals are large, with especially large losses of cows, goats, and sheep (Figure 1.3). Young et al. further confirm this process of "asset stripping" in a nearby part of West Darfur:

> One case study describes how Antonov aircraft and helicopters would "bomb everything that moved," including water points, markets and herds/flocks of animals. Lorries were used to transport looted household contents – radios, clothes, pots and pans, mattresses and furniture. Once emptied, houses were burned down. The armed militia looted livestock in the surrounding areas, and there were also many rapes.[13]

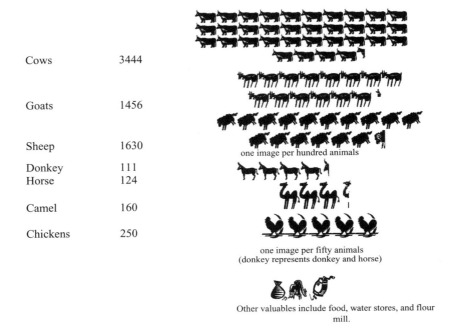

| Cows | 3444 |
| Goats | 1456 |
| Sheep | 1630 |

one image per hundred animals

| Donkey | 111 |
| Horse | 124 |
| Camel | 160 |
| Chickens | 250 |

one image per fifty animals
(donkey represents donkey and horse)

Other valuables include food, water stores, and flour mill.

FIGURE 1.3. Number of Lost Livestock Reported in the ADS Data.

This study concluded that these attacks resulted in a loss of livelihoods that is unprecedented in its scale in Darfur.

The Coalition for International Justice (CIJ) calculated the scale of the loss of sheep alone in Darfur:

> Adding up the numbers – 1.8 million internally displaced [persons], 200,000 refugees, add CIJs estimate of 400,000 deaths – one comes to a total of 2.4 million people who are directly affected by the conflict: they have been either displaced or have died as a result of the violence. With the rough estimate of two sheep per person and a livestock-loss ratio of 90 percent for displaced populations, one can calculate the high estimate of the number of lost sheep at 4.32 million. That number is over a third of the pre-conflict sheep stock.[14]

The scale of this loss of livestock was both massive and difficult to dispute. The CIJ also analyzed shifts in export volume and prices from

Darfur and concluded that the thefts of livestock probably were part of an evolving market in stolen animals that involved millions of dollars.[15] It concluded, "Once the violence was underway…, livestock looting may have been a lucrative by-product of the government's counter-insurgency campaign."[16] Thus livestock as well as land constituted incentives for the killings and displacement of Black African groups from Darfur.

## Crime Scenes of Group Destruction

The Sudanese government and the Janjaweed militia created circumstances and conditions intended to destroy the group life of Black Africans in Darfur: not only by killing but also by raping, stealing livestock, looting food, destroying food stores and seeds, poisoning wells, displacing people from their homes and villages, and then, in many cases, preventing or interfering with follow-up humanitarian care and assistance.[17] The cluster of settlements around Masteri was a massive crime scene.

As noted, the International Criminal Tribunal for the former Yugoslavia found related evidence of genocide ten years earlier in the Bosnian Muslim enclave of Srebrenica. The death toll in the cluster of settlements including Masteri may or may not rival the genocidal killing of Bosnian Muslims in Srebrenica in the mid-1990s, but the wholesale destruction of the conditions for Black African group life in Masteri and elsewhere in Darfur is parallel to what happened in Srebrenica. The Black farmers and villagers fled their homes and sought refuge in Sudanese internal displacement camps and refugee camps in Chad. The size of these camps indicates the success of the Sudanese government in removing Black Africans from their homes, lands, and group-linked lives and livelihoods in Darfur.

The Genocide Convention, quoted earlier in this chapter, purposefully includes in its definition making collective life unsustainable as a means of destroying a group in whole or in part. From the Warsaw ghetto in World War II to Srebrenica in the Balkan wars, this way of destroying group life is recognizable as genocide.[18] Even though he resisted until 2008 calling Darfur genocide, the ICC prosecutor remarked that "this strategy has been seen before. He continues, "In March 1995, President of Srpska Radovan Karadzic..., issued Directive 7. It specified that the Republika Srpska army was to 'by planned and well-thought out combat operations, create an unbearable situation of total insecurity with no hope of further survival or life for the inhabitants of Srebrenica.' The parallel to Darfur is clear.[19]

Furthermore, the resettlement of areas of Darfur by Arabs, some of whom are being recruited from outside Sudan, threatens to make the displacement of Black African groups from Darfur permanent. A 2004 Human Rights Watch report includes this eyewitness account:

> A twenty-seven-year-old farmer called Feisal said he saw "Janjaweed families coming from the north with their tents and baggage" in the first week of April. "They arrived in Geneina in cars with government cars behind," he said. "From Geneina, they took cars south.... Big cars, with thirty to forty in each car. I counted about thirteen families. Dar Masalit is becoming an Arab area. They are going to bring their families." Asked how he recognized the travelers as Arabs, he said: "Why do you ask this? Do you think we do not know? It is their color, their language and their clothes. They are not as we are."[20]

In mid-2007, humanitarian workers in Darfur indicated that the Sudanese government had brought tens of thousands of Arab settlers to Darfur from neighboring countries.[21] We discuss this resettlement in the final chapter of this book. Destruction and replacement of group life by all these means are at the heart of the meaning of genocide.

When large-scale attacks and forced migration escalated in Kosovo in the later 1990s, the Chief Prosecutor of the International Criminal Tribunal for the former Yugoslavia, Louise Arbour, went personally to a border town. Under her UN authority, she demanded entry to Kosovo for herself and a team of investigators to do crime scene analysis and collect evidence.[22] The border guards, under instructions from the Milosevic government in Belgrade, refused to let Arbour or her investigators enter. Arbour and her UN investigators only gained entry to Kosovo several months later after a bombing campaign and in the company of well-armed NATO ground troops. The Chief Prosecutor of the International Criminal Court, Luis Moreno Ocampo, faces similar problems of access from the Bashir-led Sudanese government in Khartoum.

Yet, it is not only international criminal law that often fails the victims of genocidal violence in Darfur. Criminology also fails to fully engage these victims or to learn from their experiences. The Atrocities Documentation Survey presents a unique opportunity that we use in this chapter to introduce the genocidal violence in Darfur. We do more with these data in later chapters. The ADS is a valuable resource for the advancement of a scientific criminology of genocide. Before we use these data further, however, we address the question of why criminologists have largely neglected the topic of genocide – the crime of crimes.

# 2 The Crime of Crimes

## Naming It

"Even Kofi Annan didn't want to call it genocide," my informant confided in exasperation. I asked him to explain, if the President of the United States, his Secretary of State, and Congress all called Darfur "the crime of crimes," why so few others answered the call to second this conclusion. Neither the European Union nor Human Rights Watch backed the Bush administration's genocide declaration. My informant continued, "Kofi Annan not only didn't want to call it genocide; he wanted the newly formed United Nations Commission of Inquiry on Darfur to draw its own independent conclusions about what to call it within a month."

The Commission followed from a resolution pushed through the UN Security Council by U.S. Secretary of State Powell in the fall of 2004. Kofi Annan delegated responsibility for the Commission to the Geneva-based UN High Commissioner on Human Rights, Louise Arbour.[1] As the former chief prosecutor of The Hague Tribunal, Arbour had indicted Slobodan Milosevic for crimes against humanity rather than genocide in the former Yugoslavia. Crimes against humanity are widespread and systematic attacks on civilians. In contrast, genocide requires proof of willful intent to destroy all or part of a racial, ethnic, national, or religious group.[2] Arbour's Tribunal successor, Carla Del Ponte, upped the Milosevic charges to genocide, and she was still trying to prove the elements of this crime three years later when Milosevic died in his jail cell.

Arbour prefers what she calls "real time" to "historical" international criminal justice, but she nonetheless insisted that Annan grant her at least six months to produce conclusions about the alleged genocide in Darfur. Arbour and Annan compromised on a time of three months to complete the Commission's work. The Commission staff members hastily set off on a twenty-day field study in Sudan. They then produced the outcome that Annan preferred: They found evidence of crimes against humanity and possibly even individual acts of genocide in Darfur, but no evidence of a full-blown, state-run genocide.

Although the United States responded more strongly than other nations to what it called genocide in Darfur, it also flip-flopped on this issue. As we note in the Preface, Secretary Powell first called Darfur a genocide but then failed to suggest further action. It was only reluctantly in 2005 that John Bolton, the American UN Ambassador and longtime critic of international courts, abstained on the Security Council motion to refer the Darfur case to the International Criminal Court. Bolton was reluctant because he personally had led U.S. government opposition to the formation and existence of the International Criminal Court (ICC) for several years and likely would have preferred to veto the referral.[3]

What are the sources of this American reluctance to engage and recognize the legitimacy of "the international rule of law"? One plausible answer we consider later in this chapter is that during the Cold War the United States did not want to work with its rival superpower, the Soviet Union, to develop international institutions of criminal law. Yet, with the Cold War over, why is there so much remaining American ambivalence about the prosecution and punishment of "the crime of crimes" in Darfur, as well as war crimes elsewhere? This book is an effort to explain, if not reduce, this ambivalence, for citizens as well as scholars. The slow development of international criminal law says as much or more about the history and attitudes of the United States itself as it does about other nations. The American discipline of criminology's neglect of genocide and war crimes is a parallel concern of this book.

These concerns explain why, on a fall morning, more than a year after the American tacit agreement to refer the Darfur case to the ICC, the first author of this book sat in the cafeteria of the court in The Hague talking to an American analyst for the court's Office of the Prosecutor. She regarded the U.S. determination that a genocide was occurring in Darfur as a foregone conclusion. This only highlighted the ambivalence of the American involvement in the case and the absence of a ready criminological understanding of the subject. She told me a personal story and then made two connected points that grounded her viewpoint.

This analyst had recently attended a conference in London that included a high-level Sudanese government official. Midway through the conference she heard the Sudanese official casually use the derogatory term "zurug" for Blacks.[4] She thought it reflected a deeply entrenched and unguardedly expressed racism in this otherwise polite and deferential London setting. She then noted a fact that is little known outside Sudan: Every person in an official position in the Sudanese government is immune from criminal prosecution under Sudan's National Security Act. Finally, she noted that the previous government also joined with military militias to keep order and undertake repressive attacks, resulting in hundreds of thousands of deaths in southern Sudan. Genocidal violence in Sudan was not new, and the Defense Minister in the former government was an early architect of its use.

She said that the scenario in west Sudan's Darfur region evolved out of neglect. The government used political manipulation and coercion by local Arab militias and the military to repel insurgent attacks against Sudanese military forces led by the small but growing Sudanese Liberation Movement (SLM) and the Justice and Equality Movement (JEM). She claimed that the government instigated divisions between nomadic Arab and Black African farming groups over land use in Darfur. The government used the lure of land and livestock to pit Arab against Black, further supported by a mix of military force, legal immunity and impunity, and the cooptation, coercion, and outright bribery of tribal elites. The lethal response to the insurgency is often called a scorched-earth policy to emphasize its breadth. "They [the government] had to know and anticipate that the consequences would be genocidally violent," she concluded. "The results couldn't have been a surprise."

I met an important Black African member of the ICC investigation team in the afternoon of the same day. His self-effacing manner belied his deep knowledge of the Darfur case. He challenged the arguments made by the court analyst to me that morning. To begin, he said that race was a "red flag" in the Darfur case. He emphasized the issue of displacement, rather than race. He insisted, resolutely and articulately, that the violence in Darfur was not a genocide. "The conflict is about land, not race," he observed. "It is about a desire to control the land in Darfur and the desire to displace those who have long held and farmed this land."

When I countered that racial epithets are common in attacks on Black African tribal groups in Darfur, he repeated that the conflict was about taking the land. When I insisted that the epithets were more about race than land, he responded that it was the actual behaviors we should note. "The people get killed when they get in the way" he said, "but it is more about getting them off the land" – along with making it impossible for them to return by killing their livestock, destroying their crops and seeds, poisoning their wells, and burning their homes. I protested that this sounded like destroying the conditions for reproducing and sustaining the life of a group, which is a key part of the definition of genocide. He countered that this was not the intent of the attacks. Rather, the point was to discourage the residents' return to the disputed land, whereas conviction for genocide required proving a clear intent to destroy a group in whole or in part. "This is displacement," he reasoned, "and the widespread nature of this displacement is a crime against humanity."

Gerard Prunier calls Darfur "the ambiguous genocide."[5] This terminology is consistent with the varying positions, for example, of the U.S. government, the UN Security Council and its appointed Commission, and the International Criminal Court. What is actually most surprising is that positions are so stridently defended, given the contrasting views. The legal debate is filling law journals. A lawyer-journalist, Samantha Power, provided a landmark legal history of the topic of genocide.[6] But what of the professionals, the scientists who take crime and criminal behavior more generally as their subject matter? These are the social scientists to whom we might logically look for further understanding of this topic. American criminologists are surprisingly silent about "the crime of crimes." The criminology of genocide is only in its infancy.

## Where Were the Criminologists?

By the 1950s, American criminology was already a scholarly field with a growing recognition among the social sciences. Most American universities offered criminology courses taught by sociologists. Senior scholars like Edwin Sutherland, president of the American Sociological Association, argued that the study of crime should be scientific and respected for its relevance to social policy and reform in America.[7] He coined the influential concept of white-collar crime. Younger scholars returning to academia after serving in the military in World War II, including Jewish students such as Albert Cohen,[8] studied with Sutherland and established their own careers. Given their knowledge of the Holocaust, it is reasonable to ask how and why the crime of crimes, the criminology of genocide, continues to be largely missing in criminological action.[9]

The study of crime is strongly influenced by the personal and social contexts of the researchers. Like other fields, it is a pursuit shaped within a sociology of knowledge.[10] As Gertrude Stein famously observed from her self-imposed exile in Paris, "The answers given depend on the questions asked." In contrast to the recent intense interest in Nazi Germany and the Holocaust, surprisingly few American citizens and scholars asked questions about genocide in the 1940s and 1950s. This lack of interest might be explained by a few conveniently forgotten facts of American history.

It is estimated that at least forty million indigenous peoples lived in these lands when European explorers and settlers found their ways to our shores. Fewer than ten million of those forty million indigenous Americans remained in 1650. The current Canadian government, with mixed humility, calls some of the descendants of these peoples the First Nations. Three-quarters of these First Nations people died, as many African victims of genocide do today, of deadly disease as well as systematic slaughter. Some Americans today recognize these deaths as crimes against humanity or genocide, but of course our government still does not. This may begin to explain why we fail to recognize "the crime of crimes."[11] Fein insists that the "primary deterent is our own inhibitions and lack of boldness."[12] Yet, some were bold enough to break the silence.

## Criminology's Forgotten Voice

Even in the 1940s, some spoke with raised voices about crimes against humanity. The Harvard criminologist and law professor, Sheldon Glueck, worked tirelessly and wrote extensively on war crimes for a short period during and after World War II. Glueck's contributions flowed from both his experiences as a Jewish immigrant from Europe and his American legal education. This part of Glueck's career lasted just over three years, from 1943 to 1946. During this period, he wrote articles in prominent legal journals and books about the need to establish an international criminal court to prosecute and punish crimes of war and against humanity.[13] Yet, Glueck stopped doing this work rather abruptly, and although he is still remembered today – with a prominent award of the American Society of Criminology named in his honor – he is almost exclusively remembered for his studies with his wife Eleanor on delinquency.[14] His work on international criminal justice is barely known to criminologists. So the question is not what made Sheldon Glueck work so hard on international criminal justice, but why so few remember this work and what made him stop pursuing it.

Such questions are particularly telling, given how much Glueck accomplished in barely three years of involvement with international criminal law. In addition to his articles and books, Glueck made his voice heard in an influential statement to congressional hearings that presaged passage of a resolution "to declare a governmental policy in relation to the apprehension and punishment of war criminals."[15] He also joined seventeen participants in a 1945 London planning conference for the Nuremberg Trial.[16]

Glueck did not do this work in an easy environment. No more than a day after Glueck and the trial planning team settled into their quarters in London's Claridge Hotel, battles began over trial strategy and the preparation of evidence. The battles contained hints of major problems to come for both Glueck and international criminal justice. Significantly, the planners immediately dismissed a role for Jewish refugee groups in providing evidence for the prosecution of Nazi war criminals. The minutes of an early meeting summarily concluded that "their materials are mostly gossip and that their evaluations are very emotional. It was considered that they were not a very useful source for evidence."[17] The team rejected even the University of Chicago psychiatrist Bruno Bettelheim's accounts of his own experiences at Dachau and Buchenwald concentration camps, calling them of "questionable value."[18]

Undeterred and realizing that the trial required systematic evidence, Glueck devised a comprehensive "Control System" built around compactly designed "Digest Forms" that summarized interrogation reports and documentary proof. Supreme Court Justice Robert Jackson, who headed the American prosecution team, acknowledged that Glueck's "system" was "essential to the Nuremberg Trial."[19] The influence of Glueck's work is further reflected in a series of early positions he took in his congressional statement and writings.

Glueck's approach sidestepped the popular support that the pollster George Gallup found for Churchill's and Roosevelt's initial position that, in dealing with the Nazi leadership, "the United Nations have a perfect right to do as they please.... They can shoot them without any legal proceedings."[20] Glueck acknowledged this right, but he argued that "solemn arraignment followed by trial in an international court is to be preferred...in order to inform public opinion...and to fix the record of history."[21] Roosevelt gradually accepted this view. In so doing, Roosevelt had to overrule his Jewish Treasury Secretary, Henry Morgenthau, who wanted not only to execute the Nazi leadership but also to deindustrialize Germany by turning it into a nation of farmers.

Glueck also opposed the arguments of Gordon Allport, his famous colleague from Harvard's Psychology Department.[22] Allport advised that leaders like Hitler should be put in institutions for the criminally insane in Allied countries. Glueck insisted that these leaders should instead be treated as criminally responsible (i.e., rather than as criminally irrational). Glueck backed Roosevelt's white-shoe Wall Street lawyer and war secretary, Henry Stimson, who wanted trials of Nazi leaders to assign this criminal liability.

Glueck articulated a series of positions that later earned wide acceptance in contemporary international law. First, Glueck anticipated the need for a forceful response to the assertion, made for the defense at the opening of the Nuremberg Trial, that war crime prosecution and punishment was ex post facto or retrospective law (i.e., created and imposed after commission of the acts). Glueck insisted in his congressional statement that "as citizens of a State and members of an army or navy, the defendants are presumed to have had notice of...provisions of civilized law. And their governments have on several occasions been solemnly warned by official spokesmen...that their subjects will be held to strict legal accountability for their atrocities."[23]

In a subsequent *Harvard Law Review* article, Glueck further dismissed the retrospective law defense with this commonsense as well as common law response:

> Surely,...Hitler, Himmler, Goering, Ribbentrop, Frank, Keitel, Doenitz, and the rest of the unholy alliance and supreme authority in Nazi Germany knew full well that murder, whether wholesale or retail, whether committed in pursuance of a gigantic conspiracy to

disregard all treaties and to wage lawless wars or of a smaller conspiracy evolved by a group of domestic murderers. Surely, also, the accused knew that they could be executed for their deeds without being granted the privilege of any trial at all. Can they now be heard to complain that they had no notice that they would have to stand trial under an interpretation of international law which they do not like because they deem it to involve retroactivity?[24]

This retort is today recognized by the prominent Nuremberg scholar, Michael Marrus, as the definitive resolution of this issue.[25] Yet, few criminologists know about Glueck's role in resolving this issue or his other contributions to Nuremberg.

Second, Glueck indicated his clear preference for an international criminal court over a military tribunal, noting that "it would be preferable for the United Nations to establish a special international criminal court, with its own statute and with uniform procedure." He recommended that this special court "should consist of a simplified combination of the best features of the Anglo-American and Continental systems."[26] The Allies adopted this combined approach at Nuremberg, setting the foundation for the UN's international criminal tribunals for the former Yugoslavia and Rwanda and, most recently, for the Rome Treaty establishing the International Criminal Court that received the Darfur case.

Third, Glueck recognized and rejected the resort to sovereignty as a defense against the prosecution of crimes against humanity within a nation. He saw that national sovereignty was a convenient privilege of power. Glueck argued that "to allow the fact that many atrocities were committed inside Germany – some against non-Axis nationals, others against Axis nationals – to prevent the trial of Germans for such atrocities, would be a triumph of bookish legalism and the death of both common sense and justice. There is nothing sacrosanct about the territorial theory of jurisdiction."[27]

Fourth, Glueck addressed the issue of what are called "superior orders." This is the defense that an accused must act in obedience to orders from his superior. He simply responded that "an unlawful act of a soldier, sailor or officer in obedience to an order of his government or his military superior is no defense if when he committed it he either actually knew, or considering the circumstances, had reasonable grounds for knowing that the act ordered is unlawful."[28] The logic of this position is recognized as the well-known "Nuremberg principle" regarding individuals who are issued illegal orders.

Glueck's four contributions influenced the Nuremberg Trial and international criminal law of this era. However, his work was also surprisingly important in theoretical terms that are even less well recognized today. Glueck laid the groundwork for an implicit theoretical and macro-sociological approach to the explanation of genocide and war crimes. We outline this approach here and in conjunction with Sutherland's theory of white-collar crime at the end of this chapter. This contribution is unexpected because Glueck is widely known in criminology for his assertively atheoretical research on delinquency. However, Glueck insisted on the need for a structural understanding of the politics and business of war crimes.

First, Glueck argued for a sweeping definition of war crimes that included crimes of preparation – including knowing and allowing, without attempting to prevent, preparations for war crimes – by persons in political and military positions of authority. Inclusion of these crimes of preparation was an explicit recognition of the role of the state and its agents in the instigation of war crimes. By the 1970s, criminologists such as William Chambliss and Robert Seidman, responding to events like the Vietnam War, again insisted we recognize war crimes as "crimes of and by the state."[29] Their work followed Glueck's earlier characterization of the prosecution of Nazi politicians and military leaders for their involvement in such crimes as "the vindication of the laws of civilized humanity."[30] This characterization anticipated the concept of crimes against humanity.

Second, Glueck emphasized the importance of a definition of war crimes that went beyond politicians and the military to incorporate the crucial role of powerful industrialists and bankers, manufacturers, and businessmen "who, directly or indirectly, participated in or conspired to commit crimes (largely wholesale thefts and receipt of stolen goods) as part of a general scheme of economic conquest and looting to go hand in hand with the military."[31] The confiscation of land and loot is a large part of the Darfur war crimes we investigate in this book, as it has been in many other settings. There is special irony, which will become more meaningful when we discuss Sutherland's contributions later, that when Glueck discussed this kind of organized war crime by businesspeople he invoked the terminology of "respectable criminals," observing that "all these more 'respectable' scoundrels are just as surely involved in the black calendar of crimes as are the militarists."[32]

Third, and most controversially, Glueck proposed that simple membership in designated "criminal" organizations is evidence of war crime activity. His position, adopted at Nuremberg and implemented more broadly in Germany thereafter, was that "membership in certain organizations notorious for their policy and program of cruelty, such as the Gestapo and employees of concentration and extermination camps, should create a presumption of guilt and throw the burden of proof of innocence upon the accused."[33] This procedure expanded the possibilities for prosecuting and punishing whole collectivities of participants in war crimes, for example, by using the charge of conspiracy.

The same Nuremberg scholar who credited Glueck for disposing of the retroactivity defense, Michael Marrus, argued that "the conspiracy charge... did not serve the cause of history well."[34] This conclusion is partly based on the fact that conspiracy charges are not popular in European jurisdictions. Yet, today, the conspiracy charge is a feature of more than 25 percent of all federal prosecutions in the United States, including use of the famous RICO statute to prosecute organized and white-collar crime figures. A conspiracy formulation was a central part of the ICTY prosecution of Slobodan Milosevic along with others for a "joint criminal enterprise" that included genocide. A recent article highlights the novelty of this use of the concept of conspiracy by comparing and contrasting

> ...the function of conspiracy law in the prosecution of international crimes before the International Military Tribunal (IMT) at Nuremberg, where the concept gave rise to a remarkably innovative and highly controversial conspiracy theory that revolved around the concept of "criminal organization," and the function of conspiracy law in the prosecution of international crimes before the International Criminal Tribunal for the former Yugoslavia (ICTY) at The Hague, where the concept has left a mark on a similarly innovative and equally controversial conspiracy theory that revolves around the concept of "joint criminal enterprise."[35]

Glueck spearheaded this innovation at Nuremberg. As explained later in this chapter and book, this use of the conspiracy approach infuses contemporary prosecutions of war crimes with an inherently sociological emphasis on collective processes that define the very nature of the charges and evidence of crimes against humanity and genocide.

Glueck specifically outlined how the conspiratorial theory could be applied in dealing with organizations like the Gestapo. He did this in a July 1945 memo written to Justice Jackson for the London planning meeting. He first acknowledged that the conspiratorial concept was controversial. Nonetheless, he then recommended that "separate defendants should be prosecuted as members and participants in a conspiracy... among them setting up of an organization known as the Gestapo." In turn, "the judgment would then be that the accused are guilty of this conspiracy. To support its verdict and judgment, the Joint Military Tribunal... would then set out a series of numbered findings of fact that the Gestapo (which in itself is a conspiratorial organization) was an organized association of torturers and murderers, a partnership in wholesale crime."[36]

Ultimately, Glueck suggested that smaller military commissions should prosecute the members of the Gestapo not named in the main trial for conspiracy to murder, as well as for overt acts of murder.

Because the lesser commissions could take "judicial notice" of the main trial finding of conspiracy, which was the resource-intensive and consuming preliminary task, these later trials could then be conducted more quickly and in large volume. Marrus worried, however, that these trials could become contagious in a manner like the witchcraft hysteria in Salem, Massachusetts. The contemporary best-selling German novel, *The Reader*, describes a "minor" trial of this kind in the aftermath of Nuremberg.[37] However, the feature of the conspiracy formulation of particular interest for this book is that Glueck was clearly building on ideas about criminal social organization. These ideas are still highly relevant to the development of major international prosecutions. Yet, Glueck's contribution was the isolated exception, rather than the beginning of a tradition of criminological work of this kind on international criminal law.

## Nuremberg and the Postwar Period

Because Glueck's work was in many ways farsighted, and because there was much to be done in that area, it may be difficult to understand why he did not himself continue in this field. However, Glueck stopped this work almost immediately after the first Nuremberg Trial ended. Working largely with his wife, who served as a "research assistant," and otherwise in relative isolation as a criminologist in a law school, he failed to develop either a field of study or a collection of students to continue his international war crimes work. In a much broader sense, because the Nuremberg Trial is such a celebrated part of American history, it may also seem anomalous that the United States after the war became and remained ambivalent about international criminal law and the prosecution of war crimes. Between Nuremberg and the creation of the international criminal tribunals for the former Yugoslavia and Rwanda, the United States essentially stonewalled for a half-century all efforts to advance international criminal law. Austin Turk is one of the few American criminologists who has offered a plausible explanation for this inaction.

Turk's explanation for the short life of Nuremberg and the ensuing failure to create successor institutions is based on the concept of "spheres of influence."[38] Even as the Nuremberg Trial was unfolding, the Western Allies and the Soviet Union were already developing separate and opposing spheres of influence. This separation led to a tacit and mutual recognition that the United States and the Soviet Union were dividing the world into competing regions in which neither world power particularly thought it plausible or advantageous to have international rules of law. The concept of spheres of influence held that each superpower best served its respective interests by forbidding the other power from interfering in its respective area of control. Instead, each claimed within its own sphere a right of forceful intervention for itself.

Turk points to the Monroe Doctrine for Latin America as a classic example of this concept. Under this doctrine, American governments frequently intervened conspicuously (for example, in the Nicaraguan, Dominican, and numerous other invasions) as well as covertly (in the overthrow of Allende's elected government in Chile) in Latin America. The Soviet Union used the spheres of influence concept to justify its invasions of Hungary and Czechoslovakia.[39] The shift in the balance of power in the aftermath of World War II, with the Soviet Union emerging as the key adversary of the West in general, and of the United States in particular, prevented the serious contemplation of international law enforcement beyond Nuremberg.

Nearly a half-century later, with the end of the Cold War at hand, the legally dubious "spheres of influence" understanding weakened, and the role of international criminal law gained renewed plausibility. Most criminologists took little notice of this shift. However, the breakup of the Soviet Union and the end of the Cold War, the murderous outbreak of violence in the former Yugoslavia, and the scrambling of the Western Allies to formulate a legitimate response to the post–Cold War challenges all joined in strengthening the opportunity for international criminal law enforcement that involved a more universal and less nation-based jurisdiction. This enforcement occurred first through the location- and time-specific International Criminal Tribunals for the former Yugoslavia and Rwanda, and then in the more comprehensive and permanent International Criminal Court.

Yet, we still must explain why the United States continued for so long to be at best ambivalent and more often obstructionist in its approach to the development of these institutions of international criminal law. This continued ambivalence and obstructionism imply that there is more to be said about the United States itself and in a parallel way about the slowness of American criminology to take up study of this topic. To learn more, it is useful to consider the conflict between Sheldon Glueck and Edwin Sutherland in the postwar American context.

## Postwar Origins of the Sutherland-Glueck Debate

Glueck's 1946 book on the Nuremberg Trial was his last major contribution on this topic, and he is today better remembered for his longitudinal research with his wife Eleanor on the adolescent lives of delinquents.[40] The postwar period included a major debate between Glueck and Edwin Sutherland, whom we briefly introduced earlier in relation to his famous research on white-collar crime. The irony is that this debate was not about war crimes and white-collar crime, but rather about the use of quantitative research methods in the study of more ordinary delinquency and crime. The further and more consequential irony of this debate is that Sheldon Glueck and Edwin Sutherland never acknowledged that they shared important views about the role of social hierarchy and social organization in the explanation of war crimes and white-collar crimes. They also struggled against some similarly repressive practical and societal pressures in developing their respective concepts and careers. Their scholarship would have been better served by cooperation than by competition.

To better understand the political environment that Glueck and Sutherland confronted in the peak of their careers in the 1940s, and that their successors struggled with in the 1950s and well into the 1960s, it is instructive to introduce another crucial figure: Raphael Lemkin. Like Glueck, Lemkin was a Jewish immigrant. Both came from families that experienced the rise of the Nazi movement in Europe, and both benefited enormously from the opportunity to pursue their adult lives in the United States. But whereas Glueck devoted only about three years of his adult career to international criminal law, Lemkin devoted most of his life to this endeavor. Glueck may actually have outlived Lemkin by more than twenty years as a result.

Lemkin coined the term "genocide" and saw it institutionalized in the 1948 UN Convention on the Prevention and Punishment of Genocide. Yet, Lemkin died nearly penniless and of apparent exhaustion without seeing the Genocide Convention ratified by the United States. Indeed, both Glueck and Lemkin died before the United States ratified the convention in 1988. The United States was no faster in ratifying the genocide concept than most criminologists were in studying it.

Lemkin literally worked himself to death in the cause of genocide, whereas Glueck decided to terminate the war crimes and international law phase of his career. The essence of this story is in part that it was not a good "career move," personally or professionally, to make issues surrounding the Holocaust the center of one's life at the turn of the mid-twentieth century.

Peter Novick gives the background for this story in his historical account, *The Holocaust in American Life*.[41] Although today it is widely estimated that from six million to eight million Jews died in Nazi Germany during the Holocaust, by late 1944 most Americans still believed the number was at most 100,000, and perhaps even lower. Even by the end of the war, when Glueck decided to end his concentration on the topic of war crimes, most Americans believed that fewer than one million people had died in the Holocaust, and this figure included non-Jews as well as Jews. Latent anti-Semitism remained common during this period, even if it was not a deeply felt or dominant prejudice.

Novick notes that an older generation of Jewish immigrants in the 1940s still warned their American children that "a Jew did not 'make rishis'": "To 'make rishis' was to stir up a fuss of some kind, and it was a cardinal sin, for it supposedly made Jews vulnerable to the potential wrath of the Christian world."[42] Anti-Semitism still existed in American life, even if in a more muted postwar form.

Sheldon Glueck accepted this point and was not surprised when he encountered his London colleagues' skepticism of Jewish refugees, and even of Bruno Bettelheim, as the assembled team of advisors began to plan the Nuremberg Trial. Justice Jackson, a consummate politician as well as a judge, articulated this point when he noted, with regard to his limited use of Jewish lawyers in the trial, that "most of them felt...they ought to do their work in the background and not be put forward into places of great prominence in order to avoid the impression that it was a Jewish enterprise."[43] Glueck was not a reticent personality, and although he was not surprised by this attitude, it is doubtful that he agreed with the decision to pass him over and not allow him to participate in the Nuremberg Trial itself.

Yet, Glueck understood the parameters of his situation as a Jewish immigrant, albeit also a Harvard professor. As a Jew, as an immigrant, and even as a criminologist, he was a marginal figure in the Harvard Law School.[44] Glueck was careful not to articulate his positions in terms of the victimization of the Jews in the Holocaust. Justice Jackson initially wanted the Nuremberg Trial to be about the war of aggression waged by the Germans. It was only when the overwhelming evidence of the scale of the Holocaust unceasingly accumulated, and was finally confirmed in the devastating films of the concentration camps, that Jackson shifted ground and made charges of crimes against humanity a focus of the trial. Glueck worked pragmatically within this context, for example, framing his arguments about conspiracy theory in terms of the criminal organization that made possible the waging of an aggressive war. Glueck's files at Harvard documented the dimensions of the Holocaust and its cost in Jewish lives, but Glueck did not make this his focal point.

The postwar period was also problematic in terms of acknowledging the Holocaust. Novick notes that, after the war, a prominent anti-communist journalist charged that the desire for revenge against the Nazis prolonged the war crimes trials. The American Military

Government in Germany purged Jewish refugees from work as civilian investigators because of doubts about their objectivity. The headline of a *Saturday Evening Post* editorial – "Nuremberg Verdicts Cool Ardor of Germany for Defending West" – reflected growing fears about the Soviet Union and the desire to redevelop Germany as an ally in the fight against communism.

An historical association was sometimes even noted between the immigration of Jews to America and the Bolshevik Revolution. Novick concludes, "There was a . . . serious constraint on public Jewish discourse about the Holocaust and Nazism in the early Cold War years: fear of seeming to confirm a less ancient but potentially more threatening stereotype." This stereotype linked postwar American Jews to the new and rising enemy threat of communism.[45]

The emerging Cold War with the Soviet Union therefore restricted references to Jewish victimization and the Holocaust. Glueck observed this restriction in his work, and his own Jewishness likely played a part in his decision to terminate his work on war crimes. Raphael Lemkin also understood this aspect of the postwar period, but he persisted in his work on genocide by a different means. The very purpose of the term that he coined was to emphasize the association between the extermination and nonlethal as well as lethal targeting of a specific racial, ethnic, religious, or national group. Yet, even Lemkin framed his arguments about genocide in an eclectic fashion that elided the specific ethnic intent of the Holocaust: the annihilation of the Jewish people.

Thus, Lemkin described the Nazi movement in Germany in terms of the diversity of its targets, insisting that "the Nazi leaders had stated very bluntly their intent to wipe out the Poles, the Russians; to destroy demographically and culturally the French element in Alsace-Lorraine, the Slovenians in Carniola and Carinthia. They almost achieved their goal in exterminating the Jews and gypsies in Europe."[46] In fact, Lemkin received much of his financial support from Lithuanian American and Ukrainian American groups.[47]

The point for our purposes is not just that the Holocaust itself received so little recognition in American and Jewish public discourse from the end of the war through the 1960s. More relevant is that racial, ethnic, and religious prejudice and bigotry were not emphasized in the study of war crimes and genocide. The purging from public discourse and criminology of the role of anti-Semitism in the Holocaust meant that a key causal factor was downplayed. Moreover, potential major figures in the development of this field, such as Sheldon Glueck, could find little opportunity or incentive to meaningfully and successfully build a career around the topic of war crimes. Thus, a supression of the role of anti-Semitism (and the connection of this denial to the Cold War with the Soviet Union) was likely a major part of the failure of public discourse and criminology to develop an early and sustained pursuit of the topic of genocide.

It is a small conceptual move from recognizing the role of suppressed anti-Semitism in delaying attention to the Holocaust to seeing a parallel role of racism in downplaying the genocide in Darfur. Before making this point, however, it is useful to appreciate the full irony of the debate between Sheldon Glueck and Edwin Sutherland during the founding years of American criminology.

## White-Collar Crimes and War Crimes

Sheldon Glueck pursued his quantitative studies of the "multiple factors" involved in the causation of delinquency before, during, and after his work on war crimes; this work on delinquency causation therefore occupied the larger part of Glueck's career. Throughout the war and after, from the late 1930s and throughout the 1940s, Glueck was the target of a withering and unremitting critique by Edwin Sutherland of these quantitative studies of delinquency. John Laub and Robert Sampson chart the course of this encounter and conclude that "the Sutherland-Glueck exchange became heated and took on the trappings of an intellectual shoot-out that lasted some 15 years."[48] The dispute did not cease until after Sutherland's death in 1950; from beyond the grave, Sutherland published a final review critiquing a biological determinist position that he wrongly associated with Glueck's position.[49]

The irony is that both Glueck and Sutherland developed theoretically compatible contributions on war crimes and white-collar crimes. The politics of their confrontation enhanced Sutherland's career, but simultaneously undermined the legacy that both of these scholars together could have contributed based on their overlapping understandings.

Glueck is widely recognized and remembered for his rough and overbearing manner. His manner may have resulted from his insecurity about being an immigrant Jew in a Harvard University that was anything but immigrant or Jewish. Sutherland, in contrast, was the white, Anglo-Saxon son of a Protestant minister who moved with relative ease through a highly successful career. He chaired the sociology department at Indiana University and was elected president of the American Sociological Association. Laub and Sampson summarize Glueck and Sutherland's differing personas this way: "The Gluecks suffered from social awkwardness and a severe difficulty in public relations. Whereas Sutherland was well liked and perceived to be 'humble' and 'gentle' . . . , the Gluecks were stubborn and pompous."[50]

The American theorist Erving Goffman would have said that Sheldon Glueck lacked the "impression management" skills of Sutherland. The French theorist, Pierre Bourdieu, would have said that Sutherland understood "the rules of the game" in his emerging field of sociology, whereas Glueck did not. Sutherland used Glueck as a foil to establish his claims that only his field of sociology and his theory of differential association could provide the necessary and sufficient explanation for delinquency and other forms of crime. Laub and Sampson note that, in the 1930s and 1940s, Sutherland reviewed almost all of the Gluecks' books on delinquency. He nonetheless insisted in a personal note to Glueck that he "did not desire to acquire an institutional status as a critic of your work."[51]

It is difficult to avoid the conclusion that Sutherland knew exactly what he was doing and that he believed he was doing it in the role of what Laub and Sampson identify as "the warrior of sociology's coup of criminology... linked to his social position and rising influence in the sociological discipline."[52] Sutherland's influence and position explain part of why his differential association theory of white-collar crime is today so well remembered and Glueck's work on war crimes is largely forgotten. Sutherland probably understood that this would be the outcome and that Glueck's attention to war crimes would likely be his undoing. Sutherland understood and moved effectively within the social milieu of 1950s America.

Sutherland nonetheless faced his own challenges. By addressing the topic of white-collar crime, Sutherland took his sociological perspective to important new ground that required attacking protective barriers of class, power, and status. His original manuscript on white-collar crime boldly identified by name the corporations he called criminal. He persisted in his desire to reveal these names, thereby dramatizing the heights of white-collar crime in America, until his publisher's lawyers warned that they and he, and his university as well, could be sued.[53] Sutherland ultimately deleted the corporations' names, and they were not revealed until the republication of *White Collar Crime: The Uncut Version* by Yale University Press in 1983.

Sutherland also broached the topic of war crimes in his original book, but he was cautious. His war crimes chapter is restricted to illegal war profiteering by corporations, whereas the Holocaust, the Jews, and the Nuremberg Trial go unmentioned. Sutherland understood that his attacks on powerful corporations risked angering not only the corporations but also their powerful boards of directors and executives. Still, there was popular support for this kind of critique, which was in the muckraking tradition of American journalism and the populist tradition of American politics.

In the immediate postwar period, enthusiasm quickly waned for pursuing the fate of Jewish victims and punishing the perpetrators of the

Nazi Holocaust. Attention shifted to rebuilding Germany as an ally against the Soviets. There was declining support for prolonging the prosecution of German war crimes, much less considering the possibility of war crimes by the Allied Forces.

We noted earlier the questions that the study of war crimes could pose for our understanding of America's foundational encounters with its indigenous peoples, as well as our national history with race and slavery. Even in Sutherland and Glueck's time, critics questioned the Allies' methods of submarine warfare and the carpet firebombing of German cities, not to mention the use of the atomic bomb in Hiroshima and Nagasaki. More recently, the images of a Lieutenant William Calley, Robert McNamara, Henry Kissinger, or Donald Rumsfeld being indicted, detained, and placed on trial outside the United States in an international court raise further questions.[54] These are reasons enough to imagine why ultimately neither Glueck nor Sutherland staked their careers in the 1940s on the investigation and explanation of war crimes and why the United States did not ratify the Geneva Convention on Genocide until 1988.

Yet, there is also reason to think about what Glueck might have accomplished through a collaboration – building on his access and contributions to the planning of the Nuremberg Trial – with Sutherland, working within the framework of his developing theory of differential association and his understanding of the link between white-collar crimes and financial war crimes. Glueck's wartime work brought attention to the concept of conspiracy as an explanation for the combined involvement of political, military, business, and industrial groups in war crimes. Sutherland's writing brought attention to the differential social organization of a range of such groups in crime and its control, as well as the role played by differential definitions or ideals and ideology in organizing such crime and state responses to it.[55] Social and political limitations – on considering anti-Semitism and racism in these differential definitions and on acknowledging American involvement in its own war crimes – restricted the possibilities for the kind of theoretical synthesis and theoretical advances imagined here.

We are still coming to terms with the meaning of race as a social construct. These limitations and the connected, ideologically coercive, sociopolitical context of the 1940s and 1950s clearly affected the careers of both Glueck and Sutherland. More encouraging signs of theoretical innovation and synthesis awaited the civil rights era with its expressions of Black consciousness, the end of the Cold War, and a more reflective post–Vietnam war political environment.

Yet, Glueck clearly recognized that the Nazi war machine perpetrated the biggest white-collar crimes of the twentieth century in the process of reorganizing Germany around the destruction and extermination of the Jews. His arguments made specific reference to the fortunes amassed by German industrialists and financial elites. Sutherland's differential association theory did not address the state support that this kind of activity involved. Yet, his focus on associations between these ideas and with the persons who advanced them explained how otherwise ordinary people became involved in highly organized as well as financially rewarding crimes, including war crimes.

According to his differential association theory, Sutherland argued that persons become involved in activities like white-collar crime because they are immersed in cultures that define illegal practices, including illegal business practices, as acceptable. He focused on the facilitating role of commercial clichés like "business is business" in advancing and implementing differential definitions and associations. In the same way, he today no doubt would have highlighted the more contemporary notion that "greed is good" and its role in encouraging enterprising innovation, especially when the innovative practices covertly and even overtly involve cutting legal corners. Sutherland explained that such ideas become influential because they are transmitted within business groups that are isolated from competing viewpoints and because "the persons who define business practices as undesirable and illegal are customarily called 'communists' or 'socialists' and their definitions carry little weight."[56]

Imagine that Glueck and Sutherland decided to join their ideas about the criminal organized conspiracies involving collaborations between the

Nazi military and industrialists. It is plausible that they could have found common theoretical ground. Who better than Glueck and Sutherland to have explained the significance, for example, of Albert Speer's work as the "architect" of Hitler's military-industrial complex? Speer designed and masterminded the expansion of the industrial base of Germany and ran the arsenal that made the war and the Holocaust possible. Speer harnessed the labor of twelve million German and foreign workers. He simultaneously organized and choreographed the annual Nuremberg rallies celebrating Nazi ideals. These events were held in "a massive stadium that held a quarter of a million people arrayed in ranks of hypnotizing precision, shouting themselves into an orgiastic frenzy at the words of Adolf Hitler."[57] The master filmmaker propagandist Leni Riefenstahl first captured for Germans the deadly mesmerizing force of Adolf Hitler in *Triumph of the Will*, and then sanitized his "New Germany" for the world in *Olympia*.[58] This fusion of business organization, war crimes, and cinematic propaganda was a once-in-a-century subject matter for a differential organization theory of genocide. But this collaboration was not to be.

Such a collaboration by Glueck and Sutherland would have given a criminological relevance to the explanation of the genocidal violence and victimization of the Holocaust. Sutherland acknowledged the need to elaborate his theory of differential association in terms of the differential social organization of crime within and across the various strata of the American social structure. However, Glueck abandoned his work on war crimes and international criminal law for the study of delinquency, and Sutherland persisted in his critiques of Glueck's quantitative studies of delinquency while largely limiting his own writing about white-collar crime to its domestic economic implications.

Were Gluck and Sutherland simply the mired captives of petty academic jealousies? Did lingering latent postwar anti-Semitism impede both Glueck and Sutherland's attention to war crimes and genocide? Did America's tortured history of mistreatment of its indigenous and minority populations and its militaristic foreign policies deter Glueck and

Sutherland from extending their substantive agendas to include international implications? Whatever the answers to these questions, Glueck and Sutherland left much work undone. For several decades following the 1940s, American criminologists predominantly followed Glueck and Sutherland's leads in focusing their attention on domestic forms of crime. Others eventually took up international and humanitarian work on the enormous problems associated with war crimes, but, as we see next, in ways that neglected some of the most important possibilities of a criminology of genocide and war crimes.

# 3 While Criminology Slept

*with Heather Schoenfeld*

## Finding the Victims

From Vietnam to civil rights and baseball, there is perhaps no more revered chronicler of recent American history than the late David Halberstam.[1] So it is striking that the index of Halberstam's exhaustive account, *The Fifties,* does not contain a single entry for international criminal law, war crimes, Nuremberg, or the Holocaust. Americans in the middle years of the twentieth century simply gave little thought to these issues. Criminologists joined other Americans in moving on with the postwar baby boom and its concerns about the next generation's rather than the last generation's problems. In the case of criminology, this meant a preoccupation with postwar adolescence and the problems of juvenile delinquency. Edwin Sutherland's student Albert Cohen spoke to these new concerns with his landmark book, *Delinquent Boys,*[2] and Sheldon Glueck began and ended the decade with research monographs on delinquency.[3] Audiences flocked to see *West Side Story* and *Rebel without a Cause.* Americans in the immediate postwar period feared the threats posed by communism and delinquency more than crimes against humanity and genocide.

Yet, Sutherland awakened Americans to new problems of white-collar crime. At about the same time, Sutherland's neighbor and colleague at Indiana University in Bloomington, Alfred Kinsey, fascinated Americans with his interviews with samples of college students and adults about their sexual behavior.[4] This work provided an entertaining as well as informative diversion from memories of World War II; it also popularized new social scientific methods of population sampling and survey research.

Within a decade of Kinsey's first probing survey interventions into America's bedrooms, criminologists adapted similar self-report survey techniques to the study of delinquency and criminal behavior.[5] Junior and senior high schools provided systematic samples of students whom criminologists questioned with anonymous paper-and-pencil surveys about illicit behaviors and their presumed causes. Government researchers soon also asked household samples of adults about their experiences as crime victims.[6] These annual surveys eventually charted the long upward arc of U.S. violent crime for most of the last quarter of the twentieth century, followed by the prolonged downward trajectory beginning in the 1990s and lasting into the early years of the twenty-first century. This innovation in data collection ultimately provided a tool used worldwide to document war and human rights crimes.

Although Alfred Kinsey studied sexual behavior exclusively, his surveys institutionalized a methodology finally adapted in the 1990s for research on morbidity and mortality in concentration, displacement, and refugee camps. This research exposed the extensiveness of war and human rights crimes, including the use of sexual assaults, enslavement, and rape as instruments of genocide and crimes against humanity. Yet, criminologists did not lead the way in this research, even in the 1990s. Instead, it was public health researchers who recognized the possibilities of these survey tools for the study of humanitarian emergencies – nearly a half-century after Kinsey began his work. The government criminologists came to this research even later.

Thus, the U.S. State Department in 2004 launched one of the first large-scale victimization surveys designed specifically to substantiate charges of genocide, the Atrocities Documentation Survey (ADS), in Chad refugee camps. The State Department collaborated on the ADS with the U.S. Agency for International Development (USAID) and the Coalition for International Justice (CIJ), an international nonprofit advocacy group. This survey of refugees who fled from Darfur to Chad overcame problems of access to Sudan's western region of Darfur by focusing on the bombings, killings, rapes, property theft and destruction, and related victimizations experienced by fleeing refugees. We introduce this survey in greater detail in Chapter 4. In 2004, Colin Powell charged Sudan with genocide in Darfur on the basis of this survey.[7]

Powell acted in the context of a renewed concern about genocide. Americans reawakened to the horrors of the Holocaust in the early 1960s. At first, reminders of these events sparked only limited and wavering attention. *The Diary of Anne Frank* attracted a modest audience as a Broadway play.[8] Hannah Arendt generated some discussion and debate with her *New Yorker* magazine essays and book about Israel's capture and trial of Adolf Eichmann, *Eichmann in Jerusalem*.[9] The public displayed both curiosity and ambivalence about revisiting these murderous events.

The founding of Amnesty International in 1961 signaled a new awareness of war crimes, but this organization did not become fully active in the United States until the 1970s, and even then it refrained from direct lobbying efforts. The awarding of the Nobel Peace Prize to Amnesty International in 1977 symbolized the growing recognition of the activist potential of this organization.

Israel's Six Day War in 1967 and the Yom Kippur War in 1973 reminded American Jews that the Holocaust survivors and descendants of the Holocaust experience were still at risk.[10] In these same years, the Vietnam War spawned a broad-based opposition movement, a form of activism that was spurred on by the revelation of war crimes committed by American forces, most notably in the My Lai massacre.[11] Conflict theorists of crime made these events a part of their theoretical accounts,[12] but criminologists did relatively little research on the events themselves.

The Carter administration made human rights a part of its political agenda in the last half of the 1970s, and this paved the way for the construction of the U.S. Holocaust Museum on the Mall in Washington. Carter appointed Elie Wiesel to the U.S. Holocaust Commission that oversees the Museum. Wiesel's Holocaust memoir, *Night*, which had only a small readership when first published in 1960, had sold more than ten million copies by 2007.

A global human rights movement universalized concerns about war crimes, crimes against humanity, and genocide through the 1970s and 1980s. The United Nations expanded its work on human rights through such institutions as the High Commission on Human Rights, the High Commission on Refugees, and the World Health Organization. Although the Reagan administration rejected the priority given by the Carter administration to human rights, it nonetheless selectively pursued human rights charges of anti-Semitism in the Soviet Union.[13] The broader policy reversal on human rights by the Reagan administration and its suspected violations of these rights and international law in Latin and South America stimulated leading human rights figures like Aryeh Neier to expand their legal activism from domestic to international settings.

Aryeh Neier acknowledged, in his memoir, his belated realization of the roots of his activism in his own neglected Holocaust experience. In 1939, at the age of two, Neier escaped the Holocaust by emigrating with his parents to England and eventually to the United States. In his memoir, he writes,

> Today, the bookshelves of my apartment in New York City are laden with books about the Holocaust – diaries, memoirs, biographies, histories, polemics, and a few novels – but they include only a handful of works published in the 1940s and 1950s. Though I was not aware of the absence at the time, in retrospect I find it bizarre and now believe that it contributed to a somewhat distorted political consciousness in which I failed until much later to appreciate the nature and extent of evil in the twentieth century. Though I had a closer brush than most of my peers with the defining events of the era, my knowledge and understanding of what took place remained at best superficial.

It took more than a half-century for one of Germany's most gifted writers about the Holocaust, Günter Grass, to acknowledge in his autobiography his own service in the Waffen SS – the force Glueck helped to outlaw en masse at Nuremberg. The Jewish European writer Ivan Nagel expressed empathy for the long silence of Grass, noting that for fifty-five years he could not speak about his own persecution.[14] These biographical insights reflect, at the individual level, the larger collective lag in public awareness that retarded the development of a societal and criminological understanding of the importance of international humanitarian and criminal law and universal human rights.

Human rights activists like Neier refused to ignore the widely suspected role of Henry Kissinger in facilitating the Pinochet coup in the 1980s in Chile. Neier led the American Civil Liberties Union for many years and next moved into international work with Helsinki Watch, Americas Watch, and ultimately Human Rights Watch.[15] This expanding domain reflected the decline of the Cold War doctrine of the separate spheres relationship between the United States and the Soviets discussed in Chapter 2. The demise of the Soviet Union by the end of the 1980s dramatically reduced, if not entirely eliminated, the rationale for the separate spheres inhibition on international law and human rights enforcement. The British and Spanish governments now tried, albeit unsuccessfully, to bring Pinochet to trial for his crimes against humanity in Chile.

In the following decades, nongovernmental organizations (NGOs), such as Amnesty International, Human Rights Watch, and Physicians for Human Rights, expanded their budgets and intensified their work on human rights issues.[16] These groups collected innovative quantitative and qualitative documentary evidence that stirred public awareness of human rights abuses. Because Human Rights Watch emerged out of the older Helsinki Watch organization that focused on the Soviet Union, skeptics could not question its opposition to communism. Human Rights Watch emphasized the collection of hard source evidence, especially incriminating documents and riveting visual images of killings and abuse. It pursued an aggressive use of the media to disseminate

shocking findings about human rights abuses through newly internation-
alized communication outlets such as CNN.

Although some criminologists recognized the importance of this
changing political environment[17] and the innovative work of groups like
Amnesty International and Human Rights Watch, few did actual empirical research on genocide and other war and human rights crimes. In the
absence of criminologists, the empirical study of the casualties of war
and civil conflicts found its most active engagement in the 1990s from
demographically and epidemiologically trained health researchers working alongside and with human rights groups. This research helped pressure the United States and the United Nations to establish the International Criminal Tribunal for the former Yugoslavia and a parallel
International Tribunal for Rwanda.[18] Of course, these courts did not prevent genocide in either setting.

The field of public health research conceptualized its work on
human rights under the rubric of "complex humanitarian emergencies." Although this research tradition played an essential and ground-
breaking role in initiating the systematic empirical study of conflicts
resulting in war crimes, crimes against humanity, and genocide, we take
issue with several health science research practices, findings, and the
overall orientation of this field.

Our argument is that a criminological perspective can succeed where
a health perspective failed to provide a full empirical foundation, theoretical understanding, and legal assignment of responsibility for violence
and victimization that violate international criminal law. Even when
health researchers paid increasing attention to violence as a health problem, these researchers usually chose to emphasize disease, illness, and
nutrition. Although attention to these health problems did not preclude a
focus on criminal violence and victimization, public health research often
ignored and neglected the serious international law violations involved
in these events.

Thus, public health specialists framed issues of crime and justice
in vaguer terms of health and well-being, whereas criminology largely

ignored war and human rights crimes and still bears a disciplinary responsibility for this neglect. Columnist Nicholas Kristof succinctly observed during a trip through Darfur and Chad that "after more than three years of ... brutality, it seems incredibly inadequate for the international community simply to hand out bandages when old women are roasted in their huts and young men have their eyes gouged out. What we need isn't more bandages, but the will to stand up to genocide."[19] The terminology of the public health approach obscured this message.

## "Complex Humanitarian Emergencies"

Public health researchers coined the concept of a "complex humanitarian emergency"[20] in the early 1990s to refer to forced migration and subsequent increased mortality in many parts of the world. These emergencies arise out of situations in which efforts to drastically restructure a state, society, or social group cause civil conflict or international war, resulting in the violent deaths of large civilian populations and in their displacement – typically to overflowing internal displacement or refugee camps. These camps often are breeding grounds for disease, dehydration, starvation, malnutrition, and other sources of excessive mortality.[21] The attention to the radical restructuring of populations, with resulting civilian casualties – drawing both from the international criminal law concept of crimes against humanity and from the health research concept of complex humanitarian emergencies – makes findings in the latter area of study especially relevant to our concerns.

There is substantial evidence that humanitarian emergencies have worsened over the last century,[22] especially since the end of the Cold War, with a particularly lethal increase in direct violence between racial, ethnic, and religious groups.[23] As a proportion of all war casualties, civilians increased from about 14 percent in World War I, to 67 percent in World War II, to 90 percent by the end of the twentieth century.[24] Between 1989 and 1999, the number of complex humanitarian emergencies in the world more than doubled from fourteen to thirty,[25] and the number of humanitarian refugees nearly doubled worldwide in the last third of the twentieth century.[26]

In addition, the public and population health research literature revealed specific changes in the tactics of warring parties within and between nation-states that resulted in major increases in civilian casualties. Warring groups increasingly targeted women and children. These conflicts often involved child soldiers, direct attacks on civilian populations, destruction and looting of civilian homes and institutions, abductions and the use of rape as an instrument of terror, and massive forced migrations.[27]

The identification of humanitarian emergencies as "complex" reflects several concerns of public health researchers about the political complications of initiating and sustaining humanitarian relief and assistance.[28] The first concern involves the priority these researchers attach to the work of relief agencies in improving the chances that refugees survive emergency conditions in the face of the "complex social, political, and economic issues" confronting them.[29] The second concern reflects the desire to understand neutrally, if not euphemistically, the contexts and arrangements that relief programs adapt to as "by nature complex."[30] The third concern involves an understanding that relief agencies nonetheless cannot and should not ignore "complex and political" arguments about providing sufficient medical services to communities in refugee camps.[31]

The hard and intrusive political realities of the complex humanitarian emergencies lead health researchers such as Toole and Waldman to call on the international community to intervene at early stages in "the evolution of complex disasters involving civil war, human rights abuses, food shortages, and mass displacement."[32] A crucial element of Toole and Waldman's health-initiated agenda is their recognition that, once health-oriented practitioners gain access to a humanitarian emergency situation and begin to prevent excess mortality, they can also begin to play a role in empirically documenting the unfolding course of the emergency as well as its composition and magnitude.[33]

Mortality constitutes the common thread of health and crime, and along this dimension can be traced the course of complex humanitarian emergencies. The related study of famines identifies a paradigmatic sequence of mortality and related problems marked by the onset of the crisis, followed by its rise to a peak, the arrival of emergency assistance, and a potentially rapid if belated stabilization.[34] The calculation of crude mortality rates (CMRs) is the key to assessing the occurrence of deaths for the population affected by the emergency and its duration.

CMRs typically enumerate deaths per 10,000 population per day to allow comparisons across settings and situations. These rates classically rise and fall across the stages noted earlier, tracing an inverted U-shaped curve of mortality that can include protracted onset, followed by a peak, and then a quickening rate of decline in deaths. At least "standard" rural famines unfold this way. The forced migration and subsequent increased mortality at the end of the twentieth century in Kosovo, the contested southernmost province in the Republic of Serbia, illustrate this pattern, as we describe later.[35]

The U.S. State Department identifies a CMR of 1.0 as a baseline threshold of elevated mortality in complex humanitarian emergencies.[36] This 1.0 level is two to three times the level of mortality that is regarded as "expected" or "normal" in sub-Saharan Africa. The Centers for Disease Control (CDC) recommends a program of response once this threshold is crossed. The response prescribes the use of sample surveys to establish a baseline mortality rate in a setting, followed by the implementation of an information system to collect ongoing health data, including mortality.[37] Epidemiologically trained health researchers use this procedure to provide crucial information about the mortality and morbidity surrounding humanitarian emergencies. If criminologists were to study such emergencies, they would give added attention to the sources and responsibility for these emergency situations. However, as we have noted, criminologists did not take up this work during the early post–Cold War period.

Population health researchers studying complex humanitarian emergencies bring a methodological tool kit to assist in the provision of relief (food, medicine, and shelter) for conflict-affected populations suffering elevated mortality levels. The goal of this research is to chart and plan relief efforts, rather than retrospectively assign criminal responsibility. Organizations such as the CDC gather data as a means to prevent further death and disease. As a result, they often neglect the need to assess the state-led criminal violence that occurs before victims gain access to refugee status and protection. Still, this epidemiologically and demographically guided research provides insight into the patterning of politically instigated violence.[38]

Perhaps most importantly, this research reveals that internal and external politics, including the reaction (or lack thereof) by the international community, can radically alter the form and scale of humanitarian and human rights emergencies. For example, in the Democratic Republic of the Congo, mortality rates remained at an average of about 0.7 deaths per 10,000 population per day for years, but increased up to 75 percent higher in conflict-prone regions of this country.[39] Overall, less developed countries experience higher CMRs and are more vulnerable to upward variations from baseline rates than are developed countries, making their humanitarian and human rights emergencies quantitatively and qualitatively distinct. In Zaire in 1994, CMRs for Rwandan refugees reached levels as high as 35 deaths per 10,000 population per day.[40]

Again, although not specifically designed to do so, this body of research further reveals that the population most at risk varies according to the specific roots of the conflict. In the Congo, infants and children under age 5 experienced the most highly elevated mortality rates.[41] In contrast, the elderly died most frequently during the siege of Sarajevo.[42] The Srebrenica massacre hit military-aged males the hardest.[43] Women are everywhere most at risk of rape during politically instigated violence, even though, as the Abu Ghraib prison scandal illustrated, sexual assaults against males are probably also everywhere undercounted.

The health research literature on complex humanitarian emergencies increasingly focuses on the role of age–sex dimensions and the global North-South divide of development in shaping the form and scale of humanitarian emergencies. However, we still lack comprehensive data on the age–sex composition of elevated mortality in these emergencies, and this kind of data and analysis needs to be better connected to our understanding of the North-South dynamic of development that slowly but increasingly is the focus of thought and attention in the post–Cold War world.[44] Although not actually the case, the public sees Africa as a relatively recent focus of public health research, and it is still the case that criminologists give little or no attention to international human rights and war crimes within and between African states.

## Critiquing the Health Research Paradigm

A criminological perspective on war and international human rights crimes can broaden the response to the humanitarian emergencies explored in health research. A conflict theory of crime emphasizing "crimes of the state"[45] and the need for a political criminology provides a starting point for this criminological perspective.[46] The foundation of this perspective is built on the rough outlines of a general theory of genocide[47] and attention to the theoretical forces of power and control in the causation of genocide.[48] Perhaps the most significant but ironic contribution of criminologists so far, however, is the belated but growing awareness of the unwillingness of the field and the public to entertain questions, much less answers, about some of the most momentous contemporary criminal atrocities committed against humanity.[49]

Criminology nonetheless brings an essential perspective to the understanding of war and human rights crimes. Epidemiologically and demographically trained health researchers focus mainly on health outcomes, whereas criminologists prioritize issues of political and legal responsibility. A common sequence in these emergencies is the onset of violent attacks, the flight of the resulting victims, and ensuing health problems, all of which contribute to mortality. Within this sequence, however, "the root cause of most complex humanitarian emergencies is that governments and other combatants use violence and deprivation to seek solutions to political problems."[50]

A comprehensive criminological perspective requires simultaneously keeping in mind the (1) cumulative and multiplicative effects of violence, flight, and displacement to concentrated encampments and the (2) political state and nonstate origins of and responses to these disastrous consequences. The public health perspective makes methodological and conceptual choices that obscure links between these consequences and causes. These choices include the treatment of the "missing," of those who die from pre-camp violent attacks and in the flight to camps, of "excess as distinct from normal and expected mortality," and, even more fundamentally, the substitution of the concept of "complex humanitarian emergency" for "war and human rights crimes."

We begin with the treatment of the missing in the calculation of CMRs from population-based surveys. We introduced CMRs earlier as a central concept of the health approach. CMRs are calculated by dividing (a) the number of household members reported as deceased for a specified period (usually expressed per day) by (b) the estimated size of the sampled population (with the number of respondents multiplied by average household size) and (c) multiplying the dividend by 10,000. The denominator in this calculation represents the population at risk of death.

The convention in the health literature on complex humanitarian emergencies is to include in this denominator the sum of the sampled population and one-half of the reported dead, missing, and absent from this population. This convention reduces, but still includes for the purposes of calculation, the risk represented by "the dead, missing, and absent." Meanwhile, health surveys of these emergencies conventionally do not include consideration of the missing in the numerator of observed deaths. These surveys instead treat these persons as missing data in the numerator. Often, if not usually, the missing persons in these surveys disappear in the chaos of the emergency. Family members typically fear or presume they are dead. However, health studies more selectively focus on deaths that are identified as resulting from disease and nutritional or other specified causes, thereby omitting the missing from consideration.

At times, those who study complex humanitarian emergencies add a category for injuries and violence to their health surveys. However, this category often only covers a restricted recall period of risk or the period while the individual is displaced or in a refugee camp.[51] Health researchers often treat violence that results in deaths and disappearances preceding and during flights to those camps as of secondary importance. For example, in Darfur, health studies often disregarded deaths from pre-camp violence in their surveys. Rather, health researchers focused on saving the lives of those who survived long enough to get to the camps. Yet, acknowledging and analyzing those who died and became missing pre-camp, as well as in displacement and refugee camps, becomes important for the purposes of assigning legal responsibility and understanding the root causes of conflicts.

The concept of excess mortality raises related concerns. Analysts of complex humanitarian emergencies often construct a baseline estimate of mortality by identifying an expected mortality rate for the population of interest and at risk, assuming the absence of the humanitarian emergency. That is, health researchers estimate those expected to die during "normal" circumstances. This can be difficult, because circumstances in settings like sub-Saharan Africa seldom if ever become "normal." The researchers nonetheless construct a "counterfactual" estimate of "normal" mortality and then subtract the expected or normal mortality from the level of mortality observed during the period of the humanitarian emergency. Health researchers treat the difference between the "expected" and "observed" mortality as "excessive" mortality in determining the extent and duration of the emergency.

This approach raises problems from a criminological perspective. Imagine yourself in the following circumstances. You are expected in actuarial terms to die for health reasons within a given period, but during this period you die as a result of a criminal human rights violation; for example, you are forcibly displaced from your home. Dying at home it is one thing, but it is quite another thing to be forced from your home and to die in a displacement camp. Forced displacement can constitute a war crime. Designating deaths by and during displacement as normal or expected can distort the legal documentation of the form and extent of human rights crimes and war crimes.

The problems considered for illustrative purposes here – the neglect of missing persons, the failure to consider pre-displacement or pre-refugee camp violence, and the treatment of expected and excess mortality – anticipate a broader difficulty with the concept of complex humanitarian emergencies. This concept, although helpful in encouraging the creation of population- and public-health-based methods for the study of these disasters, often blunts and obscures the meaning of much that happens in such emergencies. As noted next, health researchers' use of the concept of complex humanitarian emergencies reflects some of the politics of humanitarian relief work and explains a lack of interest in much health research in documenting or counting conflict-related violence.

To facilitate their access to and ability to work with affected populations, humanitarian organizations often seek to engage in nonthreatening and unobtrusive methods for addressing human rights abuses. Even these organizations' use of what is perceived as threatening nomenclature sometimes prevents their access to settings and people in dire need of humanitarian assistance. The same states and groups that create these emergencies also restrict access to their victims. A criminological perspective challenges this public health approach, but first it is important to appreciate the scale of this problem.

### The Humanitarian Strategic Embrace

Alex de Waal's book, *Famine Crimes: Politics and the Disaster Relief Industry in Africa*,[52] provocatively exposes issues of cooptation that emerge in the public health approach to human rights abuses. De Waal argues that what he calls "Humanitarian International," the complex of NGOs and relief agencies that respond to humanitarian emergencies, often engages in a compromised strategic embrace with states that commit the human rights abuses and war crimes whose consequences they seek to alleviate.[53] This strategic embrace often obscures if not obstructs efforts to identify and hold abusers and instigators responsible. The Darfur experience highlights differences in health and criminological perspectives.

The tension between health and crime priorities broke into brief public view when the British House of Commons International Development Committee received testimony from Mukesh Kapila in early 2005. Kapila served as the UN Resident and Humanitarian Coordinator for Sudan.[54] Kapila asked through the media in October 2003 that the violence in Darfur be referred to the International Criminal Court. The United States finally agreed to abstain in the UN Security Council, belatedly allowing this referral to go forward in early 2005.

Kapila previously worked for the UN during the Rwandan genocide and was determined to prevent another genocide in Darfur. Yet, the UN removed Kapila from Darfur in March 2004, with the killing still near its peak. Kapila testified to the British parliamentary committee in early 2005 that the death toll continued to mount because "fundamentally the issue was that the Sudan government refused to allow us access when we needed it most."[55] This summary comment only scratches the surface of Kapila's account. He described in disturbing detail the conflicted nature of the UN's work with the Sudanese government in response to the killing and resulting health problems in Darfur.

A committee member asked Kapila how effectively the humanitarian and human rights – or health and crime – parts of the UN Sudan mission worked together in Darfur. He answered that these efforts competed with one another, reporting that "we had a real struggle to overcome" and that a "culture of distrust" existed, preventing the creation of "one UN approach."[56] He explained that those charged with the "humanitarian emergency" of an aid operation typically find themselves "burdened with the task of doing something about it and when they inevitably fail the blame is put on the humanitarians."[57] Kapila saw the violence in Darfur as ethnic cleansing, a form of genocide. Yet, he reported that the response from the international community fit into the Sudan government's strategy of demanding that he and his staff simply work harder to find humanitarian solutions.

Kapila emphasized another side of this dilemma – the competition for scarce resources – by saying, "This happens in organizations that are funded in a way which is reliant on what sort of image you can present and so on. That means that we had $100 million available for food aid but we had only $1 million available for human rights."[58] Still, he concluded, "Even if twice the money came in from the world … the arguments would have been the same"; the real problem was "the systematic obstruction by the Sudanese government of humanitarian access."[59]

Kapila's testimony starkly highlights the difficulty of responding to both health and crime issues in humanitarian emergencies. Humanitarian relief workers often pursue different goals than human rights and war crimes investigators, and external and internal politics and uneven funding distribution make cooperation unlikely. In many ways, the Darfur conflict exemplifies these problems, which partly result from the politics of the global North-South divide in health, security, and development that is only beginning to be more fully apparent to the world. As another way of making this important point, we next consider a somewhat more successful response to the humanitarian and human rights challenges presented by the Serbian government aggression in Kosovo in the late 1990s.

## The Criminology of Kosovo

The Serbian province of Kosovo experienced a humanitarian and human rights emergency between March and June 1999 when Serbian military and paramilitary forces forcibly displaced the majority of the Albanian population in Kosovo across international borders to Macedonia and Albania. Within months, a military intervention allowed this population to return to their homes in an extensively documented manner. International organizations responded relatively swiftly to the underlying human rights issues, probably because this emergency happened in the developed global North and within the domain of Europe, which still feels the responsibilities of the crimes of the Holocaust. These organizations responded to the forced migration and mortality in Kosovo in ways more consistent with a criminological victimization perspective, which addresses issues of legal responsibility more directly than the complex humanitarian emergency approach.

By the beginning of the twenty-first century in Europe, at least some authorities recognized the relevance for victims of war and state violence of a war crimes survey approach, using the victimization survey methods first applied in the United States in the 1960s and 70s.[60,61] Initially, the two main international organizations in Kosovo – the Organization for Security and Co-operation in Europe (OSCE) and the North Atlantic Treaty Organization (NATO) – resisted undertaking a victimization research approach. However, several other organizations cooperated in developing a consensus about the criminal dimensions of the humanitarian emergency in Kosovo. The consensus emerged in part in response to the availability of agreed-on methods for estimating the number of deaths and the size of the refugee flow. The legally oriented American Bar Association's Central and East European Law Initiative (ABA-CEELI) played a guiding role in nurturing this consensus.

Using population-based sampling techniques, the human rights organization Physicians for Human Rights (PHR)[62] and the Centers for Disease Control (CDC)[63] surveyed refugees first in Macedonian and Albanian camps and then in Kosovo after their return to their homes. Relatively few of the deported Kosovars experienced severe health problems, again probably because these events occurred in the global North and on the doorstep of Europe, and because of the well-organized relief work in the camps and on the return home of the refugees. This allowed the interviewing to focus more directly on the experiences and consequences of the violent attacks leading to displacement, in the format of a victimization survey rather than a health survey.

PHR and CDC, respectively, estimated that 9,000 and 12,000 killings had occurred. The ABA-CEELI and the American Academy for the Advancement of Science (AAAS) generated a third estimate, which joined the PHR data with two data sets from Human Rights Watch (HRW) and ABA-CEELI listing the names, locations, and timing of deaths gathered from refugee interviews. ABA-CEELI/AAAS[64] estimated that there were 10,538 killings, with a lower and upper bound confidence interval between 7,449 and 13,627. These estimates approximate those noted by the PHR and CDC, but are higher than a U.S. Department of State estimate of 6,000 people killed and placed in mass graves.[65] The combined PHR, HWR, and ABA data also demonstrated that the majority of the killings happened during the refugee flight of Kosovars to Albania and Macedonia.[66] This provided further evidence of the criminal connection of these deaths to the Serbian-instigated forced migration.

Working with ABA-CEELI and the AAAS, Patrick Ball also used data on refugee flow recorded by the Albanian border guards, the office of the UN High Commissioner for Refugees, and the Albanian Emergency Management Group to determine that this flow followed from Serbian-instigated ethnic cleansing operations in Kosovo. His data indicated a lack of connection between refugee flow and NATO bombing raids, a connection alleged by Slobodan Milosevic in his defense at the International Criminal Tribunal (ICTY). In a later analysis of interviews collected by the OSCE and records of exhumations by investigators for the ICTY, Ball and his colleagues used models with estimates of killings and refugee flow to disconfirm the link between the NATO bombing and the forced migration.[67] The fact that ICTY investigation teams entered Kosovo with NATO security so soon after the forced migration and mortality ensured a further crime emphasis in the data collection.

Ball later offered important testimony in the Milosevic trial, where he summarized his analysis of data from the previously described sources. Milosevic questioned "the invented figure of 10,356" deaths.[68] When Ball described the statistical procedures involved, Milosevic responded, "So you distributed the assumed dead into assumed time points by applying some kind of statistical methods. How can this be a serious way of doing it? Tell me."[69] Ball patiently explained that he and his colleagues used established methods to compensate for missing data, with cautionary warnings wherever noteworthy doubts arose. Of course, Milosevic's death ended this trial without a conviction. Nonetheless, Ball's criminological analysis played an important role.

## From North to South, from Kosovo to Darfur

The criminological analysis of Kosovo probably unfolded as well as it did for several reasons. Kosovo was the last of three fronts in the Balkan wars. This allowed the outside parties to resolve this conflict based on their previous experiences in Croatia and Bosnia. The European location of the conflict further allowed direct involvement of the OSCE and NATO, along with the U.S. government, and all played intervening roles in the Kosovo phase of the conflict. The United States sent twenty-two lawyers and investigators to work at the ICTY and assumed responsibility for more than half of its budget. The United States directly and indirectly played a leading role in bringing a legal criminological perspective to the data collection effort in Kosovo.

More specifically, the NATO bombing campaign and American participation in the indictment of Slobodan Milosevic by the ICTY paved the way for the initial interviews with a sample of refugees in Albania and Macedonia. The entry of NATO troops into Kosovo presented the opportunity for in-country interviewing of samples of returning and remaining residents in Kosovo. The fact that the forced migration and mortality took place primarily in a short time period also enhanced the efficiency of the data collection and analysis.

The convergence of these factors allowed for what the chief prose-cutor of the ICTY at the time, Louise Arbour, called "real-time" inves-tigation and prosecution.[70] Arbour often cited Nuremberg as a point of reference for the ICTY.[71] However, Kosovo differed from Nuremberg in significant ways. ICTY prosecutors in Kosovo presented freshly acquired evidence of state officials' guilt, instead of piecing together historical data to assign criminal responsibility for mass atrocities, as happened after World War II and at the beginning of the conflict in the Balkans. This cooperation around real-time data collection and analysis made obvious sense as a tactic for preventing new humanitarian emergencies or lessen-ing their impact.

The AAAS and the ABA-CEELI initiated the development of a "violations documentation database" after their positive experience in Kosovo. They provided free database software that enabled interested NGOs all over the world to process their data in formats suitable for subsequent statistical analysis. They reasoned that "these analyses could serve a variety of purposes, such as providing a reliable picture of the events for the international community or aiding in the prosecution of perpetrators, and they would therefore be beneficial for all organizations involved."[72] Going forward, the prospects for a criminological analysis of war crimes looked somewhat promising or at least improved.

But Africa is not Europe, and Darfur is not Kosovo. NGOs did not use the violations documentation database just described in the displace-ment camps in Darfur. Neither the U.S. government nor the Interna-tional Criminal Court collected data inside Darfur. The media sometimes call Darfur the first genocide of the twenty-first century, but it marks a step backward rather than forward in terms of human rights and legal criminological strategies. It may still be true, as the former UN Secretary-General has said against the backdrop of Rwanda, that "A genocide in Africa has not received the same attention that genocide in Europe or genocide in Turkey or genocide in other parts of the world. There is still this kind of discrimination against African people and the African problems."[73]

The UN initially approached the Darfur emergency as a health emergency, rather than as a human rights issue, and certainly, Darfur presented a far graver health emergency than Kosovo. The overwhelming majority of able-bodied Kosovars fled across the borders into refugee camps in Macedonia and Albania and received sufficient medicine and food to avoid large-scale mortality from disease or nutritional problems. In contrast, the vast majority of those attacked in Darfur fled to internal displacement camps inside the borders of Sudan. Sudan allowed neither health nor human rights organizations to provide assistance in the beginning of the emergency.

When organizations like the UN's World Health Organization (WHO) belatedly gained access to the internal displacement camps, they confronted a massive health emergency, involving outbreaks of contagious disease combined with shortages of food and clean water. The survey work by the WHO in the Darfur camps required cooperation with the Sudanese Ministry of Health and concentrated on near-term health and nutrition issues. Although some organizations, such as Médicins Sans Frontières (MSF), undertook important survey work that included more attention to criminal violence and victimization inside the state of West Darfur, no comprehensive "violations documentation database" consistently covered the displacement camps in the three Darfur states. In contrast with Kosovo, the victims of violence and displacement remain in the camps, which allows little opportunity for survey work in the more representative home settings.

There was, however, a further important element of the Darfur story. Several hundred thousand refugees fled across the border from Darfur into refugee camps in Chad. The major survey introduced earlier, the U.S. State Department's Atrocities Documentation Survey (ADS), involved a sample of 1,136 Darfur refugees in the Chad camps. This survey shared much of the same motivation as the proposed violations database; that is, to develop information for criminal prosecutions. The American Bar Association advised and helped organize the ADS. Unfortunately, the American government did not maintain its support of the ADS, despite an enormous financial investment in it and even though the survey initially played a major role in the State Department and Colin Powell's determination that genocide occurred in Darfur. By the time Condoleezza Rice replaced Powell as Secretary of State, the ADS lost its priority in the formation of State Department policy on Darfur.

Yet, by using the ADS data from refugees in Chad, and also the MSF survey work done inside Darfur as noted earlier, it is possible to effectively estimate and analyze much of the violence and victimization in Darfur. We present the basic descriptive features of this genocide using these sources in the next chapter. That account raises unsettling questions about our progress since Nuremberg.

# 4 Flip-Flopping on Darfur

## with Alberto Palloni and Patricia Parker

It's [the low mortality estimate] a deliberate effort by the Bush Administration to downplay the severity of the crisis in order to reduce the urgency of an additional response. I find that to be disingenuous and perhaps murderous.

– John Prendergast, International Crisis Group
April 26, 2005

## The Atrocities Documentation Survey

*Documenting Atrocities in Darfur*[1] is the title of the eight-page report based on a survey of Darfur refugees in Chad and published by the U.S. Department of State in September 2004. The report's chillingly cogent tables, charts, maps, and pictures – derived from interviews with 1,136 refugees in Chad – speak volumes. Our recording from the Atrocities Documentation Survey (ADS) identified more than 12,000 deaths and many more rapes and atrocities that the respondents personally witnessed or heard about before fleeing. The report opens with a chart listing these statistics[2]:

- 81 percent reported their village was destroyed.
- 80 percent reported their livestock was stolen.
- 67 percent reported witnessing or experiencing aerial bombing.
- 61 percent reported the killing of a family member.
- 44 percent reported witnessing or experiencing a shooting.
- 33 percent reported hearing racial epithets during attacks.

Secretary of State Colin Powell made headlines when he presented these findings to the UN Security Council and the U.S. Congress as evidence of Sudanese-sponsored genocide in Darfur.

The preface to this book includes Powell's statement made to Congress, followed by this separate statement from President Bush, also built on the ADS findings:

> I sent Secretary of State Powell to Darfur and Khartoum to demand that the Sudanese Government act to end the violence.... Secretary Powell later sent a team of investigators into the refugee camps to interview the victims of atrocities. As a result of these investigations and other information, we have concluded that genocide has taken place in Darfur. We urge the international community to work with us to prevent and suppress acts of genocide. We call on the United Nations to undertake a full investigation of the genocide and other crimes in Darfur.[3]

This was the first time that an American president had rebuked a sovereign nation by invoking the Genocide Convention, and it was certainly the first time that a crime victimization survey had shaped U.S. foreign policy. This victimization survey recorded crimes previously ignored in health surveys. The findings outlined the criminology of a genocide.

Yet, beyond offering humanitarian health assistance, before and after issuing its report, the Bush administration did relatively little, especially given the massiveness of the atrocities: Secretary Powell requested more African Union troops, and President Bush called for a UN investigation. These actions signaled the administration's ambivalence about Darfur, and in fact, Powell in his congressional statement explicitly argued that "no new action was dictated by this determination." This undercut the potential force of his genocide charge.

We demonstrate in this chapter that the administration's use of survey evidence, including its own victimization survey, involved flip-flop diplomacy. To understand the confusing politics of these events, it is important to first understand the genesis of the ADS.

## Surveying Hostile Circumstances

In June 2004, Andrew Natsios, who became the U.S. Special Envoy to Sudan, appeared before a conference in Geneva and discussed satellite images of the destruction of a village in Darfur. At the same presentation, David Springer, a State Department analyst, pointed to a pair of pictures that recorded the fate of the village of Shattay – before and after a militia attack.

This presentation placed the government of Sudan on notice about its activities in Darfur. The American analyst who described this event nonetheless cautioned that the images "are not hard evidence until they are corroborated by testimony of witnesses on the ground."[4] Under increasing pressure to provide a reliable assessment of the situation, the State Department established an Atrocities Documentation Team to survey the refugees fleeing from Darfur.

Stefanie Frease of the Coalition for International Justice (CIJ) and Jonathan Howard, a research analyst with the State Department's Office of Research, conducted the survey. Howard developed the research design, and Frease assumed the role of field supervisor. The State Department wanted Frease to complete the survey in just two months.[5] This was an audacious demand, but Frease is an unusual person. A few years earlier, working inside what she called "the Srebrenica ghost team," Frease brought to the International Criminal Tribunal for the former Yugoslavia (ICTY) tape-recorded "smoking gun" evidence for the genocide trial of General Radislav Krstic.[6] The trial climaxed with those in the courtroom hearing a chilling recorded voice giving deadly orders to "kill them all, kill them all." Frease was the ICTY investigator who led a search through reams of intercepted communications to find this evidence.

The current challenge was to develop a survey instrument, recruit interviewers and interpreters, plan the logistics of conducting surveys in nineteen remote locations in eastern Chad, implement a sampling plan, move the research team in and out of the survey locations, and organize the coding and analysis of more than one thousand interviews – all in two months. The team was able to complete several hundred interviews in time for Powell's appearance before the UN Security Council in July, and it finished the full survey of 1,136 refugees in Chad before Powell's congressional testimony in early September.

The two groups who worked for two-week periods each in July and August 2004 included fifteen interviewers. The interviewers were area experts, social scientists, lawyers, and police investigators. The survey mixed the closed-ended format of a crime victimization survey with the semistructured format of legal witness statements. The interviewers worked with interpreters in ten camps and nine settlements. They randomly selected a starting point in each camp or settlement and then, from within this designated sector, selected every tenth dwelling unit for interview. They randomly chose one adult from each household for a personal interview, resulting in the final 1,136 sampled households. Interviewers coded up to twenty crime incidents per household with sufficient detail to support potential courtroom claims.

We use the ADS data in this chapter to elaborate a preliminary estimate of mortality in Darfur. In the following chapters, we use the more detailed background information to test a model of the distribution and causes of the violent victimization across twenty-two clusters of settlements in Darfur from which the refugees fled.

Of course, there are other sources of data about the conflict in Darfur. Probably the best-known data collected on this conflict come from surveys conducted by the World Health Organization (WHO) in the internal displacement camps inside Darfur. The breadth of the WHO survey work is important because of the absence of census or hospital data from which to calculate Darfur mortality. However, the differences between the ADS and WHO survey data reflect important distinctions described in the previous chapter between the crime and health research paradigms. The ADS design is a cutting-edge example of a crime victimization approach, with its emphasis on incident-based reporting of criminal events before and in the refugee camps. In contrast, the WHO survey applies the health research approach to complex humanitarian emergencies, with a subsequent emphasis on mortality linked to disease and nutritional problems inside the displacement camps.

The French human rights group, Médecins Sans Frontières (MSF), also conducted surveys in West Darfur. Although the MSF surveys covered a small number of camps, this initiative uniquely combined attention to pre-camp and in-camp deaths. This research is crucial for conclusions we reach later in this chapter. First, however, it is important to learn more about the findings of the WHO and ADS studies.

## Early Findings from the WHO Surveys

Health organizations – especially in a setting such as Darfur – obviously focus on immediate and ongoing challenges of disease and malnutrition. They are less concerned with the past violence that leads displaced persons to flee to camps in the first place. This is a key reason why Powell's State Department and its ambassador on war crimes needed a crime victimization survey and initiated the ADS.

At about the same time as the ADS was launched, during the late summer of 2004, the WHO conducted surveys of mortality and other health and nutrition issues with the cooperation of the Sudanese Ministry of Health (hereafter referred to as the WHO/SMH survey). This work allowed estimates of crude relative mortality (CMR) rates of the kind introduced in Chapter 3. Thus, a WHO retrospective survey conducted during two summer months in 2004 produced a CMR of 2.14 for the states of North and West Darfur. This level of mortality is from four to seven times the "normal or expected" mortality in sub-Saharan Africa. This CMR is a meaningful estimate of mortality (following displacement) due to health problems in the camps, with some added deaths resulting from violence experienced during refugee forays outside the camps to collect firewood or other necessities. However, violent attacks that occurred before displacement accounted for few of these deaths.

The survey work of WHO led to an early estimate of 70,000 Darfurian refugees deaths in just seven months of 2004, again almost entirely from malnutrition and disease.[7] David Nabarro, who announced this estimate, is a self-described British "public health bureaucrat" who "can translate complex facts in a way that makes emotional sense to those receiving them."[8] Development of this estimate required going beyond the original retrospective survey by linking the CMRs with separate estimates of the larger population at risk in Darfur. WHO estimated the size of that larger population at risk based on counts in the camps of displaced persons. Obviously, both the CMR and the displaced camp population varied from month to month. However, the death toll probably peaked in the summer months of 2004. Nabarro concluded that from 5,000 to 10,000 persons died in Darfur per month during this period, but we will suggest that the peak number of deaths per month was even higher.

UN emergency relief coordinator Jan Egeland returned from Darfur in March 2005. After his latest visit to Darfur, Egeland, who regularly spoke for the UN, was asked by reporters to provide an updated estimate of the death toll. At first he resisted, enigmatically saying, "It is where we are not, that there are attacks." Then when asked to comment on the outdated 70,000 estimate, he responded, "Is it three times that? Is it five times that? I don't know but it is several times the number of 70,000 that have died altogether."[9]

Egeland decided several days later to provide a more complete answer. He extrapolated from the UN's WHO survey by multiplying Nabarro's 10,000 per month figure by eighteen months (i.e., instead of seven). The UN estimate then jumped to 180,000.[10] Even though this latter estimate involved no further data – simply multiplying the 10,000 per month figure by eighteen – Egeland's new number took hold. Although it is doubtful that deaths remained at an unvarying level of 10,000 per month in Darfur for the full eighteen months that Egeland considered, there are also reasons to think the monthly death toll actually peaked at higher than 10,000 persons per month.

## A Gathering Consensus

Among the mortality estimates receiving attention in the media at the beginning of 2005, the projection of 180,000 deaths from the WHO survey work was at the low end. Jan Coebergh, a British physician, noted the absence of violent deaths from the WHO survey and estimated in the British periodical, *Parliamentary Brief,* that the true death toll was nearer 300,000.[11] The scale of this estimate echoed that offered by the American activist-scholar, Eric Reeves of Smith College, who offered similarly large estimates based on parallel assumptions.[12] In a *Boston Globe* op-ed piece, Reeves projected a death toll of 400,000. Coebergh and Reeves' estimates both added deaths from violence recorded in the ADS to the deaths caused by disease and malnutrition in the WHO survey. Thus, these estimates bridged the crime and health paradigms.

At about the same time in the spring of 2005, we issued a press release in conjunction with the CIJ detailing a mortality estimate based on a combination of the WHO and ADS surveys.[13] We examined each of the 1,136 ADS surveys, retracing all of the steps necessary to make this projection completely transparent. We concluded that as many as 350,000 persons had died, with nearly 400,000 persons either missing or dead in Darfur. Around this time, the *New York Times* and *Washington Post* reported, with frequency, an estimate of 300,000 or more deaths. Kofi Annan wrote in a *New York Times* op-ed piece of 300,000 "or more" Darfurian deaths.[14] Marc Lacey similarly cited our nearly 400,000 dead and missing figure for the first time in the *New York Times* in April 2005.[15] A consensus formed that there were hundreds of thousands of deaths in Darfur, with the estimates ranging from 180,000 to 400,000.

## The Consensus Breaks

Assistant Secretary of State Robert Zoellick, the deputy to the new Secretary of State, Condoleezza Rice, paid a personal visit to Darfur in the early spring of 2005. The *New York Times* described Zoellick as "a diplomatic lone ranger with $3 \times 5$ cards," and he described himself as a mixture of an economist and a diplomat.[16] He later left the Bush administration to join the Wall Street investment firm Goldman Sachs and in July 2007 was appointed president of the World Bank. Condoleezza Rice spoke to the press before Zoellick's departure for Sudan to emphasize the importance she attached to his trip. Zoellick's visit produced a revised and remarkably upbeat assessment of events in Darfur.

Zoellick first startled reporters in Khartoum by declining to reaffirm Powell's earlier determination of genocide in Darfur. When asked about the genocide, he said he did not want to "debate terminology." He then disputed the prevailing consensus estimates of hundreds of thousands of deaths in Darfur. Zoellick instead reported a new State Department estimate of as few as 60,000 and at most 146,000 "excess" deaths. The State Department posted a new report on its Web site, *Sudan: Death Toll in Darfur*, which asserted that "violent deaths were widespread in the early stages of this conflict, but a successful, albeit delayed humanitarian response and a moderate 2004 rainy season combined to suppress mortality rates by curtailing infectious disease outbreaks and substantial disruption of aid deliveries."[17]

The reference to as few as 60,000 "excess" deaths indicated that the new State Department estimate tilted toward the public health side of the disciplinary divide and marked a step away from the ADS victimization methodology. It relied on the health paradigm of "complex humanitarian emergencies," rather than the human rights and war crimes framework. In particular, the new estimate relied on the false assumption that the kind of survey work done by the WHO could fully measure the scale of mortality in Darfur. In effect, the State Department was ignoring its own ADS findings.

Yet, public statements by the WHO's David Nabarro (discussed later in this chapter) acknowledged that its survey provided only a partial picture of the death toll. According to Nabarro's own carefully framed remarks, the WHO survey did not count those killed in the attacks on the Darfur villages that provoked the flight and subsequent displacement and refugee camps in the first place.

Zoellick's visit came just one week after the United Nations gave the names (undisclosed) of fifty-one persons referred by its Commission of Inquiry on Darfur to the International Criminal Court (ICC) for possible prosecution.[18] The list of suspects included high-ranking Sudanese government officials – perhaps even Sudan's vice president, who was Zoellick's host at the press conference in Khartoum at which Zoellick announced the new estimate that as few as 60,000 "excess" persons perished in Darfur.

This announcement provoked disbelief. The *American Prospect*'s Mark Goldberg called the State Department visit to Sudan "Zoellick's Appeasement Tour."[19] John Prendergast spoke for the International Crisis Group and much of the NGO community when he said, "For Zoellick to float 60,000 as a low end number is negligent criminally." He added, "It's a deliberate effort by the Bush administration to downplay the severity of the crisis in order to reduce the urgency of an additional response. I find that to be disingenuous and perhaps murderous."[20] Prendergast, who served as a National Security Council official in the Clinton administration, also provided a motivation for the low estimate, saying, "We have not taken adequate measures given the enormity of the crimes because we don't want to directly confront Sudan when it is cooperating on terrorism."

The State Department's new estimate had an immediate impact on major media news outlets. Whereas these sources previously had reported *hundreds of thousands* of deaths in Darfur, the widely reported death toll now shrunk to *tens of thousands*. Major mainstream news services – including Reuters, United Press International, and the British Broadcasting Service – now included the "tens of thousands" framing of the conflict as a stock phrase in their news stories. This "tens of thousands" estimate persisted for more than a year after Zoellick's announcement in Khartoum.

## The Osama Bin Laden Connection

An explanation began to emerge in the media of why the State Department's Robert Zoellick shifted the framing of the conflict in Darfur, and this reasoning supported Prendergast's speculation about this shift's relationship to the Bush administration's war on terrorism.

The *Los Angeles Times* revealed that the CIA had provided a jet to bring the Sudanese government intelligence chief, Major General Salah Abdallah Gosh, to Washington at about the same time that Zoellick was delivering his new mortality assessment in Khartoum. It quoted State Department sources attesting to the importance of the Sudanese visit for increasing Sudan's cooperation in the war on terror. These sources highlighted Sudan's role in the early 1990s in providing sanctuary to Osama Bin Laden and a base for Al Qaeda operations, as well as the State Department's interest in learning more about these activities. During his 2005 visit to Washington, Sudan's General Gosh, who had served as an official "minder" of Bin Laden during his time in Darfur,[21] boasted, "We have a strong partnership with the CIA."

The *New York Times* reported that the CIA flew Gosh from Khartoum to Baltimore-Washington International Airport on April 17, returning him to Khartoum on April 22. The *LA Times* indicated that Gosh met in Washington with CIA officials on April 21 and 22. Zoellick arrived in Sudan on April 14, and his low mortality estimate appeared in the *Washington Post* on April 22. Thus, Gosh's trip coincided with Zoellick's stay in Sudan.[22]

Observers charged that Gosh directed or at least knew of the role of the Sudanese military in the attacks on Darfur villages. Indeed, Gosh held a prominent position in the Sudanese government chain of command responsible for Darfur, as described in the following chapters. That the U.S. government knew of his role in the violence in Darfur is evident in a follow-up *LA Times* story, which indicated that the Justice and State Departments disagreed about Gosh's Washington visit, with some in the Department of Justice suggesting that the trip presented an opportunity to detain a war criminal.[23] Alex de Waal wrote, "The real power in Khartoum is not President Bashir, who is a pious, tough soldier, but a cabal of security officers who have run both the Sudanese Islamist movement and the Sudanese state as a private but collegial enterprise for the last 15 years.... And the members of this cabal are serial war criminals."[24] In addition, Congress had cited Gosh in 2004 as playing a key role in the Darfur genocide.[25]

Later, the *LA Times* reported links between the CIA and Sudan's security service, the Mukhabarat, noting that "Gosh has not returned to Washington since, but a former official said that 'there are liaison visits every day' between the CIA and the Mukhabarat."[26] The U.S. State Department subsequently called Sudan a "strong partner in the war on terror."

It is likely that the reduced mortality estimate in Darfur and the temporarily suspended references to genocide were part of this cooperative strategy. President Bush did not mention the genocide in Darfur for a period of more than four months in 2005. In May 2005, the columnist Nicholas Kristof wrote in the *New York Times*, "Today marks Day 141 of Mr. Bush's silence on the genocide, for he hasn't let the word Darfur slip past his lips publicly since January 10 (even that was a passing reference with no condemnation)."[27] The nonpartisan Congressional Research Service reported that, although Gosh and other Sudanese officials played "key roles in directing...attacks against civilians," the administration was "concerned that going after these individuals could disrupt cooperation on counter-terrorism."[28] This silence and inaction actually marked a return to a policy dating at least to the first Bush administration, when "Washington bureaucrats turned a blind eye towards the policy of the authorities in Khartoum, mainly in the hope of securing their support for American goals in the Middle East."[29]

Gosh's visit to Washington reaped benefits both for his country and personally. The administration allowed Sudan to enter into a $500,000 public relations contract with a Washington-based lobbying firm, C/L International, to improve its image and increase its influence. This contract violated Executive Order 13067, which prohibited American companies and citizens from doing business with Sudan.[30] Congress forced an end to this deal in February 2006. Still, Sudanese Foreign Minister Mustafa Osman Ismail met with Secretary Rice in Washington and negotiated a review of economic sanctions, at nearly the same time as Deputy Secretary Zoellick was attending Sudan's July 2005 presidential inauguration.

Even though General Gosh reportedly ranked number two on the widely leaked UN list of senior Sudanese officials blamed for the ethnic cleansing in Darfur, his positive dealings with the U.S. government no doubt enhanced his status and encouraged other countries to meet with him. Gosh also visited London and met with British officials in March 2006.[31] One year after Gosh's visit to Washington and Zoellick's announcement of his low mortality estimate in Khartoum, in April 2006, the UN belatedly imposed sanctions on four men for Darfur war crimes, but the most highly ranked and only government official was a Sudanese Air Force officer.[32] A senior State Department official Donald Steinberg, explained that our interests "cut on the side of not offending the regime in Khartoum." The Bush administration pushed to keep Gosh off the sanctions list.[33]

## State Department's New View of Death in Darfur

The State Department reoriented its approach to Darfur by outsourcing an analysis of mortality to the Centre for Research on the Epidemiology of Disasters, a research group in Brussels based at the School of Public Health at the University of Louvain. Working with a new State Department liaison, Mark Phelan, and using surveys done outside the department, the Brussels group in May 2005 reported the background details for a new, lower mortality estimate, but did not follow the scholarly practice of referencing the primary sources on which it relied. Its findings are summarized in a working paper posted on the Web titled *Darfur: Counting the Deaths*.[34] Oddly, the working paper underwriting Zoellick's low estimate was not posted until one month after his comment in Sudan.

The *Washington Post* reproached Zoellick about the validity of his new mortality estimate in an April 2005 editorial titled "Darfur's Real Death Toll." The *Post* insisted that "the 60,000 number that Mr. Zoellick cited as low-but-possible is actually low-and-impossible" and concluded that "next time he should cite better numbers." The editorial instead cited our estimate of more than 300,000 deaths.[35]

Zoellick protested the editorial in a letter to the editor that defended his actions and referred to parallel charges that administration officials had fabricated and exaggerated intelligence data.[36] The characterization of the population-based survey mortality estimates as "intelligence" was unusual, but perhaps understandable when viewed in conjunction with the Washington visit of the Sudanese security and intelligence minister, General Gosh. In his letter, Zoellick wrote,

> I did not invent intelligence or stretch it. I did not recommend that the analysts change their assessment. I did indicate that estimates varied widely and that many were higher. Our estimate was based on more than 30 health and mortality surveys by public health professionals, and it was corroborated by a World Health Organization research center.

To support Zoellick's claim, the State Department posted on its Web site the earlier noted and very brief report, *Sudan: Death Toll in Darfur*.[37] This report again relies heavily on unreferenced sources.

A follow-up *Washington Post* article quoted a "senior State Department official" who said the report was "less scientific than you would think."[38] Why was the State Department now relying on a review with a health and nutrition approach and based on uncited sources that reported results substantively at odds with its earlier report issued under Colin Powell? What were the unreferenced sources, and what could they tell us about the numbers of deaths in Darfur during this continuing lethal conflict? How could scientific studies of such a lethal and protracted conflict produce such different conclusions? What can this experience tell us about the place of criminology in science and diplomacy? The answers to these questions may not definitely tell us whether outsourced scientific research was, to use Zoellick's words, "invented or stretched intelligence," but they do reveal ways in which scientific research can flip-flop in response to demands of diplomacy, in this case involving a denial of the deaths of many Darfurians.

The answers again involve the application of the health, not the crime, perspective in surveying the events in Darfur. The tension between these approaches appears at the outset of the outsourced British report. In a broadside against the State Department's ADS work from the previous summer – the survey that was the foundation of Colin Powell's testimony about genocide to the UN and U.S. Congress – the Brussels report complained that "these interviews...were not designed in any way to function as a mortality survey nor was there an overall systematic sampling methodology used that could make it representative of the roughly 200,000 refugees that fled to eastern Chad, much less of the entire 2.4 million people affected of Darfur."[39] Yet, the ADS survey applied a probability sampling methodology based on a two-stage random selection in all nineteen identified Chad camps and settlements.[40] Why would the Brussels report suggest otherwise?

The answer at least partly involves the criminal victimization (as contrasted with public health) approach followed in the earlier State Department/CIJ work. Despite the overlap in the social and political causes of the health and crime outcomes of such humanitarian emergencies, epidemiologists and demographers focus mainly on health outcomes,[41] whereas criminologists prioritize issues of legal responsibility for violence.[42] As we noted, a common sequence that these emergencies follow is to begin with violent attacks, followed by the flight of the victims and ensuing health problems. The violent attacks, flight, and health problems all contribute to mortality. The challenge is to simultaneously keep in mind the cumulative and multiplicative effects of violence, flight, and displacement to concentrated encampments, and the political state and nonstate causes of these disastrous consequences.[43] This is not possible given the limitations of health and nutrition surveys that ignore pre-camp violence leading to displacement – no matter how pristine their population sampling techniques may be.

## Reexamining the Surveys

We previously suggested that the WHO survey work underestimated mortality in Darfur by ignoring almost all of the pre-camp killings that led survivors to flee to the camps. To address this problem, we reexamined each of the 1,136 surveys from the ADS to arrive at an estimate of the number of killings that occurred in Darfur. This reexamination established that, during the period before the refugees arrived in Chad, 360 persons *specifically identified as husbands, wives, sons, and daughters* died or went missing. Only deaths of nuclear family members that were specifically referred to in the original interviews were included in the total of 360. This requirement of explicit nuclear family membership eliminated duplicate reports of deaths by extended family members. The count of 360 dead or missing persons formed the basis for the calculation of a CMR of 1.2 deaths per 10,000 people per day, or more than 98,000 persons presumed dead for the first eighteen months of the conflict. Note that this figure exceeds by more than 50 percent the low estimate reported by Zoellick, even though it does not cover the full period of the conflict and does not include deaths from malnutrition and sickness in the camps, the focus of the WHO survey. How could there be such a large disparity on such a fundamental matter of life and death?

From a criminological perspective, the key is the difference between the State Department's victimization survey methodology and the studies done for health-focused organizations in Darfur. Recall that, although Colin Powell wanted to testify on the basis of reliable evidence about the genocidal killings that led Darfurians to flee their villages and seek refuge in camps, the public health organizations worked with a different purpose. Because their goal is to stop those living in the camps

from dying of starvation and disease, public health organizations undertake population surveys of mortality, morbidity, and nutrition to establish the health risks posed in camp settings. These organizations – such
as the World Health Organization, the World Food Program, and the
Centers for Disease Control and Prevention – focus on these immediate and ongoing risks, rather than the past violence that led refugees to
the camps. This is why Powell needed his own victimization survey to
substantiate his congressional testimony about genocide.

The State Department had to conduct the ADS with the refugees in
Chad because the Sudanese government would not allow this kind of
violence-based investigation within its national borders. The Sudanese
government wanted to blame the deaths in Darfur on problems of health
and nutrition resulting from failed relief efforts of the international
health organizations.[44] Powell's State Department therefore developed
its own alternative victimization survey methodology. Because the
refugees in the Chad camps had fled from Darfur, they could provide a
retrospective view of the violence. Increasingly, demographers are using
this kind of indirect estimation approach for inaccessible settings; for
example, to learn about North Koreans' family histories of nutrition and
health problems, surveys have been conducted of North Koreans who
have taken refuge across the border in China.[45]

In contrast, the WHO jointly conducted its survey inside Darfur with
the cooperation of the Sudanese Ministry of Health (WHO/SMH) as
a health rather than a legally oriented crime victimization survey. The
different foci of the State Department/CIJ and WHO/SMH studies are
complementary, but their separate criminal law and health purposes led
the State Department to flip-flop misleadingly in its conclusions. Yet, the
State Department must have been aware of the limitations of the WHO
survey. When he made his seven-month estimate of 70,000 deaths, David
Nabarro of WHO explained that "these projections have not sought to
detail deaths due to violent incidents within Darfur communities."[46] The
CNN coverage of Nabarro's press conference indicated that "the figure
does not take into account deaths from direct violence in the conflict-torn
region."[47]

However, as recently as February 23, 2005, the British Secretary of State, Hilary Benn, testified to a parliamentary committee that "it is my best information that the WHO estimate...did include deaths from injuries and from violence."[48] Later in the same hearing, the Member of Parliament who raised the issue contradicted that statement, saying, "I am since told that the Committee has been advised by the WHO that that 70,000 does not include deaths due to the violence from which people have fled."[49] The parliamentary committee report concluded in bold print, "The only violent deaths which the WHO's estimate includes are those which took place in the camps for Internally Displaced Persons (IDPs)....Cited without clear explanation of its limitations, the WHO's estimate is extremely misleading."[50]

Amazingly, the issue arose yet again in the late May 2005 report from the Brussels group and provided further insight into Zoellick's low State Department estimate. The Brussels report, co-authored with the State Department's Mark Phelan, asserted that "the WHO mortality survey and the WHO mortality projections have often been confused and misguidedly used interchangeably. This has led some to misinterpret a WHO statement indicating exclusion of violent death from the WHO estimate, as also meaning violent deaths were not included in the WHO mortality surveys."[51] This assertion was made despite the fact that the WHO's Nabarro and the British parliamentary committee both made the point that violent deaths in the WHO/SMH survey represented only the less frequent instances of violent mortality in and around the camps and did not include deaths from attacks on the villages that led individuals to flee to the camps.

## Complementary and Combined Approach

The different foci of the State Department/CIJ and WHO/SMH surveys on pre- and in-camp experiences, respectively, make their results potentially complementary. The WHO/SMH survey indicates the health- and nutrition-related deaths in the Darfur IDP camps in the late summer of 2004, whereas the State Department/CIJ survey informs us about the violent deaths from attacks that led victims to seek sanctuary in Chad refugee camps.

We recalculated a CMR estimate based on the combined results from the two surveys. We noted earlier a CMR of 2.14 reported for North and West Darfur in the WHO/SMH survey. We took this figure as a meaningful estimate of mortality following displacement due to violence in and around the camps, but excluding deaths due to violent attacks before displacement. To complete the picture of Darfur mortality, we simply added the WHO/SMH estimate to the State Department/CIJ survey CMR due to violence and flight, which is 1.20, yielding a combined estimate of 3.34.

It is dubious in legal terms to call any of this mortality "expected" or "normal." Still, it can be useful to compare the CMR of 3.34 to the "normal" mortality rate of from 0.35 to 0.50 (per 10,000 per day) in a sub-Saharan African country in the affected period of 2003–04. The CMR exceeded expectations by a multiple of six or more. At this rate, 15,000 or more Darfurians died per month during the peak period of the genocide.

It is uncertain how long the peak period lasted, but the conflict in Darfur has been ongoing for more than five years. The WHO estimated 10,000 deaths per month, but recall also that Jan Egeland of the UN extrapolated this figure over eighteen months, a period that is almost certainly longer than the peak of the violence. In this sense, the WHO projection of constant mortality was both too low and too long, with offsetting consequences.

According to our calculations, it is much more likely that the Darfur death toll is between 200,000 and 400,000 than between the 60,000 to 160,000 estimate of Zoellick's State Department. This is a difference of hundreds of thousands of deaths. Yet, the very low estimate held sway in much of the media for more than a year after it was proclaimed by the State Department.

The downward bias of Zoellick's State Department estimation of deaths likely resulted in largest part from an overreliance on health-based nutritional studies. Yet, rather than further belabor existing estimates, we designed a new strategy to estimate mortality in Darfur with attention to both pre- and post-camp violence and health.

## A New and Alternative Approach

Our final estimation is based on a unique study that bridged the concerns of the crime and health perspectives. Médecins Sans Frontières (MSF)[52] published this study in the journal of medical research, *Lancet,* in October 2004.[53] MSF reported on four displacement camps in West Darfur between April and June 2004. The use of a limited number of sites resulted from the Sudanese government's restrictions of access placed on the researchers.

Like the WHO/SMH study, the MSF study found within-camp violence accounting for only 6 to 21 percent of deaths. Yet, the MSF study also asked about the period leading to flight to three of the four camps. Nearly 90 percent of the deaths before and during flight resulted from violence. In these three camps, the village and flight CMRs (5.9–9.5) were much higher than the in-camp period CMRs (1.2–1.3). Overall, the average mortality rate was 3.2 across the four MSF camps – with pre-camp violence included in three of the camps. *Note that this combined CMR approximates our estimate above resulting from combining the CMRs of the State Department/CIJ and WHO/SMH studies.*

Still, we concluded that it would be more persuasive to develop a new and alternative calculation that estimated mortality in Darfur on a month-by-month basis during the different time periods included in the MSF camp surveys. The MSF surveys used essentially the same sampling design as the WHO/SMH survey. The strongest feature of the WHO surveys was the number of camps included, whereas the strongest feature of the MSF surveys was the coverage of both pre- and in-camp mortality. We combined the MSF and WHO/SMH surveys to draw on the strengths of both. We narrowed the focus initially to nineteen months of the conflict and to the state of West Darfur, and later drew broader conclusions. The risk population figures for these months came from the UN humanitarian profiles. We included UN refugee camp counts in Chad to complete the estimate.

Our new estimate involved calculations of *direct* and *indirect* monthly estimates of CMRs to better take into account sources of over- and underreporting of deaths. We reasoned that doing so would allow us to balance upward and downward biases. We developed this approach in collaboration with Alberto Palloni, a recent president of the Population Association of America. The first author of this book is a former president of the American Society of Criminology. This collaboration explicitly bridges the population/health and crime/law paradigms.

The direct estimation method included CMRs calculated for all age groups in the surveys. We noted earlier our concern that respondents might use extended definitions of their families in their reports of deaths. The indirect estimation method alternatively included CMRs calculated only for family members younger than 5 years of age. We expected these reports would be less likely to include extended family members because respondents would focus more narrowly on their own children.[54] We then used life tables for sub-Saharan Africa to indirectly estimate the full age distribution of mortality.[55]

We present the directly and indirectly estimated results of our new alternative approach on the two sides of Figure 4.1. CMRs are presented on the left side of the figure for the nineteen months of 2003–04 considered by the surveys in West Darfur. The numbers of estimated deaths are presented for the same months on the right side of the figure. Some further detail results from the use of 95 percent confidence intervals to select the final upper and lower bound death estimates.[56] The peak in the death estimates on the right side occurs later than the peak CMRs on the left, which trend downward despite a relatively level period between ten and twenty months. The delayed peak followed by the decline in deaths estimated on the right side of the figure results from the expanding scope of the conflict in this period, as reflected in the growing numbers of the conflict-affected population.

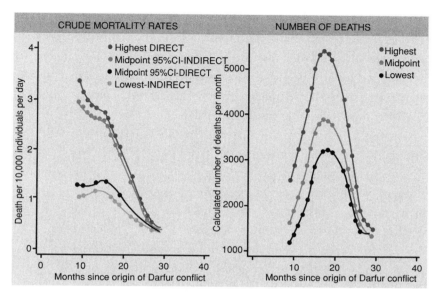

FIGURE 4.1. Estimated Deaths during Darfur Conflict.

The overall rise and decline in estimated deaths in West Darfur follows the classical pattern of complex humanitarian emergencies. Perhaps most interestingly, the peak monthly level of deaths estimated for West Darfur is about 4,000. We argue that there is good reason to believe that deaths are distributed approximately evenly across the three Darfur states. If this is so, the death toll in Darfur peaked in early 2004 at about 12,000 per month. Note that this figure lies between the 10,000 estimate of WHO/SMH and our earlier 15,000 estimate that combined the findings of WHO and ADS. This 12,000 peak monthly death estimate does not include missing persons and thus provides a cautious baseline figure.

Let us now say something more specifically about the nineteen months surveyed in West Darfur in 2003–04 and then suggest some broader conclusions. When we sum the mid-points between the high and low monthly death estimates on the right side of the figure over nineteen months, the estimated deaths total 49,288. When we extend the right tail of this distribution to May 2006, using additional data from a subsequent

WHO/SMH survey, the death toll reaches 65,296 in West Darfur alone. This estimate covers thirty-one months of the conflict, which has been under way for more than five years. If we estimated further years of the conflict or if we included all or most missing or disappeared persons, the death estimate would be much higher. Sudan currently blocks surveys of deaths or missing persons inside its borders.

Largely as a result of the violence, the UN indicates that more than one million individuals are now displaced or affected in West Darfur, with about one million people similarly displaced in each of the adjoining states of North and South Darfur. If the same ratio of death to displacement applies across states, this implies that about 200,000 deaths occurred over thirty-one months in Greater Darfur. This calculation divides the difference between the potential upward and downward biases of the direct and indirect methods, yielding estimates of 170,000 and 255,000 deaths, respectively. The number of deaths would range between 300,000 and 400,000 or more by extending the estimate to include subsequent years and missing and disappeared persons.

## Crime and Diplomacy

We demonstrated in this chapter a tendency for health-oriented researchers to underreport violent deaths in what these researchers designate complex humanitarian emergencies. The U.S. State Department in April 2005 shifted its focus from its own ADS study of criminal violence and victimization in Darfur to an outsourced review of studies that emphasized health-related deaths from disease and malnutrition and produced a low estimate of mortality in Darfur. Major news organizations such as Reuters and the British Broadcasting Corporation followed the State Department lead and reported tens of thousands rather than hundreds of thousands of deaths. The State Department stopped describing the Darfur conflict as genocide during this same period. Although the President and the State Department subsequently reasserted the genocide charge, we concluded that policy on this issue was biased by an alliance with the Sudanese government in the war on terror.

The findings of this chapter underline the importance in violence-driven disasters such as Darfur of considering the difference between crime- and health-oriented research and both the political and humanitarian purposes of this research. Yet, we can easily understand the cautious approach taken in health-oriented research. Two events in the spring and summer of 2005 highlighted the problems of sustaining important working relationships that make research possible in countries like Sudan.

In the first event, two senior MSF officials were arrested after their NGO published a study reporting hundreds of rapes in Darfur. The second event occurred at a meeting convened by the MacArthur Foundation of ICC representatives and NGOs doing aid work in Darfur. An NGO representative observed that "nobody wants to do anything that will compromise the security of workers on the ground or their ability to do their job," another remarked that "gathering information for war crimes investigations is not part of our mission," and a third said that "security for our staff and beneficiaries is totally dependent on how we are perceived in the area."[57] These kinds of problems restricted MSF's mortality study to a handful of camps, limited the WHO/SMH mortality survey to deaths occurring in the camps and not before, and finally led the State Department/CIJ to undertake its own survey in Chad refugee camps.

Our final estimate of mortality presented in this chapter was published in the journal *Science* in September 2006. The conclusion – that hundreds of thousands rather than tens of thousands died as a result of the conflict in Darfur – appeared in more than 100 newspaper articles worldwide.

As a final check on media reporting of mortality in Darfur, we conducted a content analysis of news articles by the two largest international news services, Reuters and the BBC. We included articles appearing in 2006 that cited numbers of deaths in Darfur. We summarize results of this analysis in Figure 4.2. Reuters consistently reported "tens of thousands of deaths" prior to publication of the September 2006 article in *Science*. The BBC reported fluctuating numbers. However, both news

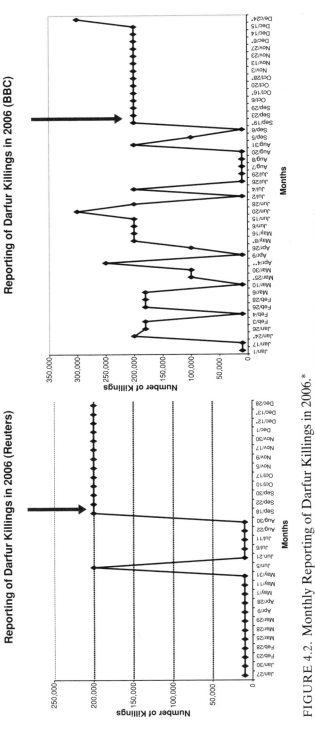

FIGURE 4.2. Monthly Reporting of Darfur Killings in 2006.*

*Each month includes two to four articles (depending on availability) for Reuters and BBC.

organizations began to consistently report the 200,000 number following the appearance of the *Science* article in September. Nearly all news organizations now report hundreds of thousands of deaths – in excess of 200,000 deaths – during the conflict in Darfur.

Oddly, the U.S. Government Accounting Office (GAO) published a review of Darfur death estimates in November 2006 that did not include the *Science* estimate.[58] The GAO review's critical conclusions were reflected in its subtitle, "Death Estimates Demonstrate Severity of Crisis, but Their Accuracy and Credibility Could Be Enhanced." It included the observation that "many experts believed that the lower end of State's estimate was too low and found that published documents describing State's estimate lacked sufficient information about its data and methods to allow it to be replicated and verified by external researchers."

The GAO found strengths and weaknesses in all the estimates, but it indicated greater concern about the higher than the lower estimates. Even though our estimate was the most recent one, was published in a journal that is among the most highly regarded in the world, and appeared two months before completion of the GAO report, it was not included.

The GAO insisted it did not have time to include the *Science* estimate. However, the two-month interval between the *Science* and GAO publications and the importance of the issue make this explanation implausible. We suggest two alternative explanations. First, the GAO did not want to probe the assumptions of the population health paradigm that guided its report. Second, the GAO did not want to more directly confront the background and timing of the April 2005 State Department estimate and its neglect of its own ADS data on the violence that substantiated Secretary Powell's determination of genocide in Darfur. Nonetheless, as shown in Figure 4.2, the State Department's low estimate was ignored when major news organizations reported and adopted our *Science* estimate of 200,000 or more deaths in the fall of 2006.

# 5   Eyewitnessing Genocide

## The Prosecutor's Brief

In February 2007, four years after the outbreak of atrocities, the new U.S. Special Envoy to Sudan, Andrew Natsios, corrected the State Department's low mortality estimate and reaffirmed Sudan's genocidal responsibility for hundreds of thousands of deaths in Darfur. "Arming the Janjaweed," Natsios told the U.S. House Committee on Foreign Affairs, "led to the launching of genocide in 2003 and 2004, which resulted in the deaths of hundreds of thousands of innocent civilians and the destruction of their villages and livelihoods."[1] Later, on *The Nightly Newshour*, Natsios confirmed that additional genocidal attacks had occurred within recent months in North Darfur. The interviewer spared Natsios the vexing question of why the United States did not intervene if a genocide was continuing under the watch of President Bush, who had vowed to avoid President Clinton's neglect of Rwanda.

In early 2007, world attention focused instead on the International Criminal Court (ICC) to which the UN Security Council had referred the conflict in 2005. After investigating the two-year-old conflict for an additional two years, the ICC Chief Prosecutor, Luis Moreno-Ocampo, "named names" in February 2007. Moreno-Ocampo, who is both a courageous and calculating prosecutor,[2] identified only two individuals in his February news conference: a Sudanese government minister, Ahmad Muhammad Harun, and an Arab militia leader, Ali Muhammad

Abd-Al-Rahman, whose *nom de guerre* is Ali Kushayb. Ocampo asked
the Judicial Chambers to issue summons for them to appear before the
ICC.[3] The Judicial Chambers took the further step of issuing warrants for
their arrest. In June 2008, Moreno-Ocampo reported to the UN Security Council that in the following month he would present evidence of
involvement of "the whole state apparatus" of Sudan in "the organization, commission, and cover-up of crime in Darfur."[4]

The middle-aged Moreno-Ocampo is an affable man with darting
eyebrows, a bushy beard, and an engaging smile. He previously headed
Transparency International for Latin America, the NGO that specializes
in exposing international corporate corruption. Before that, he prosecuted the generals who directed the infamous "disappearances" in his
native Argentina. The ICC job is equally challenging, in part because the
prosecutor must pursue war criminals without the benefit of police and
arrest powers. "I'm a stateless prosecutor," Moreno-Ocampo laments. "I
have 100 states under my jurisdiction and zero policemen."[5]

Moreno-Ocampo made his initial Darfur case to the ICC judges in a
cautious and circumscribed way, specifying attacks on only four villages
in 2003 and 2004. He alleged crimes against humanity and war crimes,
rather than specific crimes of genocide: "The conclusions are that many
thousands or even hundreds of thousands of civilians have died – either
from direct violence or as a result of disease, starvation, and the conditions of life imposed by the attacks."[6] He cited others' allegations of sexual violence: "Rape is reported in open sources as a common weapon of
the conflict."[7] Perhaps most important, although Moreno-Ocampo identified the Fur, Masalit, and Zaghawa tribes as victims of the violence,
he limited consideration of race to a few descriptions of epithets in the
attacks, and he did not in 2007 charge the accused with genocide. Still,
Moreno-Ocampo's presentation stipulated that "the prosecutor's investigation has revealed the underlying operational system that enabled
the commission of those massive crimes."[8] This characterization left no
doubt that the violence in Darfur was *collective* rather than individualized violence that was committed as part of an organized enterprise.

The prosecutor's statement represented a theory of liability that explicitly involved a group acting with common purpose:

> HARUN and KUSHAYB are charged together under Article 25(3)(d) with having contributed to the commission of a crime by a *group of persons acting with a common purpose*. . . . Criminal "common purpose" responsibility is demonstrated under the Rome Statute if the contribution is made either: (1) with the aim of furthering the criminal activity or criminal purpose of the group, where such activity and purpose involves the commission of a crime within the jurisdiction of this Court, (2) in the knowledge of the intention of the group to commit crimes. There are reasonable grounds to believe that the requirements of either of these forms of "common purpose" criminal liability have been met.[9]

The concept articulated in Moreno-Ocampo's statement – group-based common purpose – is based on ideas about "criminal organization" and "joint criminal enterprise" that are of central importance in the response of contemporary international criminal law to collective violence. These ideas build on social science conceptions of group dynamics and collective action.[10] Their most notable contemporary application was in the aborted (due to his death) prosecution of Slobodan Milosevic for his involvement in a "joint criminal enterprise" to commit genocide in the former Yugoslavia.[11] The concepts of "joint criminal enterprise," "criminal organization," and "common purpose" signal the use of laws prosecuting criminal *group* processes in the collective commission of crimes. This kind of prosecution pursues both the upward and downward reach of the *organization* of the criminal activities themselves.

This focus on organization played an understandably important but sometimes controversial role in the relatively recent American law enforcement pursuit of infamous organized crime figures and their operations, as well as in the earlier prosecution of the Nazi war machine at Nuremberg. This focus is controversial because it is "conspiratorial" in nature. The legal scholar Mark Osiel questions the unreflective use of such legal doctrines in international criminal law: "An open mind would

begin not by asking what legal doctrines offer precedents to cope quickly
with this new challenge (i.e., genocide and crimes against humanity), but
rather, what kind of influence do participants in such criminality actually exercise over one another, through what organizational devices and
interactional dynamics."[12]

We use the concepts of "collective efficacy"[13] and "collective action"
to elaborate our understanding of the criminal organization of the genocidal violence in Darfur.[14] The interviews conducted with Darfur
refugees in the Atrocities Documentation Survey (ADS) reveal this
organization in remarkable detail. In the next chapter, we discuss the
broad organizational dynamics of the large-scale criminal enterprise. To
illustrate these concepts, we focus in this chapter on the notorious militia leader Musa Hilal and the social and historical context of his role
in Darfur's genocidal violence. First, however, we examine the historical background to the socially constructed and state-instigated politics of
collective violence in Darfur.

## The Racial Dynamics of Darfur

The U.S. charge of genocide in Darfur includes an assertion of racial
intent. More specifically, this assertion is that the Sudanese government
has intentionally used the divisive force of racism to collectively motivate
the death and destruction of a legally "protected" group (or groups) in
Darfur. The United States accuses the Sudanese state of joining its air
and ground military forces with less formally organized Arab militias,
commonly called Janjaweed, to attack racially targeted African farmers and villagers. What complicates this assertion of racism is that the
Africans in Darfur – who are predominantly members of the Zaghawa,
Fur, and Masalit groups – may be physically indistinguishable from their
Arab neighbors, with whom they also share the Muslim religion. However, in support of the race-based genocide claim, Chirot and McCauley
insist that "Some of the worst ethnic genocides of the twentieth century

involved targeting groups that were difficult to differentiate on physical or cultural grounds from perpetrators."[15]

Yet, some NGOs, such as Save Darfur, the academic-activist Eric Reeves, and the widely read *New York Times* columnist Nicholas Kristof insist that the Darfur conflict is racially driven. Kristof describes in a column the case of Halima, who was one of seven women recently captured and raped by Janjaweed militia outside a displacement camp.[16] This account details racial epithets like those reported in about one-third of the survey interviews we analyze from the ADS in this and following chapters:

> "You blacks are not human," she quotes them as yelling."We can do anything we want to you. You cannot live here." ... She says three men raped her, beat her and stole her clothes. Another of the seven who were caught, Aziza Yakub, 17, confirmed Halima's story, and added that the Janjaweed told her while raping her: "You blacks are like monkeys. You are not human."

Kristof's columns in the *New York Times* regularly refer to such incidents and the larger conflict in Sudan as pitting Arabs against Black Africans. Yet, other reporters for the *Times*[17] and some academics describe the same opposing parties as Arab and non-Arab; in doing so, they implicitly refer to little more than the use or nonuse of Arabic as a first language and as the characteristic dividing the opposed groups. This is not a minor editorial difference. The role played by the state in the social and political construction of racial difference is an important part of what makes these war crimes genocide.

The varying identification of the victims in this conflict as Black and non-Arab suggests that these distinctions are inherently uncertain and socially constructed. Sudanese society is made up of hundreds of tribal entities. Flint and de Waal emphasize that, historically, "Darfurians – like most Africans – were comfortable with multiple identities. Dar Fur was an African kingdom that embraced Arabs as valued equals."[18]

Furthermore, Darfurians often shifted their tribal and racial identities to match their changing social and economic circumstances in a forbidding desert environment.

For example, O'Fahey notes that, until the latter part of the last century in Darfur, when a successful Fur farmer obtained a certain number of cattle, he identified with the Arab Baggara, and in a few generations his descendants boasted an "authentic" Arab genealogy.[19] In this earlier era, the growth of Arab-Islamic influence in Darfur sometimes took the benign form of a nationalistic "Sudanization."[20] However, this era is now history, along with its fluidity of geographical and social movement and identity transformation. The implications of this change are ominous because, as O'Fahey warns, "the Janjaweed ... have a fully developed racist ideology, a warrior culture, weapons and plenty of horses and camels – still the easiest way to get around Darfur."[21] Horses and camels play important roles in a region lacking a modern transportation infrastructure.

Americans might approve of the assimilation involved in Jewish[22] and Irish[23] immigrants becoming "white," but in Africa, changed identities are often linked to outbreaks of violent conflict. In South Africa, John and Jean Comaroff note that "local relations among the peoples of the region, not to mention the distinctions and conflicts among them, were always much messier, more inchoate ... ; less black and white, less sharply dualistic, less recalcitrant and clear-cut."[24] Group conflict brought social rigidity, distancing, and separation, with the consequence that, "at moments of crisis, such subtleties ... dissolve. ... Cleavages, real and imaginary, reassert themselves."[25]

Brubaker calls this process "unmixing," which aptly describes Rwanda.[26] The Hutu and Tutsi in Rwanda, like the Blacks and Arabs in Darfur, shared a history of intermarriage that defied racial classification and made them sometimes physically indistinguishable. Yet, during the Rwandan genocide, a binary racial divide dominated the thinking of both perpetrators and victims. The state played the central role in creating and maintaining racial cleavages – the Rwandan government mandated the use of identity cards that distinguished Hutu from Tutsi.[27] This advanced a process of racially making the case for genocide.

In Darfur, as in Rwanda, the state constructed racial and tribal distinctions that empowered the Arab Janjaweed. The Janjaweed are members of Arab pastoral groups with livelihoods built around raising and herding animals. These Arab pastoralists relied historically on seasonal access to grazing land and water on property settled by African agriculturalists. Intertribal traditions of negotiation, cooperation, and dispute resolution made this nomadic lifestyle possible. However, grazing land and water became scarce and contested with the advent of climate change and the intensified desertification of sub-Saharan Africa. Access to arable land now represented the opportunity for life itself in Darfur. Group-linked settlements on this arable land therefore became prominent places of conflict.

By the mid-1980s, intertwined processes of desertification and famine aggravated disputes over land and water and contributed to a socially constructed, racially tinged division between Arabs and other Africans. Differences of language and livelihood associated with perceived skin tone were increasingly defined as racial. Traditions of cooperation and accommodation evaporated in a desert terrain that offered up major new scenes of bloodshed. African farmers resented Arab herdsmen who moved intrusively through their pastureland. Group relationships shifted from what Oberschall calls a more "normal" to a "crisis" frame.[28]

Race and ethnicity emerged as the driving forces of this conflict. El-Battahani concludes, "The longer a conflict persists, the more these ethnic, religious and cultural factors come into play. In an old conflict, when even the initial causes have petered out or died away, that 'abstract,' ideological ethnicity becomes an active material and social force."[29]

Major clashes led to hundreds and then thousands of deaths in the late 1980s. More Africans than Arabs died in these fever-pitched battles, as if in rehearsal for more one-sided conflicts to come. Indigenous forms of dispute settlement disappeared, and the central government in

Khartoum imposed no new or more successful mechanisms to resolve the conflicts. A dismissive Arab supremacist ideology magnified rather than mitigated these bloody, unresolved conflicts.

The "Arabization" of the conflict dates in Darfur to the mid-1980s. One source involved the activities of the Libyan strongman Muammar Qaddafi, who during the famine of 1985 brought food and guns into Darfur as part of his larger ambition to create an "Arab belt" across sub-Saharan Africa. The newly available weapons made intergroup clashes more lethal, and the new import market in weapons kept growing, even when Qaddafi lost enthusiasm for this military adventure.

Sadiq al-Mahadi, who was elected prime minister of Sudan in 1986, developed a plan to create an "Arab and Islamic Union." The al-Mahadi government intensified Arabization policies. These policies became more brutal following the military coup led by al-Mahadi's successor, Omar al-Bashir, in 1989. Both administrations played on Arab/African tensions and justified their continuing neglect of Darfur with the new racially infused excuse that its problems resulted from insufficient Arabization.

A group of Arab intellectuals wrote Prime Minister al-Mahadi a well-publicized letter in 1987 that celebrated the "Arab race" for the "creation of civilization in the region ... in the areas of governance, religion and language."[30] The letter warned, "If this neglect of the participation of the Arab race continues, things will break loose from the hands of the wise men to those of the ignorant, leading to matters of grave consequences." From this period on, an Arab-Islamic supremacist ideology prevailed, and Arabs replaced Africans in the civil service of Darfur. The extent of this displacement spurred a highly controversial underground report, *The Black Book: The Imbalance of Power and Wealth in Sudan*. A group called "The Seekers of Truth and Justice" published and distributed the report in 2002. This group opposed Arab domination of the government and evolved into the rebel Justice and Equality Movement (JEM) in Darfur. *The Black Book* challenged an Arab leadership that excluded Black Africans from government positions.

The changed interethnic environment further allowed long-entrenched racist attitudes associated with Sudan's history of slavery to gain new life. Slavery had persisted largely unchallenged as an institution in Sudan until the 1920s.[31] It played a major part in Sudan's twenty-year North-South war, during which an estimated 10,000 people were enslaved.[32] The old racism of slavery, with its roots in the nineteenth century, gained a furtive foothold through abductions during the Darfur conflict.[33] As discussed in Chapter 6, a Khartoum court received evidence of the abduction of as many as forty women and girls from the Wadi Saleh area of West Darfur.[34] Kwame Appiah notes, "Because people almost always think of slaves as belonging to a kind – a race, a tribe, a class, a family – that is suited to enslavement, the slave status tends to survive the abandonment of the formal institutions of slavery."[35] References to Blacks as slaves are a mainstay of the racial epithets heard during attacks on African villages in Darfur.

Samantha Power rightly warns that depicting the Darfur conflict that began in the mid-1980s as the product of "a racist conspiracy" may not tell the full or complete story.[36] Still, Nicholas Kristof remarks that, although "shorthand descriptions are simplistic, they're also essentially right."[37] "Thus was racial polarity constructed," the journalist Sebastian Mallaby observes, "where none had previously existed."[38] Prunier argues that the 1984 famine sharpened the divide between the nomadic herders and farmers and that now this dichotomy is superimposed on an Arab versus African dichotomy. He concludes, "This marked the beginning of years of low-intensity racial conflict and harassment, with the 'Arab' Centre almost automatically siding against the 'African Periphery.'"[39] The Sudanese government defined "Arab" as good, and "African" as bad.

## The Racial Dynamics of Contemporary Sudan

The Sudanese state socially constructed and intensified the Arab/Black African divide in Darfur over a period of at least twenty years. During this time, some African groups in Darfur slowly organized a resistance effort. By early 2003, the Fur had organized a small-scale Darfur Liberation Front (DLF) that joined with the Zaghawa and renamed itself the Sudan Liberation Movement/Army (SLA/SMA). The SLA/SMA formed links with the Sudan People's Liberation Movement (SPLM) in South Sudan, where the United States played a major role in brokering a peace agreement between them and the government of Sudan. U.S. Christian evangelical groups, who had worked in this region of Sudan for years, converting large numbers of Africans, successfully prevailed on the Bush administration to advance a major peace agreement for South Sudan.[40]

The contesting North and South parties signed the Comprehensive Peace Agreement (CPA) in early 2003 with the hope of ending a twenty-year conflict that had its own genocidal dimensions. Meanwhile, the conflict escalated in the Darfur region of western Sudan, probably in part because the United States focused its attention on the North-South agreement, but also because of the U.S. preoccupation with the oncoming war in Iraq. In 2003, the other prominent and previously noted rebel group in Darfur – the Justice and Equality Movement (JEM), which had published *The Black Book* – joined the conflict. Rebel groups drew members from the Zaghawa, Fur, and Masalit tribes, although the rebel forces remained relatively small and the Zaghawa and Fur were more involved than the Masalit in this initial rebel activity.

These still modest-sized rebel groups mounted organized attacks against government forces in Darfur during the early months of 2003, including a surprisingly successful ground attack that destroyed a number of planes at a government air base in April 2003. Flint and de Waal report that, as a result, "the security cabal in Khartoum was fired by rage: its instinctive response was to crush the rebels who had done this, along with anyone else who sympathized with them. Military Intelligence took the Darfur file."[41] This security cabal included Salah Gosh (introduced in Chapter 4), Abduraheem Hussein (Minister of Interior), and Ahmad Harun, introduced in the ICC brief described earlier. Figure 5.1 goes well

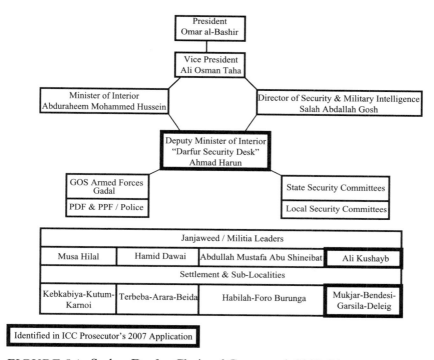

FIGURE 5.1. Sudan-Darfur Chain of Command, 2003–04.

beyond the 2007 brief in locating organizationally a number of individuals identified in the ADS survey and discussed in this and following chapters. In 2008, the Prosecutor asked the ICC to charge President al-Bashir with genocide.

The security and military intelligence sector of the Sudanese government is a powerful residual product of President al-Bashir's military coup. This group likely reasoned that the government could shift its military assets from southern Sudan to Darfur and attack with impunity, given the focus of the Americans and the international community elsewhere. The ruling Arab-Islamists in Khartoum used the Arab militias as their allies and proxies in Darfur. They proceeded to eliminate the prospects of African rebellion by not only killing but also removing Blacks from their farms and villages and resettling their lands with nomadic Arab tribes. This plan, in the words of the Genocide Convention, involved "deliberately inflicting on the group conditions of life calculated to bring about its physical destruction in whole or in part."

We concieve the genocide charge as follows: The government of Sudan knowingly mobilized and collectivized a racially constructed division between the Arab and Black African groups to intentionally motivate the death, destruction, and displacement of the latter groups from their farms and villages in Darfur. We assume authorization from the highest levels of the Sudanese government, as implied in Figure 5.1, for the coordination of Government of Sudan (GoS) military forces with Arab militias in attacks on African farms and villages. As one refugee respondent surmised, "They come together, they fight together and they leave together."[42] The Sudanese government used Arab militias to crush African tribes in Darfur much as they did in southern Sudan.

Numerous writers about genocide, beginning with Raphael Lemkin,[43] who coined the term, emphasize the energizing role of race or related ethnic, national, and religious constructs in conjunction with more material motivations for genocide. As Hinton notes in the context of the Cambodian genocide, although sociopolitical changes create an environment in which genocide occurs, "for genocide to take place ... these changes must be accompanied by a violent ideology that adapts traditional cultural knowledge to its lethal purposes."[44] Similarly, Scheper-Hughes and Bourgois observe, in their analysis of the material and symbolic origins of genocidal violence, that "conflict between competing groups over material resources – land and water – can sometimes also escalate into mass slaughters when combined with social sentiments that question or denigrate the basic humanity of the opposing group."[45] Brannigan and Hartwick cogently conclude, "What are required are techniques of provocation and incitement."[46]

Essential but perhaps underemphasized in some of these accounts is that such "ideologies, sentiments, provocations, and incitements" require a collective organizational force that rises above simple individualized expression. In the case of Darfur, this collective expression is distinctively racial, although it is also powerfully associated with ethnicity and the settlement of land and property claims. Prunier concludes, "Since Darfur had been in a state of protracted racial civil war since the mid-1980s, the tools were readily available; they merely needed to be upgraded. It was done and the rest is now history."[47] Demonstrating the application of such tools and their upgrading in a joint genocidal criminal enterprise, however, requires conceptualization of a collectively organized racial intent. Past and more recent theoretical contributions of sociological criminology provide the required concepts.

## The Criminal Organization of Collective Action

One of America's most famous criminologists, Edwin Sutherland, understood the need for a theory of crime that explained how and why individuals who were subjected to differing group influences often engaged in quite distinctive forms of criminal behavior. These crimes could be as distinctive as the "street" and "suite" crimes committed under quite different collective or group influences: in the former case, in some of America's most desperately disadvantaged urban neighborhoods, and in the latter case, in America's most ethically segregated corporate boardrooms.[48] Thus, Sutherland created a highly versatile theory that explained a wide range of criminal behaviors, from common law crimes to corporate crimes. Yet, it was not until the recent work of Robert Sampson and his development of the concept of collective efficacy that sociological criminology's theories and methods strongly emphasized group processes while simultaneously and systematically taking conventional individual-level processes into account.[49]

The concept of collective efficacy builds on the foundation of the psychologist Albert Bandura's conception of self-efficacy, but it differs in emphasizing that individuals are collectively organized in neighborhoods that have their own distinctive qualities. Sampson and his colleagues observe, "Just as individuals vary in their capacity for efficacious action, so too do neighborhoods vary in their capacity to achieve common goals."[50] The community and surrounding society value this communal capacity, even if or because subgroups might rebel against them. The point is that these evaluations are socially shared. For example, shared goals can promote a "neighborhood efficacy" based on the communal supervision of children and the collective maintenance of social order. Sampson emphasizes that efficacy occurs not just as a result of the actions of individuals within families but also as a consequence of processes at the level of neighborhoods. His research demonstrates that, even when individual-level factors are held constant or removed, some neighborhoods can still be seen as enhanced in their capacity to perform monitoring and order-maintaining tasks in ways that prevent and reduce crime. Sampson's work on collective neighborhood efficacy supports the well-known African aphorism that "it takes a village."

Sutherland (1943) would regard this neighborhood-level process as a form of "differential social organization" among citizens that is mobilized to counteract organization around criminal opportunities within communities. Recently, Matsueda added the concept of social efficacy to refer to the capacity of particular individuals to mobilize others in realizing shared goals such as collective efficacy.[51] Thus, the concept of social efficacy is a linking mechanism highlighting the acts of individual initiative or "agency" that inspire others to join together in collectively organized communal action; for example, mobilizing individuals within a neighborhood for the joint supervision of children and the collective maintenance of public order. Social and collective efficacy are powerful concepts that explain how some communities are well organized to control crime.

This discussion leads to parallel questions of whether similar but opposing processes can socially organize crime itself, again as part of a versatile and generalized theory of crime, and whether collective genocidal violence can be explained by collective processes. In the next section, we explore whether Musa Hilal, an infamous Arab militia leader, acted as an agent of social efficacy in the collective organization of genocidal violence in Darfur. At a theoretical level, the question is whether the protection and destruction of village life are *both* collective processes, despite their diametrically opposed purposes.

## The Differential Social Organization of Genocidal Victimization

Matsueda advances the use of the concepts of social and collective efficacy,[52] collective action,[53] and frame analysis[54] in explaining both group-based patterns of crime and its control. To do so, he borrows from a prominent collective action theory that (i) defines key processes collectively or as group based, rather than simply as actions of individuals; (ii) defines opposing organized groups of actors as "us" and "them"; and (iii) emphasizes the perception and definition of injustices caused by "them" that can be corrected or altered through the organized actions of "us."[55]

This formulation incorporates a premise common in classical American structural and cultural theories of delinquent gangs and crime. This premise is that disadvantaged American youth often confront shared problems of status frustration that they organize to solve together.[56] These theories argue that, when these youth "frame" their shared frustrations as following from a status system that is unjustly stacked against them – as an "us" versus "them" framing of injustice – they often begin to collectively pursue socially organized solutions to reduce their frustrations by illegal means, for example, through organized gangs.

A parallel conceptualization informs our understanding of the socially organized perpetration of genocide. Scheper-Hughes and Bourgois similarly note that, in genocidal contexts, "extreme forms of 'us' versus 'them' can result in a social self-identity predicated on a stigmatized, devalued notion of the other as enemy."[57] This kind of framing can instigate and organize large-scale collective violence in a manner analogous to smaller group conflicts involving fights between youth gangs.

Thus, we suggest that a "joint criminal enterprise" – to use the language of international criminal law – is also a socially framed collective action or solution that encompasses an "us" and "them" ideology.

Although this enterprise is often a process pursued outside formal institutional settings, such as in street gangs, it can also be instigated through the agency of state-supported groups and actors. State-supported groups and agents can provide the social efficacy that Matsueda describes as leading from individual initiative to collective action. As criminologists emphasize, these collective actions often are the product of intertwined, legitimate (e.g., national or local governments), and illegitimate (e.g., gangs or militias) opportunity structures.[58]

Social actors work with the opportunities immediately available to them, whether they are gang members or politicians and military officers. This point is as important in understanding international war crimes in Darfur as it is for domestic street crimes in Chicago or Stockholm.[59] In Darfur, the Sudanese state worked with its military and through its government security apparatus to mobilize the leadership of a genocidal criminal organization that most notably involved Janjaweed militias. Sutherland anticipated how such criminally organized processes can be fostered by governments, for example, even in the more familiar wartime environments of developed countries like the United States. Think for a moment about a familiar American historical context described by Sutherland.

Writing about theft in America during World War II,[60] Sutherland explained, "The meaning of property ownership and of property rights was confused by governmental appropriation of private property, by radical departures from the previous system of determining values and distributing property, and by general use of public property with little attention to its ownership." The American government used its special powers to seize private property to mobilize for the war effort. Sutherland emphasized in this context the role of the state in using definitional language – through what would later be called "techniques of neutralization"[61] and "vocabularies of motives"[62] – to redefine the seizing of citizens' property. The U.S. government redefined private property as collectively available for the war effort. Sutherland reasoned that individuals also now felt freer to take property for their own purposes, and therefore, property crime increased.[63]

In Darfur, the Sudanese state and its agents went much further in generating a genocidal process, redefining not only property norms but also the holders of the settled property – the racially identified Black African farmers and villagers – as appropriate targets for displacement and death. The settlements of African farmers and villagers constituted occupied "lands of opportunity" and, as such, presented a potential solution to the shared impoverished circumstances of landless Arab tribes. Matsueda writes of crime more generally that "such social organization is the result of collective action and entails building consensus over a problematic situation, and then translating that consensus into action."[64] In Darfur, the problem of the Arab pastoralists was that they needed to graze their herds on the arable land settled by the Black African agriculturalists.

The state-instigated solution authorized the victimization of the settled Black African groups that farmed and thereby controlled the land. The Sudanese state used the social efficacy of its agents to collectively define the Black African groups and settlements in "us" and "them" racial terms. This definition of the situation encouraged taking African villagers' property, destroying their villages, raping their women, killing their men, and displacing their people.

## Racializing Collective Violence in Darfur

Analysts trace the recent conflict in western Sudan to the rebel attacks against government forces in the early months of 2003 that we briefly described earlier. Yet, the roots of this conflict ran deeper, as illustrated by the example of the agency and social efficacy of the militia leader, Musa Hilal. Hilal is one of the Sudanese state's principal agents in North Darfur. Several other important militia leaders, named in Figure 5.1 and discussed in the next chapter, participated in the organization of this genocide.

Recall that Prosecutor Moreno-Ocampo's 2007 brief to the ICC judges named only one militia leader, Ali Kushayb. We identify four militia leaders active in Darfur in Figure 5.1, but they are not the only leaders; our goal is nonetheless to describe the criminal organization and the role of race in the genocide in Darfur. To begin, it is important to point out that Hilal's leadership role probably was limited to the nomadic Arab groups called the Abbala in North Darfur; he was not involved with the Arab groups called the Baggara in South Darfur.

Four of the large Arab Baggara tribes in South Darfur own land and probably, as a result did not participate in the recent Darfur conflict. In contrast, a number of the smaller Abbala Arab tribes in North Darfur – who historically relied on seasonal access to the Black African farmers' lands – became increasingly impoverished as desertification, drought, and famine diminished their herds, restricted their access to grass and water, and generally undermined their nomadic lifestyles. "To this day," Flint and de Waal report, "many Abbala Arabs explain their involvement in the current conflict in terms of this 250-year-old search for land, granted to the Baggara but denied to them."[65] This was and is a shared source of collectively framed injustice. It is important to locate Musa Hilal within this context.

Musa Hilal is the son of Sheikh Hilal, an important leader among the proud but increasingly poor Arab nomadic groups in North Darfur. Until recently, the Arab nomadic groups traversed a changing landscape of diminished life chances and opportunities, in ways analogous to classical criminology's emphasis on differential opportunity and limited mobility prospects. Yet, Musa Hilal, as their leader, today exploits the enhanced opportunities he enjoys as a newly empowered agent of the Sudanese state.

Hilal insists that he is "a big sheikh...not a little sheikh."[66] He is as well a reputed leader in the semisecret and supremacist pan-Islamic organization called the "Arab Gathering." Yet, Hilal also makes no secret of being an agent of the Sudanese government. He boasts that beginning in the summer of 2003, "when the government put forward a program of arming all the people, I will not deny I called our sons and told them to become armed, and our sons acquiesced.... Those who became armed were no less than 3,000."[67] Hilal explains, "Our job is to mobilize people – the government has told us to mobilize people."[68] This role is further confirmed by Salah Abdallah Gosh, the head of the National Security and Intelligence Service discussed in Chapter 4 and identified in Figure 5.1, who reports that Hilal "was invited by the government to back the government Army, and he gave the people guns and leadership."[69] In this way, the Sudanese state provided Hilal with the opportunity to build a militia that capitalized on his own past exploits.

For Hilal is not merely an authorized agent of the Sudanese state; he is also a convicted repeat criminal with a lengthy record that extends from robbery to murder. Hilal is an imposing figure in his late forties and is well over six feet in height. By 2002, he was already a powerful and well-armed militia leader associated with widespread killing and looting in Darfur. Hilal is a personal embodiment of the kind of mobility that can follow from the integration of legitimate and illegitimate opportunity structures.[70]

A *New York Times* account reported that a past governor of North Darfur, Ibrahim Suleiman, summoned Hilal during this period and warned him, "If I decide to kill you, I will kill you, and nothing will happen to me." Hilal is reported to have simply smiled in response, thinking that he was untouchable.[71] The governor nonetheless arrested Hilal, reportedly for tax evasion, and sent him to a prison in far-away Port Sudan. Four months later, however, the government in Khartoum removed Suleiman from office and brought Hilal back to the Sudanese capital under "house arrest." In June 2003, Hilal flew back to Darfur and organized the Janjaweed with government support, reportedly due to the intervention of Vice President Ali Osman Taha (see Figure 5.1), a known supporter of Hilal.[72] The deposed governor of North Darfur later cited the decision to bring Hilal back to Darfur as a turning point: "When the problems with the rebels started in Darfur, we in the government of

Sudan had a number of options. We chose the wrong one. We chose the very worst one."[73]

In the past, the Sudanese government recruited young men from the Black African groups of Darfur, including the Masalit tribe, for their campaigns of death, destruction, and displacement in southern Sudan. Now, the government excluded these same Black African groups from militia recruitment in western Sudan and targeted them as victims. Flint and de Waal[74] describe the revised racial order of the Darfur conflict:

> Darfur's new army... closed its doors to the "African" tribes who were traditionally its mainstay. But in everything else it was undiscriminating, accepting – even seeking out – the criminal element that was a defining feature of the pre-war Janjawiid. Musa Hilal set the example. Shortly after returning to North Darfur, he visited Kutum jail, and ordered the staff to bring all prisoners before him. One of the wardens remembers him saying, "Why are Arabs in prison?" and ordering that they be released. Many such men found a safe haven in the Janjawiid, whose own behavior was defined by its unbound criminality. The Janjawiid stole, burned, mutilated, killed, and raped – subjecting tiny communities to unimaginable horrors.

Musa Hilal rallied his recruits to attack Black African villages with a vocabulary framed around racially inspired exhortations and justifications.

## Hilal's Place in the Criminal Organization of Genocide

As already noted, Hilal frequently emphasized in interviews with reporters that the government authorized his mobilization and recruitment work in Darfur. Ahmad Harun served as Deputy Minister of the Interior in charge of the "Darfur Security Desk" and has been identified by the ICC Prosecutor as the intermediary between the leadership of the Sudanese government and Arab militia leaders such as Musa Hilal (see Figure 5.1). Harun is in his early to mid-forties and is a former judge with a degree from Cairo University.

Perhaps more significantly, before assuming responsibility for Darfur, Harun mobilized local tribes in response to an insurgency during the 1990s in the Kordofan area to the east of Darfur in Sudan. Julie Flint summarizes the well-known strategy the Sudanese government used repeatedly in such areas:

> The strategy is the same as used in the twenty-one years of war in southern Sudan and the Nuba Mountains: (1) finding an ethnic militia with existing rivalries with the targeted group (the ethnic group related to the rebels); (2) arming and supporting that militia, and giving it impunity for any crimes; (3) encouraging and helping it to attack the civilians of the targeted group, with scorched earth tactics often backed up by government ground troops and air power; (4) killing, raping, abducting, or forcibly displacing the targeted group and destroying its economy; and (5) denying humanitarian access to needy civilians. This pattern of attack has been used, again and again, in southern Sudan.[75]

In Darfur, Harun mobilized local tribal militias that included the Janjaweed and integrated them into the Public Defense Forces (PDF), a citizen paramilitary and reserve component of the Sudanese Armed Forces.[76]

Harun directed civilian and military activity in Darfur in mid-2003, at or about the same time as Hilal returned to North Darfur and Khartoum removed Ibrahim Suleiman, Hilal's nemesis, as governor of North Darfur. Harun spearheaded a major recruitment effort implemented through local leaders like Hilal, explaining that "practically speaking the GoS [i.e., Government of Sudan] can never have sufficient numbers of soldiers."[77] Harun offered this judgment after a period of several months in early 2003 when the Sudanese military was losing several hit-and-run battles with small rebel groups. The rebels capitalized on the element of surprise, but they also benefited from the unwillingness of some Government of Sudan forces to carry out "scorched-earth" attacks on African farmers and villagers. Some of these government soldiers came from Black African tribes in Darfur and therefore refused to join in attacks on their own groups. Harun needed a more readily motivated group for local purposes, and this led him to form the Arab Janjaweed militias.

Harun energetically pursued his Darfur mission. He visited Darfur at least six times in July and August 2003 for meetings,[78] including one attended by a refugee interviewed in the ADS. The refugee recalled, "I was at the meeting where he announced that those that disrespected the government should be 'cleansed away' by the government." This refugee served as a representative to the West Darfur Council before fleeing the violence. He reported that the meeting was part of a government program of propaganda "which tried to show that all blacks are rebels and should be fought."

Harun spent more than four months altogether in Darfur.[79] At another meeting near Nyla, Harun listened as a militia/Janjaweed leader boasted that the Arab tribes "can wipe out the areas of the Fur, Zaghawa, and Masalit in a matter of one month." In a July meeting in Al Geneina, Harun said that he held the power "to kill or forgive whoever" in Darfur. His speech encouraged attacks on *civilian* populations he associated with rebels, rather than the rebels themselves, and he said they were ready "to kill three-quarters of Darfur in order to allow one-quarter to live." When asked about the indiscriminateness of this policy of killing, his defense was that the "rebels infiltrate the villages," and thus, the villages "are like water to fish." Harun regularly encouraged taking from "all the Fur and what they had," which he characterized as "booty," and further identified the primary targets of attacks as the Fur, Zaghawa, and Masalit.[80]

Harun repeated most if not all of the previous statements in a July 2003 speech in Al Geneina, in the company of Musa Hilal and another local militia leader, Hamid Dawai, whom we introduce in Chapter 6 (and see Figure 5.1):

> On that day, Harun's speech was preceded by that of the notorious Militia/Janjaweed leader Musa Hilal. Hilal's speech was characterized by the witness who heard it as "very racist." Hilal was enthusiastic about unifying to fight the enemy and characterized the

conflict as a "holy war." Hilal's remarks were followed by Harun's announcement that the President had handed him the Darfur Security Desk and that he had the power and authority to kill and forgive whoever in Darfur. It was shortly after the meeting in Al Geneina that Harun travelled together with Hamid Dawai.[81]

Harun not only recruited Janjaweed but also distributed weapons and money for training camps. He controlled an "unlimited and unaudited budget" for these purposes.[82]

### Eyewitnesses of Hilal's Role from the ADS Interviews

ADS interviews confirm the role of Hilal in carrying out Harun's initiatives by establishing and operating training camps, making speeches in market settings, and leading violent attacks. There are at least eight eyewitness and six hearsay accounts of Hilal's activities in the ADS surveys, beginning with descriptions of the training camp operations.

Two of the training camp accounts are from the area near Kebkabiya. Both date from the time of Harun's July 2003 Al Geneina speech given in the presence of Hilal. The first respondent drew a map (see Figure 5.2) of Hilal's training camp in North Darfur near Masteria, locating the camp in relation to nearby Fur and Arab villages. The second respondent described how she feared the threat the training camp posed to her safety. The interviewer recorded the following racially explicit account of this women's experience:

> She lived in a village within walking distance from the Arab village of Midop, where Musa Hilal trained his men. They trained for twenty-five days with weapons....Musa Hilal is the Sheikh of Midop....During the training, the Arabs shopped at the market in the black villages and said they were going to kill all the blacks. She didn't see the training, but she saw the bullets and fragments from the shooting. People were not hurt during the training period. On the twenty-sixth day of the training, someone spoke over the microphone. He said that you have trained for twenty-five days and

now should kill the people in the nine villages nearby. The speaker spoke Arabic; she doesn't know Arabic, but others told her what the speaker said. She heard the announcement over the microphone herself. She fled after hearing the announcement, so she didn't see the attack on the village that followed. She has been told that all nine villages were attacked with camels, horses, vehicles, and that people were killed.... While she was fleeing, she was chased and caught by men with green uniforms. Their animals were taken. Clothes were taken from the women and men were killed. They said, "We killed all your men and will kill you too." Everyone began to weep.... The women were raped. It happened at night so they couldn't see individual perpetrators.... When she escaped she went to Karnoi, then to Tine, and finally to Chad.

The interviewer indicated this respondent clearly was traumatized and appeared much older than her reported 35 years of age.

Another respondent confirmed the description of the training camp and provided a second map of its location near the Wadi and Midop area. He confirmed that the training lasted about a month and that "they trained in shooting, including with...a shoulder-fired weapon (i.e., a bazooka) that makes a terrible sound." Militia leaders prohibited villagers from traveling or grazing their animals in the shooting range during this period.

Journalists who reported on the training camps recounted the salience of race in Hilal's training regime for new Arab recruits. Hilal alleged that the Black Africans settled land originally belonging to Arabs. Wax reported that before an attack on April 27, 2004, Hilal and the troops sang war songs proclaiming, "We go to the war. We go to defeat the rebels. We are not afraid of war. We are the original people of this area."[83] Another journalist wrote from Darfur that "*The Guardian* has spoken to a deserter from a training camp run by Mr. Hilal, who said the Janjaweed commander whipped up racial hatred among his fighters. When the recruits first arrived at the camp..., Mr. Hilal made a speech in which he told them that all Africans were their enemies."[84] Another interview with a defector reported that men paraded around a training

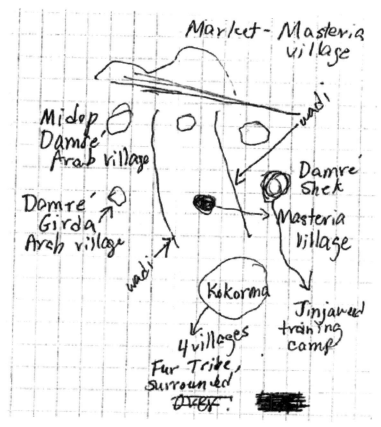

FIGURE 5.2. Janjaweed Militia Training Camp.

camp singing songs parodying the local Africans and teasing the spurned African recruits with claims that "we are lords of this land. You blacks do not have any rights here."[85] Hilal did not just convert individuals to his cause; he built militias around a collective will – a common purpose and shared intent to attack and kill Black Africans.

Hilal incited his recruits and terrorized his victims with racist speech. Two eyewitnesses saw Hilal in the marketplace of nearby Mister-iha in August 2003, where he delivered public warnings with explicit racial messages. Both eyewitnesses described the events in detail. One

appearance occurred on a Tuesday market day in June 2003. Hilal
arrived in a white four-wheel-drive car with tinted black windows that
the respondent had seen in the village on at least five previous occasions
carrying men and sometimes equipped with a doska – a large, mounted
machine gun used in attacks. Hilal appeared as part of a group and spoke
to a mixed crowd of Arab and African villagers, as described in this
account:

> The first time he saw Musa Hilal in the market...was a Tuesday.
> Musa Hilal spoke first. Musa Hilal said he was sent by the Govern-
> ment of Sudan, and he told the people that we are going to kill all
> blacks in this area, and that if you kill people, nobody will be prose-
> cuted. Also if you burn (i.e., homes and buildings), nobody will pros-
> ecute or "question" you. Animals you find are yours. But if you find
> a...a big machine gun, it belongs to the government. He said we will
> clear the land until the desert begins. Musa Hilal spoke Arabic, which
> the respondent understands. He also said, "I have come to give the
> Arab people freedom."

The respondent further indicated that an official accompanied Hilal and
explained his recent arrest and subsequent return to North Darfur:

> From his accent, he wasn't from the area. He said Musa Hilal
> had been arrested, "but we brought him back for your safety." He
> instructed the people to "understand" what Musa Hilal said, to "obey
> his orders," and to use him as a "reference."

The speeches demoralized the Black African listeners: "The Arabs were
happy with the speeches.... No Arabs objected. The Fur and Zaghawa
didn't speak and were sad." This eyewitness provided accounts of subsequent attacks and burnings not only of his own village but also of surrounding villages that he observed while fleeing. He also reported that
the Janjaweed did not attack Arab villages.

Another respondent confirmed Hilal's identity, noting that he
knew him from school and took care of his family's household. This

respondent recalled, "I was standing in the middle of the market" when Hilal entered the market with armed men at his sides and announced that "the government gave me the order and I came here. The government gave me cars and uniforms. The government gave me the order to start killing the people here – all the blacks from here to Karnoi and Tine and up." Hilal indicated that he was told to "kill all the blacks in this area" and that his forces should "give the Arab people freedom" by "clear[ing] the land."

Combined Sudanese and Janjaweed forces attacked nearby towns in the area of Kebkabiya numerous times, conducting particularly vicious attacks in August 2003 (recounted in ADS interviews analyzed in the next chapter) following Hilal's earlier appearance in the Misteriha market. One of the respondents quoted earlier described the attack on his own village. He returned from his farm work to see from a short distance away the "shooting and killing. . . . There were horses and cars with machine guns. . . . They had cars with machine guns and they started killing people." He continued,

> They had a big truck to put all the things in from the houses. It was a green army truck. There were many trees where I was hiding and I got up in the tree to see what was happening. The machine gun was mounted on the car and someone was guiding the gun. The gun had three legs (i.e., a tripod) on the top of the car. It was a Toyota (khaki colored). There was someone driving and some soldiers on the cars and someone shooting. I could not hear them except yelling like frightening [them]. All of them had uniforms on. I couldn't see if they had markings because I was too far, but they had army caps. They came from four directions. I saw there was one man who had a horse who arrived and led the attack – he just waved his arm to attack. He had a uniform, a white horse, with a red flag/cloth that he was waving.

The respondent cried when the interviewer asked about his family, expressing anguish and dismay that the government supported the

Janjaweed. The interviewer reported his exact words about going back to the village to look for his family after the attack:

> I went back and *nothing* was there. [Respondent begins to cry.] I looked under everything, and I looked for my family and for my house. I didn't find [them]. I have five children with their mother who were gone and the other wife and three children and they were gone. Until now I don't know what happened to them. Maybe they were in the fire – I don't know. [Begins to cry again.]

When asked about the fate of surrounding Arab villages, he replied, "The people who were in the villages around us were the ones who were killing us, so how can they kill themselves?"

## Musa Hilal and the Specific Role of Race

The ground attacks on African villages characteristically started with forces shouting racial epithets, which are extensively recorded in the ADS. Refugees often reported hearing the incoming forces shouting racial slurs, such as "This is the last day for blacks," "We will destroy the black-skinned people," "Kill the slaves," "Kill all the blacks," as well as references to "Nuba, Nuba" (in this context, a derogatory term used for Black Africans).

The epithets shouted in the attacks that were specifically linked to Musa Hilal usually referred to "slaves." Their uniformity suggests a common source and theme. Six of the additional hearsay interviews further reported use of racial epithets, and three of these also included explicit references to slaves. There was thus extensive evidence of "specific racial intent" in the interviews linking Musa Hilal to attacks in Darfur.

Often, the attacks involving Musa Hilal followed a similar pattern: repeated bombings, ground attacks led by Janjaweed and GoS forces, yelling of racial epithets, killing of the men who did not flee, and raping the remaining women. A woman refugee from Tine heard the attackers say, "We don't like black men or women in this area." Her account continued as follows:

> They attacked the village three times. By the last attack, her house
> was destroyed. There were eight days of bombing. They brought rein-
> forcements. After the first bombing, the men ran and left their fami-
> lies. They took the cars and left. The Arabs took women – they take
> the pretty ones. They killed any men they found behind. She saw
> twenty women taken. She was taken.

Although this woman did not report being raped, the interviewer thought that she was raped. In Chapter 7, we statistically link racial epithets
as measures of racial intent to Sudanese and Janjaweed involvement in
the death, rape, destruction, and displacement reported in Darfur.

There are allegedly documents confirming the state instigation of the
racialized attacks and the specific role of Musa Hilal:

> As a communiqué to the commander of the "Western military area"
> from Musa Hilal's headquarters in Misteriha said, citing orders from
> the president of the Republic, "You are informed that directives have
> been issued... to change the demography of Darfur and empty it of
> African tribes" through burning, looting and killing "of intellectuals
> and youths who may join the rebels in fighting."[86]

Another account reported the following:

> Hilal appears to have unlimited power in Darfur. A statement from
> local authorities in February instructed "security units in the locality"
> to "allow the activities of the mujahideen and the volunteers under
> the command of Sheikh Musa Hilal to proceed" in North Darfur
> and "to secure their vital needs." The document stressed the "impor-
> tance of non-interference" and directed local authorities to "over-
> look minor offences... against civilians who are suspected members
> of the rebellion."[87]

However, as we see next, the links between Hilal and the government of
Sudan are perhaps most vividly reflected in the joining of the Janjaweed
attacks with Sudanese bombing attacks.

Thus, one of the ADS interviews described how villagers in the Kebkabiya area early in 2004 listened to FM radio frequencies used in government communications and heard government pilots giving "orders to Janjaweed as to where to attack." Radio communications of this kind are reported elsewhere in the ADS interviews and in interviews conducted by Human Rights Watch. The latter included a man from Kebkabiya who heard a conversation involving Hilal prior to an attack in the Tawila area, on February 27, 2004: "I heard them on Thurayas [satellite phones distributed by the government to militia leaders] with someone in Khartoum, to arrange the point where the planes should land to bring the required ammunition."[88]

Racial epithets heard during the air-to-ground communications and interviews by Human Rights Watch further linked these communications (see the left side of Figure 5.1) to GoS military leaders, such as General Gadal:

> We heard the names of [government army] pilots and conversations.... That is how we know some of the pilots. One was Egyptian, because of the way he spoke in clear Egyptian Arabic.... We heard him on the radio organizing the attacks. They called him Janabo Gadal or Officer Gadal. Also, Afaf Segel, who is a woman pilot from Sudan. She said things like "Nas Karnoi na dikim fatuur" which means, "I am going to give breakfast to the peasants from Karnoi," before Karnoi was bombed. Captain Khalid was another pilot. In their communications on the radio they called us "Nuba, abid," and said things like, "I am going to give those slaves a lesson they will not forget."[89]

Gadal also was reported in the ADS interviews to be in the Kutum area where Hilal was active, as well as elsewhere:

> MIGs came first but didn't bomb – they buzzed the village. Then the Antonovs came. When you listened to the radio on FM you could hear ... I heard them say "Move! Move! Gadal Move!" (Interviewer's note: respondent speaks fluent Arabic.)....We were in the wadi and saw the army come and the Janjaweed were circling the village. Those

who could run well survived and others were killed. I took the way through the mountains to Abilina.

Human Rights Watch interviews reported Hilal's presence during several other attacks in North Darfur. He reportedly traveled by government helicopter and was present during instances of torture: "He gives orders to both soldiers and Janjaweed."[90]

## Specific Individual and Collective Racial Intent

Musa Hilal and the government of Sudan deny all charges of war crimes. As of this writing, investigators from the International Criminal Court have not filed charges against Musa Hilal. It was not until July 2008 that the Prosecutor asked the ICC judges to charge President al-Bashir with genocide. The charter filed in 2007 by the ICC Prosecutor were of a more limited nature and involved only the former Deputy Minister of Interior, Ahmad Harun, and the less well-known militia leader discussed in the next chapter, Ali Kushayb.

In a 2006 article in the *New York Times*[91] based on an interview given near the town of Kebkabiya, Hillal elaborates his denial of committing war crimes:

> He said there were no tensions here between Arabs and non-Arabs. By way of demonstration, he ordered one of his soldiers to round up a group of market women. When the women arrived, cowering under their bright robes as Mr. Hilal hovered over them, one by one [they] said there were no tensions here. Hilal then proclaimed, "See! We have no problems here. We live together in peace."

In another interview, Hilal exhibited the same sense of unwavering inevitability he displayed when Governor Suleiman warned him years earlier of the potential consequences of his actions. On this occasion, he confidently told the interviewer, "The government call to arms is carried out through tribal leaders.... Every government comes and finds us here.

When they leave, we will still be here. When they come back, we will still be here. We will always be here."[92]

Of course, for sociological or criminological purposes, it is not necessary to establish the individual legal responsibility of Musa Hilal or any other specific person for acts of genocide. We use Hilal here as an example to illustrate the roles played with social efficacy by militia leaders in mobilizing and organizing genocidal violence as a joint criminal enterprise. The broader interest for the sociological criminology of genocide is to explain the involvement of state actors as joint perpetrators in criminally organized action that – with an individually and collectively framed racial intent – resulted in the death, destruction, and displacement of Black Africans in Darfur.

Our focus is on group processes, rather than on individuals. Our premise is that a collective explanation is needed for collective violence. We noted at the outset of this chapter that international criminal law prosecutions increasingly refer to collective processes involving criminal organization, common purpose, and joint criminal enterprise. The challenge is to develop a fully elaborated collective understanding of the genocidal violence in Darfur. To this end, in the following chapters, we further analyze the unique data in the State Department's ADS survey.

# 6  The Rolling Genocide

## A Global Day for Action on Darfur

The genocide rolled on as demonstrators gathered around the world for the 2006 Global Day for Action, three years after the violence began in Darfur. Whereas the Rwandan genocide claimed most of its lives in just two to three months of unremitting violence, the Darfur genocide continued in a wave-like pattern. Former Secretary of State Madeline Albright joined demonstrators in New York City's Central Park to make this point, observing, "President Clinton and I have so many times said how horrible it was that we weren't able to do something about Rwanda, but the lesson is different. Rwanda was volcanic genocide . . . this is rolling genocide." Demonstrators also gathered in Canada, Europe, and Asia, and genocide survivors led demonstrations in Rwanda and Cambodia. The world again ignored the Canadian UN commander during the genocide in Rwanda, Romeo Dallaire, who now lamented, "We are going to witness, again with blood on our hands, the destruction of human beings who are exactly like us."[1] The whole world watched as death, rape, and destruction continued, and as a trove of evidence for that violence languished in the State Department's files.

Chapter 5 presented eyewitness evidence recorded in the ADS refugee interviews from Chad that Musa Hilal in particular exhibited, repeatedly, his intent to eliminate Black Africans from Darfur. He did this in public speeches and by personally leading attacks on settlements in Darfur. Indeed, he very publicly verbalized his racial intent in a speech given alongside the Sudanese minister in charge of the Darfur Security Desk, Ahmad Harun. Musa Hilal is an important figure because his involvement in war crimes is both longstanding – pre-dating his return to Darfur in June 2003 – and wide ranging, extending over much of the state of North Darfur and into West Darfur. In his own public statements, Hilal announced that his operations with Janjaweed militia and GoS military against Black Africans ranged north from Kebkabiya to Karnoi. Hilal's racial targeting intent was specific, and it was also socially organized and geographically dispersed.

In civil law employment discrimination cases involving charges of racial bias, verbally explicit racial epithets presented in evidence in association with statistical patterns of differential employment outcomes are often treated as highly probative by judges. Because race is so central to legal definitions, as well as to the social science theoretical perspectives introduced in the previous chapter, and because the influence of race can be analyzed in the ADS data at both the specific individual level and at more general collective levels, these epithets and their expressions of racial intent are of great importance.

We begin this chapter by demonstrating the wave-like nature of the killing in conjunction with Sudanese government offensives in Darfur. This killing pattern is well documented in 2003 and 2004, before it became difficult if not impossible to collect such data in Darfur. We then make the essential point, by using ADS interviews, that the racial intent to conduct this genocide was not specific to Musa Hilal alone. We present the documented activities of three other militia leaders and describe events in one settlement area, Bendesi, which were illustrative of the collective racial intent involved in the genocide in Darfur. This intent was part of a larger, state-led, and jointly organized criminal enterprise with a common purpose, namely the elimination of Black Africans from parts if not all of Darfur.

Thus, a collective as well as an individual form of racial intent engulfed Darfur in genocide.

## Unrolling the Genocide

Figure 6.1 presents monthly counts from two sources of the number of persons killed in Darfur from January 2003 through August 2004. The two sources are the ADS interviews and a separate survey based on news and NGO reports (henceforth referred to as "media reports") of deaths in attacks on 101 villages.[2] Neither the ADS interviews nor the media study were designed to count every death in Darfur. The ADS interviews restricted death reports largely to persons whom the respondents could identify at least indirectly, whereas the NGOs and journalists' lack of access to many sites of attacks limited the completeness of the media reports. We combed all ADS interviews to record the named and unnamed related and unrelated persons reported killed and missing. The refugees often fled from places where journalists and NGOs could

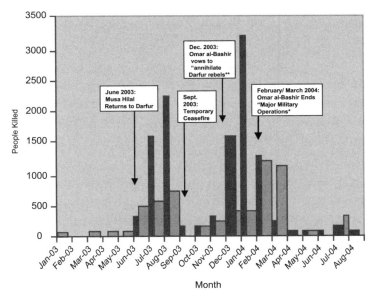

FIGURE 6.1. Chronology of Key Events and Monthly Death Estimates from Survey and News Counts of Killings, January 2003–September 2004.

not go, so the media reports are less comprehensive than the refugee interviews.

The bars in Figure 6.1 indicate for each month the survey-reported death counts and the media-reported death counts. The former numbers peak at higher levels than the latter, yet the patterns are otherwise strikingly similar. Of course, the killings and especially the rapes did not stop with the end of our time series – only our data sources stopped. In both series, deaths are highly concentrated in two intervals: from June 2003 through August 2003 and from December 2003 through March 2004. Several events in these intervals played major roles in the onset and reduction of violence in Darfur.

The first interval began with the return to Darfur of Musa Hilal and the beginning of intense recruitment of Arab militia members in June 2003. It ended with a negotiated ceasefire in September 2003 that promised a government disarmament of militias; this ceasefire proved unenforceable by the late fall of 2003. The second interval began with a December 2003 vow by Sudanese President al-Bashir to "annihilate" Darfur rebels. It ended with al-Bashir's premature announcement of the end of "major military operations," followed by the anguished warning of the UN's representative to Sudan, Mukesh Kapila, about the parallel between the genocidal killings in Darfur and Rwanda, where Kapila had served earlier. These events bracketed the same temporal peaks in deaths, albeit at different levels, in both the survey and media studies. There is no survey other than the ADS that comprehensively covers deaths resulting from violent attacks in Darfur during these twenty months, and its similarity to the media study encourages the conclusion that the ADS is representative of the rolling, wave-like patterning of attacks during this period.

We now return to a more qualitative account of the rolling genocide. This genocide extended far beyond the involvement of Musa Hilal. Map 6.1 indicates the locations of attacks led by three other Janjaweed militia leaders.

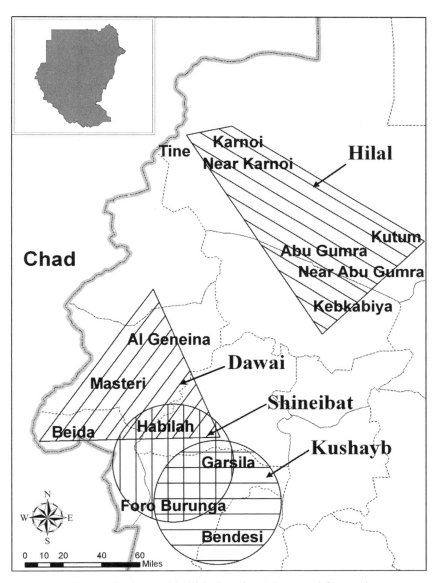

MAP 6.1. Janjaweed Militia Leaders' Areas of Operation.

## A Collectively Organized Genocide

*Dawai:* Hamid Dawai is a second important militia leader. Prosecutor Moreno Ocampo's 2007 brief identified Dawai as also participating in a July 2003 meeting in Al Geneina with Musa Hilal and then leaving on a government helicopter with the Darfur Security Desk Minister, Ahmad Harun. Neither Dawai nor Hilal is indicated in the brief as a suspect, even though the brief contains this statement: "Harun could not have carried out his responsibilities without knowing that the attacking forces intended to mount wholesale attacks upon towns and villages and their civilian populations."[3] The helicopter ride with Dawai offered Harun an eyewitness view of the destruction, as Al Geneina was a government-controlled area close to the Chad border in the central part of the state of West Darfur. Dawai's forces destroyed numerous villages and turned this area into a no-man's land along the border.[4]

Hamid Dawai is an emir of an Arab tribe, the Beni Halba, and a Janjaweed leader in the Terbeba-Arara-Beida triangle near Al Geneina, which forms the westernmost point of the Darfur border with Chad. He is a Chadian Arab and a naturalized citizen of Sudan, with homes in Al Geneina and Beida. Dawai is linked to 460 killings of civilians in this area between August 2003 and April 2004. Amnesty International indicates that Dawai is "the chief of the Arabs...gives auxiliaries to the army...[and is] the high commander of the Janjaweed...based in Al Geneina. There is a military camp called Guedera where they train people. It is not a secret. They get organized in Al Geneina and then the planes go to this camp."[5] The headquarters of the joint operations are located in the old customs yard in Al Geneina[6] and in Beida, where a government military base houses helicopters and heavy weapons, including tanks.[7] The joint government and Janjaweed training is consistent with President al-Bashir's warning as early as January 2003 that "we will use the army, the police, the mujahideen [i.e., literally meaning religious fighters], the horsemen to get rid of the rebellion."[8]

When Human Rights Watch visited the Terbeba area, it "found it deserted and uninhabitable, its food stores looted and burned, and

90 percent of its grass huts reduced to cinders. Villagers said they were attacked on February 15, 2004, at 6:00 A.M. by a joint force of Janjaweed on horses and camels and government forces in Land Cruiser vehicles. The attackers killed thirty-one people."[9] More than 500 families lived in Terbeba before the attack.

An eyewitness in the ADS interviews identified Hamid Dawai as the leader of this attack on Terbeba and reported seeing thirty-six bodies, five more than the Human Rights Watch report. He recalled, "At 7 A.M. on 15 February 2004 my village was attacked by a mixed force of Janjaweed militia and government soldiers commanded by Hamid Dawai. I saw Dawai giving orders to both groups as I ran past him. I knew Dawai as a friend of my family." This respondent also reported, as did Human Rights Watch, that "the soldiers were shouting, "'Kill the Nuba.'" (Nuba is a pejorative term usually used by Arabs in Sudan for Black people and/or slaves.[10]) He added, "The Janjaweed took about twenty-two girls between the ages of 12 and 15. They released all but one who died after two days. The girls had all been raped."

The respondent escaped during the attack. Although shot in the leg, he ran, and after watching the eleven-hour attack from about 200 meters away, he returned to Terbeba in the late afternoon, as described in this account:

> He went back to the village at about 5 P.M. after the soldiers had left. His leg wound was not serious enough to prevent him. He saw thirty-six bodies including that of his neighbor . . . who had been tied hand and foot and thrown into a burning house. The bodies were scattered everywhere. He found his houses had been burned to the ground, his livestock had been stolen, and all the goods from his shop looted. The whole village was destroyed.

From his spot just across the border, this respondent also witnessed the Janjaweed surround four villagers who were hiding among some trees in a wadi. He watched while all four, whom he named, were shot.

Sixteen ADS interviews included eyewitness identifications of Hamid Dawai in association with the attacks they recorded, and three more reported hearing others identify Dawai. Thirteen of these sixteen respondents who identified Dawai also reported hearing racial epithets during the attacks. Several more reported shouting, but could not understand the exact words. All who reported hearing specific epithets heard the word "Nuba," whereas several also heard references to Blacks and slaves. Several explained that the word "Nuba" meant Black slave.

A Masalit from a mid-sized village, who served in the Sudanese military and then returned home to become a farmer, reported another attack led by Dawai in late December 2003. Dawai had visited the village several weeks earlier. His group arrived in two pickup trucks with mounted machine guns. The respondent reported, "He [Dawai]... personally shot one passerby in the street. He then announced that this would be a very difficult year for the Masalit. He said all the Masalit in this area were Tora Bora and added he didn't want such people in Sudan. Then he drove off." (Tora Bora is a racialized term taken from Osama Bin Laden's retreat to the mountains on the Afghanistan-Pakistan border. The Janjaweed in Darfur frequently use this term to refer to rebels, as discussed further in Chapter 8.)

The interviewer reported from the interview with this Masalit man that Dawai led the attack on the town two weeks later. The description illustrated how government and Janjaweed forces worked together in this area of West Darfur and how militia leaders like Dawai drew on the authority that the government presence conveyed:

> At about 1 P.M. two military vehicles drove into our village looking for me. The vehicles were driven by Sudanese soldiers, but they were accompanied by the Janjaweed leader Hamid Dawai. Dawai had been the Chief of an Arab section of Beida and I knew him well. The soldiers told me that they wanted to have a meeting. We all walked over to the village police officer. Dawai came with us. Dawai told us that he was the government. He said the government had given him men, guns, and vehicles. He asked what did the Masalit have?... Then he asked us to leave the area. He told us we had five minutes to talk to my people and decide. He then left

with his cars. Thirty minutes later some of Dawai's soldiers came into the pastures outside the village and took eighty cows, some of which were mine, and killed four people – all men. I think they were testing our reaction. But there was nothing we could do to defend ourselves.

The Janjaweed shouted the familiar refrain, "Nuba, Nuba, out, out," during the attack, which involved about 500 troops. The Masalit man escaped uninjured and hid nearby, where he saw his fleeing uncle shot and beaten to death. He returned to the village in the evening after the attack and found his home burned and the village completely destroyed. He does not know how many persons the attackers killed, but when he was hiding outside the village he saw four children killed.

Several other ADS interviews detailed torture and rapes. The first of these interviews indicated that "after the rapes, the women [were] told…they should go tell their families that they all have to leave Darfur," whereas another interview described gang rapes by six men and mutilations with knives. Another account of an attack on the town of Korsha near Masteri illustrated the violence directed toward leaders of communities and the claims made about putative village support for rebels. The Masalit respondent described the following event involving Dawai:

> They gathered five sheikhs/imans in the village and demanded to know where is Tora Bora (interviewer's note: Tora Bora is local jargon for rebels). The sheikhs said they don't know such things. The Janjaweed tied their hands behind their backs, piled straw around them, and poured kerosene on the straw. Hamid Dawi said, "Where is Tora Bora – you are Tora Bora." Then Dawai lit the straw and burned them all to death.

About ten Janjaweed participated directly in this execution while many others watched. Dawai's men called the local villagers "Noab" (i.e., the plural for Nuba – Black) during the attack and told them that "Sudan is Arab."

*Kushayb:* The third militia leader identified in the ADS interviews is Ali Kushayb, who was charged by the ICC with war crimes. Kushayb is about 50 years old and an "Aquid al Oqada," which means "colonel of colonels," in the Wadi Salih locality where he is one of the senior leaders. Kushayb holds an officer rank in the military and is a member of the Public Defense Forces. He is known as an "Emir of Mujahideen" or a "leader of religious fighters."[11] He commanded thousands of Janjaweed militia men in the southwestern part of the state of West Darfur – stretching from the towns of Garsila and Deleij to the east; west to Foro Burunga and the Chad border, including the towns of Bendesi and Mukjar in the center of this area; and all the way to Kass in South Darfur. Mukjar is located in the central belt of Darfur near the Jebel Marra Mountains. This is the most fertile region in Darfur and is inhabited by a mixture of Arab and African tribes, among which the Fur are the most prominent.

Kushayb met with Harun frequently. Harun arrived by helicopter for an important meeting with Kushayb in the town of Mukjar in early August 2003; he also brought weapons and money for the militia at about this time. Kushayb brought Janjaweed militia from Garsila to Mukjar, where he met first in private with Harun and then with other militia leaders.

Harun delivered a speech at this meeting to army and police commanders, the governor of West Darfur, and the militia leaders, including Kushayb. Harun rallied the crowd by saying, "Since the children of the Fur have become rebels, all the Fur and what they had, had become booty for the Mujahideen."[12] He referred to the Fur in unmistakably racial terms.

A local community leader shouted from the audience that the people there "were innocent and that the government intended to kill them" and that "what Harun had said was not appropriate for a minister to say." For Harun, and the security regime he represented in Khartoum, this outburst probably constituted further evidence of the rebellion he came to repress. Ocampo, the ICC prosecutor, confirmed the protestor's judgment, saying, "Harun consistently incited attacks upon the civilian populations associated with the rebels, rather than the rebels themselves."[13] His brief cites Harun himself as acknowledging that the Janjaweed were "less disciplined," while nonetheless also saying the joined attacking forces "would go together, with one objective, under one leadership."[14]

The Mukjar speech in August 2003 came shortly after Harun proclaimed in Al Geneina that "they were ready to kill three-quarters of Darfur in order to allow one-quarter to live." Ocampo regarded this speech by Harun as a turning point that "immediately sparked the looting attack on Mukjar." The Janjaweed militia began the looting spree as soon as Harun left. Kushayb led his forces in a sequence of attacks the day after the Mukjar speech, burning all the towns and villages between Bendesi and Mukjar.

Kushayb participated in the Bendesi attack in military uniform, giving orders to the Janjaweed militia. Members of the armed forces came to the umda's (i.e., a ranking tribal figure) house in Bendesi before the attack and said they would return later to collect "Zakat" (i.e., an Islamic tax). The attack started a few hours later and included four military Land Cruisers carrying forty to fifty soldiers each and more than 500 Janjaweed. The attackers shouted, "Nuba, Nuba," and said they were sent "to kill every black thing."[15] Ali Kushayb had to have heard the Janjaweed shouting "slaves," and this was confirmed by an ADS interview with a Masalit eyewitness to this attack. He estimated that the attackers killed 150 persons, including 30 children and three of his brothers and two cousins, within the first ninety minutes. The attackers took livestock and looters loaded stolen property onto Sudanese military vehicles. They raped women throughout the night. The Masalit refugee continued as follows:

> While carrying out the rapes, the attackers were saying, "We have taken Tora Bora's wives, praise be to God." At least one of the women who was raped bled in the course of the assault. When this happened the rapists shot their weapons in the air and announced, "I have found a virgin woman."[16]

The attack lasted five days and destroyed most of the town.

Two ADS interviews identified Kushayb as leading his forces in nearby Mukjar, where further attacks took place within a day or two after those in Bendesi. Attacks continued in Mukjar from August 2003 to March 2004. One respondent reported he heard the governor say "Blacks are useless" and that "you are Negroes and we are Arabs. God made you to serve us." He saw twelve young men shot and killed, and his own parents and other relatives died in the attacks. Kushayb's forces arrested many young men and took them to police buildings.

The ICC prosecutor's brief includes accounts of frequent torture in Mukjar during this period:

> The witness...knew about a mass detention at the new police station....He had been arrested by members of the Armed Forces and Militia/Janjaweed...shortly after his arrival in Mukjar, and he was being held by members of the Armed Forces in a room with about sixty other men. All of these men were restrained in different ways. Some of them...had been tied and suspended in the air....His arms were held wide apart and tied to a plank of wood on the ceiling, while his legs were also held wide apart and tied to objects on either side...a stove was left burning between his legs....All the men had whip marks on their bodies and their clothes were torn and bloodstained...He had been repeatedly beaten, called "Tora Bora" and deprived of food....Two other men...had been badly beaten and his fingernails and toenails had been forcibly removed.[17]

The ICC brief also includes accounts by two eyewitnesses of separate instances when Kushayb led executions in Mukjar of twenty and twenty-one young men.[18] An ADS respondent recalled that the Janjaweed said "we are going to cut off your roots," a presumed reference to the alleged support of rebels.

An eyewitness ADS interview and the ICC prosecutor's brief described another set of attacks led by Kushayb in November/December 2003 in Arawala, the mostly Fur town about fifty kilometers north of Mukjar. The interview indicated that more than 400 deaths resulted from ground attacks, including 160 men killed and laid out in a ditch. The

Janjaweed attackers said they were looking for "Tora Bora." As they fled from the town to the surrounding mountains, the Jangaweed killed many with machine-gun bursts, including twenty-four people who fled with the respondent. He described a woman he buried "who resisted being raped and was shot in the genitals and killed." Those who went to the mountains found that "armed Arab nomads were sent by the GoS to stay around the wells...to keep the displaced from getting access to the water....He knows of seventeen children who died of dehydration while hiding in the mountains." Later, government planes launched a large-scale air attack on the mountains while the Janjaweed waited below to shoot those fleeing the bombs.

The prosecutor's brief included eyewitness reports of the separation of males and females during attacks, with the younger women singled out for continuous, brutal rapes. Respondents identified Kushayb as a participant in those rapes:

> According to the witness, during and immediately after the attack, the Militia/Janjaweed and members of the Armed Forces rounded up civilians and divided them into three groups: men and boys, older women, and young women. The older women were further divided into smaller groups. The Armed Forces and Militia/Janjaweed... [separated the] group of young women and took them all to the local military garrison.... After arriving at the military garrison, the young women...were stripped naked and raped. Kushayb, after being called by the soldiers, came to inspect the naked women and then left. That night, men in military uniform tied the women to trees with their legs apart and continually raped them. The fighters told the women: "Little dogs, this land is not for you."

This activity continued for nearly a week and led to the deaths of at least three young women.

*Shineibat:* A fourth Janjaweed militia leader, Abdullah Mustafa Abu Shineibat, is identified in eight ADS interviews, although he is not named in the ICC brief. All of the ADS identifications are eyewitness accounts of Shineibat's activities, and six involve racial epithets. One interview included this description: "I recognized...Abdullah Shineibat. He is Arab, short, fat with a moustache, he has a small beard and is around forty years old. He seemed to be leading the attack." Shineibat mainly operated in the area of West Darfur that stretches from the Chad border region of Arara to Habila, thirty kilometers to the east.

Like Hamid Dawai, with whom he led an attack in Kenu near Foro Burunga, Shineibat is an Arab emir from the Beni Halba tribe.[19] A Masalit ADS respondent from Kenu who reported Dawai and Shineibat's joint role in an attack on his town recalled an earlier meeting with a chief of police who warned of the violence to come. The police chief revealed that he was going to issue an order for the police to leave Kenu because it was going to be attacked. About thirty Janjaweed then called together the local sheikhs, as described in this account:

> They demanded that Kenu must pay for its protection in money, sheep, tea, and sugar....The Janjaweed set a price that could not be paid. They also stated that all guns must be collected. The Janjaweed gave the sheikhs seven days to comply....There was a Sudan National Security (SNS) unit in Foro Burunga...some sort of intelligence unit....There is also a Zaka office for Foro Burunga (i.e., interviewer's note: an office that collects Islamic taxes). The SNS obtained a vehicle and funds from Zaka to distribute guns and ammunition to the Arab nomadic tribes....The attack on Kenu started at 10 A.M. on January 1, 2004....The forces went to the most densely populated parts of the village and fired guns and grenades at the people....The forces went through the village shooting people, looting and burning houses. The attack lasted three hours and resulted in eighty-four dead and ten wounded.

The attackers killed the respondent's brother.

Another Masalit ADS respondent described an attack a month earlier on Daza, located about thirty kilometers from Foro Burunga. This respondent recognized Shineibat among a group of familiar Arabs from the area: "I recognized some of them because they used to come to our village every day to buy things. They used to shout at us, 'Nuba, Nuba.'"

They shot his brother, father, and mother in his compound. A respondent also identified Shineibat as the leader of an attack with a Masalit sheikh on the town of Mangarsa, which is about forty kilometers from Foro Burunga. The sheikh reported that seven other villages were attacked the same day.

On the basis of knowing both Shineibats, this respondent commented on the integration of the Janjaweed militia and the GoS military:

> I recognized the man heading this attack as Omda Abdullah Shineibat. I knew him because he was a sheikh of Sisi village, and I saw him at meetings of sheikhs in Foro Burunga. He had a beard and walked with a limp. His brother, Al Hadi Ahmed Shineibat, was also in the attack. He was a real military man and used to live in the military camp in Foro Burunga.

This respondent escaped the attack on his village, but the attackers shot his brother in the back and he died. Janjaweed later stopped the respondent on the road to Chad. They took him to the Sojo military camp in Foro Burunga, and this was the start of the worst part of his ordeal:

> They threw us on the ground at the camp and tied us to a tree. The Chief of the camp came to us. I knew him as [name deleted]....[He] shaved my head with his knife. He cut my scalp and there was blood everywhere. I was left tied to the tree until 10 p.m....Other men then came and untied us. They tied our wrists to our ankles in front and then threaded a stick under our knees. They then pulled us into a tree with a rope tied to the stick. I swung upside down. Four military men then beat me with sticks. This went on for one to two hours. The same thing happened every day for seven days.

The torture continued for several more days after this. They interrogated him about being a leader, and what he knew of other leaders. They eventually released him, and he escaped to Chad with his mother. The only sense he could make of the ordeal was this observation: "The military accused me of being in the Darfur militia, but I was not. I was only a villager."

Several of the ADS interviews also placed Shineibat in attacks in the area of Habilah. A Masalit resident of the town of Dambusa, about ten kilometers from Habilah, heard attackers shout, "The government wants to finish all Black men and all Darfur people." He estimated that, in December 2003, "around 150 people were killed in Dambusa and he heard that around 20 women were raped by the Arabs." The respondent heard the soldiers say in another attack in a nearby village in the same time period, "We don't need black people in this land – this is Arab land not African – Black people are only good for slaves." Another man saw about forty people, mostly men, shot and killed at about the same time near Habilah. He said the Janjaweed came and "asked me what tribes lived in the village – they figured out what tribes they wanted to eradicate and then destroyed them."

Shineibat is associated with a number of attacks on the village of Gobe, near the Chad border. One of the ADS interviews places Shineibat at the scene of the attack and provides an insider's description of the targeting of this village:

> I was a member of the Sudanese police force for about six years, when I was dismissed by the government as they were dismissing all African police officers.... I was in charge of thirty-three officers.... I moved around between the stations and lived with my wife and family in accommodations within the stations.... In March 2003, an order came from Khartoum that all weapons were to be taken away from the Masalit, Fur, and Zaghawa police officers – except Kalashnikovs.... We were no longer able to defend the villages from attack, and the weapons taken from the police were given to the Janjaweed. In April 2003, a written order came to take the Kalashnikovs from African police also. We were ordered to stay in our offices if ever an attack occurred. On December 1st 2003, I was in the police station. Although I was no longer officially a police officer, I used to go and help with the communications since I was the only one who knew how to operate the things. Twenty minutes before Gobe was attacked, I received a message on the radio...from Geneina saying, "All police are to stay inside the office." The government military and Janjaweed

attacked the village. The military were in trucks with Daska machine guns. They remained outside the village and shot into it. The militia were on horses, camels, and on foot. Those on foot stole the animals and the rest rode through the village shooting...and destroying the homes. Only the police station and homes surrounding it were not destroyed. The member of the military in charge of the attack was [name deleted]...and also present was...Shineibat, an Arab militia leader.

This respondent further indicated that attackers stole livestock in the Habilah and Al Geneina areas for resale in local and regional markets and outside Darfur as well: "Animals that were stolen in the attacks on the villages were taken to Nyala town and then were put on planes to Egypt, Syria, and Iran. I have seen property stolen in the attacks for sale in the market in Dienne, an Arab town, and Kutungan and Foro Burunga." This respondent concluded, "The government wanted to kill or send all of the black people out of Darfur and give the land to the Arabs."

## The Destruction of Bendesi

The cluster of settlements in and around Bendesi provides an instructive example of genocidal victimization in the southern part of West Darfur. The two individuals charged by the ICC prosecutor – Minister Harun and the militia leader, Kushayb – are charged in part for their roles in attacks on Bendesi. Tensions grew between Arab herders and African farmers for at least two years before intense violence broke out in this Wadi Salih locality in August 2003. A refugee interviewed in Chad reported an early attack on the village of Kaber, south of Bendesi, in December 2002 and several attacks thereafter. The Arab attackers wore khaki uniforms. They killed an umda and at least several others, including several children they threw into a nearby river. The refugee reported that during the attack, "they tried to defend themselves, and when they did they were defeated."

Attackers hit Kaber again in June and in the first days of August 2003, killing four persons and taking cattle. A plane dropped bombs on the village in the August 3 attack. A woman who fled this attack recalled, "I stopped at my father's shop and found him dead and the shop looted. I also saw the body of my ex-husband. My cousin was shot too, and died later of the injury." Sudanese planes bombed and strafed another village, Bamboi, in early July. The attacking Janjaweed militia called their victims "Nuba dogs." Another respondent reported two killings on the road to Bendesi. These "pre-attacks" led the villagers to flee. The populations of Bendesi and Mukjar swelled as farmers and villagers in smaller centers moved toward what they hoped was the safety of larger settlements.[20]

Before widespread violence broke out in the area, between seven to ten thousand people lived in Bendesi. The town itself is described as lush, and the surrounding region is a fertile growing area. In the past, Arab nomads often passed through the area and stayed with their herds near the town of Bendesi. They frequented the markets of this and surrounding towns. The town of Mukjar is located twenty-five kilometers to the northeast.

Arab herders long regarded land in Darfur as belonging to Allah, with rights of use and settlement contingent on mutually advantageous exchange relationships.[21] In the past, they kept their livestock off the cultivated land and on the traditional migration routes during the farming season, which lasted approximately from July to February. But farmers in the Bendesi area complained that Arab herders increasingly allowed their livestock to graze on their crops during the growing season. Desertification and scarcity of grazing opportunities fueled the growing tensions. In 2002, a dispute followed an attempt to negotiate grazing rights and resulted in the shooting of four African men. For the next two years, African farmers accused Arab groups of looting and shooting in this area.[22]

In response, the Black African groups of this area – who are mainly Fur but also Masalit and Zaghawa – armed and defended themselves. A resident of Bendesi remarked that negotiation with the Arab herders was futile: "Anyone who tried to dispute them was shot.... Also during this time, it became very unsafe for young women to go outside the village.... Many young women were beaten and raped and were killed if they refused."[23] The local Black African tribes armed and trained themselves as a defense measure. An umda in the Chad refugee interviews reported that arms became more readily available in the area following the civil war in Chad. Local rebels smuggled them across the border. These rebels also attacked the local police and army barracks. In early August, the Sudan Liberation Army (SLA) attacked and stole weapons and a radio from the Bendesi police station, killing two Arab men. Similar raids occurred in Mukjar and surrounding villages.[24]

Tension mounted in the early weeks of August 2003, as the government actively recruited local Arabs into more formally organized militias. The government publically called for recruits, but they only took Arab volunteers and they turned away Black Africans. Ali Kushayb, the Arab militia leader now charged by the ICC, led this recruitment effort, integrating the militia members into the structure of the Public Defense Forces of the region. The local African groups identified these militas as Janjaweed, characterizing them as highwaymen and robbers – the mirror image of the Sudanese government's depiction of the Tora Bora.

Ahmad Harun, the previously discussed middle-level Sudanese ministerial official charged by the ICC, appeared on numerous occasions during this period in the Bendesi/Mukjar area. The umda interviewed in the Chad refugee camp recalled, "I was at a meeting where he announced that those that disrespected the government should be cleansed away by the government." He further reported, "The government has a propaganda program against blacks...which tries to show that all blacks are rebels and should be fought." Harun is identified both in the interviews and in the ICC prosecutor's brief as the government architect of the strategy of "collective punishment" that held all the African civilians in the Bendesi area responsible for the scattered local rebel attacks on police stations and government installations. Harun used the analogy that these farmers and villagers were the "water" in which the rebel "fish" swam and survived.[25]

The attacks came to smaller villages surrounding Bendesi in the first weeks of August. These attacks led up to the assault on Bendesi on August 15, 2003. Reports of more planned attacks circulated in the markets and among mothers and children. For example, one woman reported, "I heard about that in the market, and also from children who heard it from Arab children while herding. They were saying, 'We're going to eliminate all the Nuba and just leave the trees – we'll even eliminate the ants.'"[26] A large government-organized attack in the Bendesi area began on August 15, 2003.

Witnesses reported to ICC investigators that the Arab militia leader, Ali Kushayb, left Mukjar on August 15 in a vehicle with Janjaweed militia. He appeared later the same day in Bendesi in military uniform, issuing orders to the Janjaweed.[27] The Janjaweed arrived at the umda's house and indicated they would be back later to collect "Zakat" – an Islamic tax. A refugee from Bendesi recalled, "At 7 A.M., six Land Cruisers with mounted guns of the Sudanese military force arrived and on a loudspeaker announced that everyone had to bring their goods and be assessed for taxes in a central area." The government troops on the Land Cruisers equipped with machine guns accompanied the Janjaweed, who were on horses, camels, and on foot. The combined force included more than 500 men.

The government troops and Janjaweed simply waited an hour or two while the people of Bendesi gathered with their possessions for "tax collection." Then they attacked. The government soldiers rode in the Land Cruisers with fixed machine guns and rockets, and the Janjaweed attacked on horseback and camels. They fired into the crowd, and a refugee remembered that they shouted "Tora Bora" and "we don't want any Blacks in this area." This respondent described seeing many people killed and injured. She fled on foot and said it felt like "running on dead bodies." This same woman saw a 12-year-old girl raped by five men in

Bendesi. When the woman saw her again in Mukjar, she was covered in blood. She died soon after.

Another refugee in Chad from a village near Bendesi counted thirty-two persons killed, with many girls abducted, raped, and then returned days later. Although some respondents offered exact counts of persons killed and raped, others emphasized that the attacks were too chaotic and terrifying to allow such counts. A woman observed, "They rode into the village and were screaming, 'Exterminate the Fur, kill the Fur!' It was total destruction. I saw people dead. I saw women raped. But I didn't have time to count how many were killed or raped."[28]

Soldiers arrested several sheikhs and called them "Tora Bora." They took them to a military base for torture: "The conditions were terrible – thirty-seven men in a small room about four by three meters. We were all lying down, tied up, some on top of each other." One of the survivors reported he was detained for seven days. He heard later that three of the men died as a result of the torture. During the attack on his village, he heard the Janjaweed shouting "Kill the Nubas" and "the young Fur and Masalit should be eradicated." Many fled from the area of Bendesi to Mukjar, but to little avail. For example, a refugee in Chad said, "We stayed in Mukjar . . . but it was very dangerous for men. I didn't leave the house because the soldiers were arresting and killing many men suspected of being rebels."

Respondents consistently recalled hearing a mixture of racial epithets along with the Tora Bora allegations. A refugee tried to flee, but was caught in Bendesi. He described the Janjaweed saying, "You were at Tora Bora," which meant to him that they thought he was from the rebel group. His captors wanted information about the sheikh and information about rebels.

The attack on Bendesi that began on August 15 continued for five days and followed a pattern repeated in many parts of Darfur. After the initial assault, members of the armed forces and Janjaweed went through Bendesi in a door-by-door fashion, searching for remaining residents and killing those they found. Then, over the following days, witnesses described seeing "the attackers divide into three groups: one burned the village; one collected animals and broke into houses; and the third chased the people who were running away." A witness in the prosecutor's brief stated that she heard the attackers say their orders were "to kill every black thing except the Laloba and Daylabe trees which are also black."[29]

The rapes and killing continued during this time, and over much of the next month. A refugee in Chad identified more than fifty young men shot and killed between August 15 and September 8 in the Bendesi area. All together, he knew of 229 men killed. Attackers repeatedly arrested and took young men into custody, often torturing them. Ali Kushayb helped organize police stations and military bases for these purposes.

A refugee in Chad also reported that more than thirty girls were abducted and raped by the Janjaweed in the Bendesi area: "Of these, two had their throats slit, one was strangled, and one was shot when they resisted being raped." He indicated that the government military took some of the women to Khartoum as a form of "booty." The al-Bashir government, as noted in an earlier chapter, authorized a court inquiry into the abduction of women and girls from the villages of Wadi Saleh in 2005.[30]

## From Specific to Collective Intent

The ADS interviews considered here and in the preceding chapter provide wide-ranging, mostly eyewitness evidence of the specific racial intent of four prominent Janjaweed militia leaders to physically destroy the conditions necessary to sustain life, in whole or in part, for three African groups – the Zaghawa, Fur, and Masalit – in settlements such as Bendesi. Of the forty-four ADS witnesses to these four militia leaders' activities, thirty-five, or nearly 80 percent, indicated they heard racial epithets during attacks on the African farmers and villagers. This reported level of racial epithets is about twice that observed overall in the ADS sample and indicates the role of these militia leaders in motivating their followers with racist ideology.

The Janjaweed leaders considered in this chapter are local agents with the social efficacy required to transform specific racial intent into collectively organized racial intent. The Government of Sudan ministerial appointee, Ahmad Harun, led and coordinated the assaults of these Arab leaders and their militias on the Black African groups. Harun and Kushayb planned and led attacks on Bendesi. The prosecutor's brief emphasized the incendiary spark that Harun struck in a speech he delivered in Mukjar before the attacks on Bendesi. Similarly, the speech given by Hilal alongside Harun in Al Geneina the month before included explicit racially driven rhetoric. Racism was the motivational vocabulary of the "us" and "them" framing of these attacks. At a minimum, this framing was known to the political leadership of the Sudanese government. More likely, it involved the high-level commitment of financial and military resources by this government's leadership.

Evidence of the *specific* intent, organization, and knowledge of the racial violence in Darfur involving the Janjaweed militias is copiously reflected in the eyewitness accounts of the ADS interviews. The greater challenge is to more fully establish what we call the *collective* racial intent of the government of Sudan that underwrites the racially targeted violence described in this and earlier chapters. The next chapter more specifically conceptualizes and empirically analyzes the operation of collective racial intent using the ADS interviews. The chapter has two goals: (1) to establish the higher-level responsibility of the Sudanese government for the proliferation of the racial intent that led to the death, rape, and destruction of African group life in Darfur and (2) to provide systematic criminological evidence of the transformation of individually experienced racial sparks into their deadly collective consequences.

# 7  The Racial Spark

## Racial Difference

In July 2004, Louise Arbour was appointed the UN High Commissioner of Human Rights, and she remains in this position as of this writing. She was also the prosecutor who in 1999 indicted Slobodan Milosevic for crimes against humanity.[1] As such, she was the first prosecutor to indict a sitting head of state for war crimes. Arbour is a fiercely independent French Canadian jurist who became known as a "real-time" prosecutor with the intention of pursuing crimes while they were still being perpetrated by high-ranking war criminals rather than years later.

Despite her example, in 2007, four years after the escalation of violence in Darfur, prosecutorial attention still focused on investigations of lower-level government and military officials. This focus risked turning back the clock of international criminal law to the era of historical prosecutions of ex-Nazis years after Nuremberg or, worse yet, of no major prosecutions at all. Arbour wanted to arouse slumbering public opinion about the real-time "massive crimes" in Darfur. In her new role as High Commissioner, Arbour appointed Jody Williams, who won the Nobel Peace Prize for spearheading a campaign that resulted in an international land mines treaty, to chair a Mission on the Situation of Human Rights in Darfur. Yet, this mission confirmed little more than the well-known fact that "numerous efforts by the international community have not been successful in ending the conflict."[2]

The "Report of the High-Level Mission on the Situation of Human Rights in Darfur Pursuant to Human Rights Council Decision S-4/101" mostly added to the sense of failure to mount a meaningful international response to this conflict, three years after Mukesh Kapila compared Darfur to the genocide in Rwanda. Nonetheless, the report provided an opportunity for Arbour to comment on whether the crimes in Darfur should be called genocide. In her position as ICTY prosecutor, Arbour had charged Milosevic with crimes against humanity, not genocide, partly on the premise that this lesser charge promised a quicker trial and conviction. Carla Del Ponte, her successor as ICTY prosecutor, decided to increase the charges to genocide, even though several ICTY judicial decisions discourage the pressing of genocide charges.[3] A high standard of evidence is required to prove "specific intent" to destroy a protected group in whole or in part (i.e., rather than more simply having a general "knowledge" of these destructive efforts).

Arbour addressed this issue in the context of Darfur: "The difference between genocide and crimes against humanity such as extermination, murder, rape, torture, and persecution is merely a matter of whether it was intended to target a specific ethnic group for elimination."[4] We believe this issue is more complicated. We argue instead that there are further collective ramifications of racial intent.

## A Collective Action Theory of Genocide

The preceding chapters lay the groundwork for the collective action theory of genocide that we now present and assess with the ADS data. Our basic premise is that the Sudanese government is responsible for the racial invective involved in the targeted violence and destruction of specific African groups in Darfur. El-Battahani,[5] an authority on Sudan at the University of Khartoum, writes, "The rulers in Khartoum have mastered a technique of divide and rule, of disrupting and co-opting ethnic, regional elites." More broadly, he concludes, "Of all ideological weapons used in African warfare,...ethnicity...has proved by far the superior." The Sudanese government fostered racial and ethnic divisions by mobilizing Arab militias for nearly twenty years in the south and then shifted that activity to the west, in Darfur. The government recruited the militias among the landless, nomadic Arab herders who were desperate for access to water and pastures for their livestock in an ecosystem of increasing desertification.[6] The government targeted settled Black African agricultural groups.

Racial targeting is by definition intentional, and intent is a legally required element of genocide. In Darfur, this intent is expressed both at specific individual and more general collective levels, from the level of individuals leading and participating in attacks to the level of organized groups – such as the government of Sudan military and the Janjaweed militia – that combine to terrorize and target clusters of settlements for attacks. The multilevel challenge is to analyze, theoretically and empirically, both the individual- and collective-level dynamics of this racially intentional and targeted violence.

Our critical collective framing approach identifies a socially, politically, and historically constructed racial division between Arab and Black African groups in Sudan as a central part of the violence in Darfur. Figure 7.1 summarizes and further elaborates our argument.

The critical collective framing approach we elaborate in this chapter posits the Sudanese genocidal state as an endogenous system that emerged as the transformed macro-level result of collective action. This approach both diverges and converges with six past explanatory approaches.

Our attention to racial symbols and identification diverges from a state insecurity approach that focuses on defensive reactions to insurgent threats.[7] We demonstrate that threats of rebel or insurgent groups are wrongly perceived and exaggerated in Darfur. Our approach similarly diverges from a second primordial explanation that emphasizes hatreds so long standing they are considered exogenous.[8] While we acknowledge past hostilities, we emphasize that their influences are contingent on time and place.

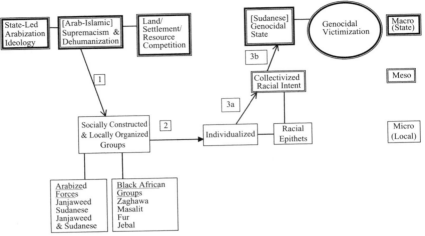

FIGURE 7.1. Transformation Model of Genocide: Macro-Micro-Macro Mechanisms

A third contextual consideration is the competition for life-sustaining resources stressed in a population perspective.[9] This perspective sees set-tlement density not simply as concentrations of people but also the pres-ence of desirable property – possessions, livestock, and the settled land itself. Densely settled areas are where opportunities and incentives are greatest and resources most strained by those that want and need them. The influence of population and resources is also contingent and further-more mediated by racial dehumanization.

Among the most important contingencies we consider are choices highlighted in a fourth instrumental perspective featuring state-based ethno-political entrepreneurs who advance their interests by cultivating public fear and disrespect of subordinate groups.[10] These feelings are often stimulated with invidious socially constructed racial attributions. Thus our approach further overlaps with a fifth constructionist approach that emphasizes racial symbols and identity manipulation by elites.[11] We draw finally from a sixth cognitive framing approach which identifies shifts noted above from "normal" to "crisis" scripts or frames during emerging conflicts.[12]

The critical collective framing approach we elaborate in this chapter identifies a socially, politically, and historically constructed racial division between Arab and Black African groups in Sudan as a central part of the violence in Darfur. Figure 7.1 summarizes and further elaborates our argument, addressing what Coleman[13] and Sampson[14] call the "transformation problem": how systems are built from the interdependent and purposively collected actions of individuals or, in other words, how systematic collective racial intent is built from the aggregated and concentrated racial intent of individuals in targeted settings.

Coleman originally described the transformation problem as "the process through which individual preferences become collective choices; the process through which dissatisfaction becomes revolution; through which simultaneous fear in members of a crowd turns into mass panic."[15] Coleman's emphasizes what he calls "type 3" relations that transform the micro-level actions of individuals into the macro-level actions of social systems.

The government of Sudan is the transformed genocidal state system produced by emergent collective action at the far right of Figure 7.1. The foundation of this state, shown on the left side of Figure 7.1, is the state-led Arabization ideology with its dehumanizing "us" and "them" collective framing we traced earlier from the mid-1980s in Sudan. This supremacist ideology justifies an Arabization policy and is played out in terms of the growing land and resource competition between settled Black African and nomadic Arab groups in Darfur. The property, possessions, livestock, and the settled land itself constitute opportunities and incentives not only for mass criminal violence but also for the massive criminal acquisition of goods and property that is often a core part of genocide.[16]

Coleman theorizes that macro-level ideology-state relationships of the kind seen in Sudan and Darfur emerge from macro-to-micro-to-macro transformative sequences involving individuals, as shown in the lower part of Figure 7.1. Link 1 in this figure depicts the role of demonizing and supremacist ideology in the social construction of the intensified division between Arab and Black African groups in Sudan. The targeted mechanisms of this transformative process form the further links labeled 2, 3a, and 3b in Figure 7.1.

Link 2 represents the role of socially constructed racial identities in stimulating use of the kinds of racial epithets in Darfur by the Janjaweed militia leaders and their followers. Schmitt emphasizes that, in a genocide, "an enemy exists only when, at least potentially, one fighting collectivity of people confronts a similar collectivity."[17] The transformation of individual expressions of racial intent requires their aggregation and concentration in particular social locations, in this case settlement clusters, where they take on a frenzied collective dimension in Link 3a. This kind of racially targeted and viciously violent collective process is a form of "fanatical fury" – involving "a mixture of panic, rage, and a wish for vengeance."[18] Minister Harun and the militia leaders used their social skills and efficacy to ignite this fury with a racial spark. Coleman argues that this kind of transformative (i.e., type 3) process, elaborated with the meso-level links in our model, is weakly developed in most theories. Link 3b indicates the importance of this process. This link depicts the culmination of the frenzied fury that connects collective racial intent to genocidal violence. This victimization is, of course, the lethal and lasting scar of this kind of *genocidal state* and *collective state of mind*.

American criminologist Jack Katz's account of the "righteous slaughter" observed in family-based domestic assaults foreshadows collective genocidal processes at the individual level. Katz emphasizes the vocabularies of motive reflected in the cursing that accompanies impassioned domestic disputes:

> Consider cursing. Most of the studies of impassioned violence reveal a great deal of attendant cursing. Although impassioned attacks sometimes occur without verbal forewarning, it seems natural to move into assaults with shouts of "bitch," "you fucking asshole," "rat bastard," "punk mother-fucker," "nickel-and-dime drunk,"..., and so forth. Why?... They curse, not in the superficial sense..., but...to effect degrading transformations....Symbolically transforming the

offending party into an ontologically lower status. . . . Curses draw on the communal language and its primordial sensibility about the relationship between the sacred and the profane. . . . Cursing sets up violence to be a sacrifice to honor the attacker as a priest representing the collective moral being.

Katz[19] indicates the transformational role curses can play in arousing residually primordial and intensely collective emotions. In this way, Katz illustrates at the individual level the collective frenzy represented in Link 3b. As Brubaker and Laitin note, "We may have as much to learn about the sources and dynamics of ethnic violence from the literature on criminology . . . as from the literature on ethnicity or ethnic conflict."[20]

When the kinds of fury and emotion Katz describes are unleashed collectively and violently on a racial or ethnic group, the violence earns the adjective genocidal. Yet, most scholarly discussions of genocide focus on modifying the content included in the use of this concept as a noun, for example, by advocating the expansion of genocide to include political conflicts.[21] These definitions are insightful in probing the boundaries of genocide, but our interest is more in understanding the collective racial and ethnic dynamics that animate the genocidal victimization. Brubaker and Laitin[22] make a related point about "ethnicization" by emphasizing the following:

> *That* political violence can be ethnic is well established, indeed too well established; how it is ethnic remains obscure. The most fundamental questions – for example, *how* the adjective "ethnic" modifies the noun "violence" – remain unclear and largely unexamined. Sustained attention needs to be paid to the forms and dynamics of ethnicization, to the many and subtle ways in which violence – and conditions, processes, activities, and narratives linked to violence – can take on ethnic hues.

The ADS data we analyze in this chapter uniquely move beyond static definitions of genocide to provide instructive narratives of the processual forms and dynamics that racial epithets play in the organization of these collective attacks.

Hinton introduces the term "genocidal priming" to refer to these processual forms and dynamics of mass victimization.[23] This concept focuses on broader processes involving more than the consequences of genocidal attacks. Hinton concludes that "specific situations will become more or less 'hot' and volatile – or more likely to be 'set off' – as certain processes unfold." We use Coleman's theory of social action to reveal the intensely collective form and dynamic of this process. We incorporate Hinton's point that "when the priming is 'hot' and genocide does take place, there is almost always some sort of 'genocidal activation' that ignites the charge that has been primed." We hypothesize that this kind of racial spark or ignition is collective in nature. Thus, we also follow Blumer[24] and Oberschall[25] in elucidating the racial forms and destructive dynamics of genocidal victimization as a collective framing process.

Similarly, Gamson's collective action framework emphasizes that "only an injustice frame ... taps the righteous anger that puts fire in the belly and iron in the soul."[26] The Arab nomadic pastoralists adopted a group solution to their landless status by pursuing an "us" versus "them" confrontation with the settled African agriculturalists about watering and grazing their livestock. These conceptualizations elaborate our understanding of the roots of this socially organized genocidal confrontation.

The collective framing approach offers an answer to the classic question of how and why ordinary people enlist in genocidal killing. In the context of ethnic cleansing in the former Yugoslavia, Oberschall writes, "Once the young man 'took out a gun' he became encapsulated in a quasi-military unit subject to peer solidarity and ethnic loyalty."[27] He explains that rationalizations and justifying norms – the dominant vocabularies of motive – then take over. In the former Yugoslavia, "They conducted war according to the crisis script." These crisis scripts in Darfur are racial and transformative in form and content.

When also encouraged by state-based ethnic entrepreneurs – or leadership with special social skills or social efficacy – such expressions of violent racism further acquire a collective organizational force that rises above their individual expression, leading to genocidal victimization. Prunier concludes, "Since Darfur had been in a state of protracted racial civil war since the mid-1980s, the tools were readily available; they merely needed to be upgraded. It was done and the rest is now history."[28] We demonstrate in the next section how the racial epithets in Darfur significantly increased the severity of genocidal victimization during attacks.

In sum, the Sudanese state and its agents bore an instrumental responsibility in Darfur – leading the genocidal process and designating the racially identified African farmers and villagers as targets. Arab herders depended on seasonal access and movement through the arable land farmed by the Black Africans. Desertification intensified their need for this access. The state-instigated solution led through the Black African groups.

We explore the transformative links in Figure 7.1 by using the ADS interviews. The sampling of Darfur refugees and the detailed recording of racial epithets heard by these refugees during the attacks in Darfur allow a unique analysis of the sources and consequences of collective racial intent in Darfur.

## Geo-Referencing and Reclustering the ADS Interviews

We now note several features of the ADS survey that make possible the analysis we present in the remainder of this chapter. The United Nations High Commission on Refugees maps its camps into lettered grids or sectors, which enabled a multistage cluster sampling of 1,136 Darfur refugees in all twenty camps and settlements in eastern Chad. The camp administrators assigned new refugees to sectors led by locally recognized sheikhs from the former villages of those refugees.

The organization of the camps around the sheikhs meant that their social geography reproduced the distribution of localities in Darfur from which the refugees fled. Our analysis focused on these pre-camp settlements of origin. The State Department's application of advanced geo-spatial technology in the ADS facilitated the reclustering of the refugees in terms of their places of origin. With the aid of cartographers and translators, the interviewers were able to designate an originating location for 90 percent of the refugees.[29] This could not be done, by way of contrast, with the health and nutrition surveys of the internal displacement camps discussed in Chapters 3 and 4.

Thus, we used an ADS field atlas to locate respondents in twenty-two originating settlement clusters with fifteen or more respondents each (see Map 7.1) representing 932 of the 1,136 respondents. This sample proportionately represented the population of refugees crossing into Chad, with sufficient respondents from originating settlement clusters to allow reliable measurement. Each of the clusters (henceforth called settlements) was designated in terms of the largest included or nearby town on Map 7.1.

The ADS interviews also provided unique measures of the violence the refugees experienced in Darfur. We know of only one other systematic study of pre-camp violence in Darfur,[30] and none that asked about sexual violence. The ADS team consisted of twenty-four investigators and six core staff, including a former sex crimes investigator with the International Criminal Tribunal for the former Yugoslavia who briefed interviewers about sexual victimization. The interviewers asked the refugees when, how, and why they left Darfur and if, when, and how they, their family, or fellow villagers were harmed.

The interviewers conducted an average of five interviews per day; at the end of each day, each interviewer and translator pair went through each interview and completed a one-page "preliminary atrocity field coding sheet" with thirty-five "event codes" that included physical and sexual violence, as well as information about perpetrators, dates, other victimization, and locations.[31] The researchers paid special attention to ensuring reliability and validity in the collection of these data."[32]

Respondents provided detailed information on the acts and perpetrators of incidents during attacks that caused them to flee their villages. In addition to background information about the households, the accounts also included reports of persons killed, raped, and abducted in attacks

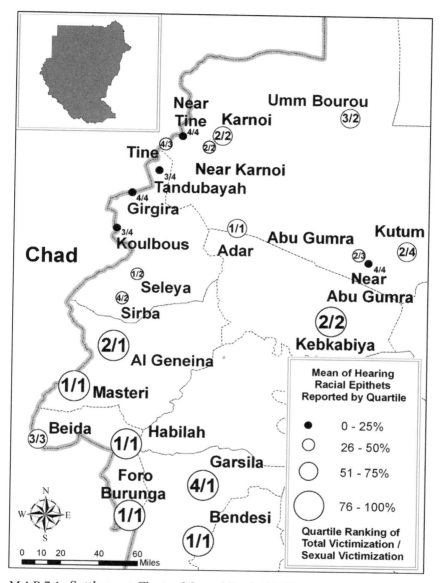

MAP 7.1. Settlement Cluster Map of Racial Epithets and Total Victimization and Sexual Victimization.

and detailed narrative descriptions (usually including names of the per-petrators) of the times, places, and circumstances of the attacks. A key part of the interview asked respondents to recall what they heard attack-ers saying during the attacks. Respondents frequently reported hearing racial epithets in this part of the interview.

The circles on Map 7.1 represent, by quartile, the proportion of per-sons who reported hearing racial epithets. This proportion ranged from about one-quarter to nearly half of the respondents in the different set-tlements.

These racial epithets, like the curses introduced earlier by Katz, com-bined elements of motivation and intent, and they were raised to cru-cially compelling collective levels, as indicated by the settings in which they were heard most frequently. The racial component of the epithets was the motivational element. The intentional element included the tar-geted references to killing, raping, assaulting, looting, and destroying group life.

Thus, refugees often reported hearing the incoming forces shouting racial slurs, such as "This is the last day for blacks," "We will destroy the black-skinned people," "Kill all the slaves," "Kill all the blacks," "You are black and you deserve to be tortured like this," and "We will kill any slaves we find and cut off their heads." These words and phrases shouted by the perpetrators provide insight into and evidence of their motiva-tion and intentions during the attacks on Darfurian villagers. We refer to these slurs as reflecting racial intent in further detail in the following sections.

## Quantifying the ADS Refugee Experience

An essential way of further understanding the experiences of the ADS refugees involves summarizing in quantitative terms who they are and what happened to them. Much of the quantitative detail of this analy-sis is presented in the Appendix and is summarized in charts and tables there. We begin with a quantitative descriptive portrait of the average refugee experience, which is presented in greater detail in Table A.2 of the Appendix.

About 40 percent of the ADS respondents are male, and these refugees are on average 37 years old. Females probably outnumber males because in Darfur males are more likely to be killed, whereas females are more likely to be raped but survive, at least physically. Just over half of the Africans in the sample self-identified as Zaghawa, with approximately one-quarter Masalit and about 5 percent each Fur and Jebal. The largest concentrations of the Zaghawa fled from North Darfur, whereas most of the Masalit and Fur fled from West Darfur, with the Jebal previously concentrated in one town, Seleya, in West Darfur.

We read each attack narrative and coded the description of the attacking group as Janjaweed, Sudanese, or combined Sudanese and Janjaweed forces. About two-thirds of the attacks involved combined Sudanese and Janjaweed forces; in nearly one-fifth, Sudanese forces acted alone (usually in bombing attacks); and about one-tenth involved the Janjaweed alone. The remaining 10 percent of cases could not be categorized, and they form a comparison group in some of the analyses.

The researchers added one item during the second two-week period of the ADS interviews,[33] asking whether rebels had stayed in the respondent's town or village. Less than 2 percent of the respondents in the sample reported a rebel presence, with these reports disproportionately located in several northern settlements such as Karnoi, near Tine, and Girgira, and with the reported rebel presence there still low, ranging from 6 to 13 percent. The media study described earlier identified seven of the settlement areas in our analysis as being the location of rebel activity.[34] We included both the ADS and media measures of rebel activity in our analyses.

Two waves of attacks in Darfur corresponded with the peak periods of refugee flight. About one-quarter of the sample fled during the three months of first-wave attacks, and about half fled during the four months of the second wave of attacks, with the remaining quarter fleeing during the other thirteen months. The second offensive was the most destructive of the group conditions of social life for Black Africans in Darfur.

The ADS interviews recorded in detail the shouting of racial epithets, our measure of racial intent, during the attacks. We examined the narrative accounts of the attacks on a case-by-case basis. We recorded the content of the epithets, detailing as precisely as possible the exact wording. We assigned a code to each respondent indicating whether he or she heard racial epithets. Respondents heard racial epithets in all settlements, as noted earlier and on Map 7.1, with about one-third of the respondents hearing them during the attacks. These epithets often invoked images of racial slavery, and they provided concrete, first-person evidence of racial intent.

We also incorporated a measure of the density of the population settlements in which respondents lived. The more densely settled areas of Darfur are often also the most fertile in providing the necessary conditions for group life. We developed a measure of density in which the numerator consists of the number of settlements in an area recorded in the UN Humanitarian Information Profiles and the denominator is based on the number of square kilometers in the area.[35]

Settlements in the southwestern area of West Darfur – including Bendesi, Foro Burunga, Habilah, and Masteri – score highest on the settlement density measure. As noted, settlement density measures more than the population at risk of victimization. It also measures criminal opportunities and incentives, including the extent of desirable property – consisting of possessions, livestock, and the settled land.[36] Settlement of a land area effectively constitutes ownership in Darfur, and access to settled land is often a crucial resource for sustaining life in a time of desertification and recurrent famine. We therefore hypothesize that the greatest victimization occurred in the densely settled areas of Darfur, in response to the increased opportunities and incentives for attacks and the increased strains on resources.

This hypothesis parallels the Malthusian view of population growth previously applied to the Rwandan genocide by Jared Diamond.[37]

According to Diamond, "Population and environmental problems created by non-sustainable resource use...ultimately get solved in one
way or another: if not by pleasant means of our own choice, then by
unpleasant and unchosen means, such as the ones that Malthus initially
envisioned."[38] Some would argue that Diamond is not a strict environmental determinist, even though he argues that "population pressure was
one of the important factors behind the Rwandan genocide."[39] Diamond
also allows an important role for racial/ethnic hatred, observing,

> I'm accustomed to thinking of population pressure, human environ-
> mental impacts, and drought as ultimate causes, which make people
> chronically desperate and are like the gunpowder inside the powder
> keg. One also needs a proximate cause: a match to light the keg.
> In most areas of Rwanda, that match was ethnic hatred whipped
> up by politicians cynically concerned with keeping themselves in
> power.[40]

His reference to the role of politicians controlling the state and molding
collective racial intent fits well with Flint and de Waal's[41] previously discussed account of a Sudanese security cabal in Khartoum that unleashed
the Janjaweed on the Black Africans of Darfur.

The final pieces of our descriptive portrait of the ADS sample
involve its genocidal victimization. The classical understanding of genocide emphasizes the intentional *taking of lives* that characterizes the
destruction of a group. In contrast, a more contemporary approach to
genocide also focuses on the deliberate infliction of *physical conditions
of life* on a group calculated to bring about its destruction.[42] Article II of
the original Genocide Convention definition includes both elements.[43]

A report section, which was part of each survey, recorded incidents
of victimization. Respondents reported attacks on themselves, their families, and settlements involving bombing, killing, rape, abduction, assault,
property destruction, and theft leading to becoming a refugee. Each
respondent therefore reported attacks on him- or herself, as well as on
his or her settlement.

We consider bombing both as a means and a form of victimization. We therefore analyze bombing separately from other forms of victimization. Because only the Sudanese state possesses planes and bombs, bombing provides a unique measure of state involvement. As one refugee account notes, the bombing in Darfur is crude: "Government troops firebomb villages with barrels of gasoline," usually simply rolling the barrels out of the open cargo hold of the plane.[44] Individuals report their settlements being bombed up to a maximum of seven times, with a mean of about one bombing run per settlement. All of the settlements whose refugees report more than one bombing were in North Darfur (i.e., Abu Gumra, Karnoi, Tine, Umm Bourou, Adar, Girgira, and Tandubayah), where the conflict began in earnest in 2003.

Finally, we created a victimization severity score based on the common law seriousness[45] of the incidents reported during attacks on the settlements. We aggregated reports of specific incidents experienced or witnessed by each respondent in the settlement. We assigned values of five to reported killings, four to sexual violence or abductions, three to assaults, two to property destruction or theft, and one to displacement.[46] The severity scale is nearly normal in its distribution. The maximum victimization severity score is 56, with an average score of just over 34.

To the extent that genocide victimization encompasses a group "in whole" – as, for example, a scorched-earth policy implies – there might be little within- or between-settlement variation in numbers of deaths or total victimization. All are victimized. On the other hand, to the extent that attackers victimize a group "in part," there is variation in both within- and between-settlement outcomes. For the legal and criminological reasons indicated earlier, we are particularly interested in the role that racial intent plays in explaining variation in Sudanese state-organized victimization along with that perpetrated by Janjaweed forces of the Black African groups and settlements.

Our interest is thus in the victimization of the settlements as much as of the individuals who are the victims of the Darfur conflict and represented in the ADS sample. There is, of course, a long tradition in both sociology and in criminology of studying group and institutional as well as individual-level processes. For example, the literature on the sociology of education[47] focuses on the effects of student- and school-level variation in socioeconomic status – as measures of individual- and institutional-level resources – on educational achievement. The questions asked in this tradition of research involve the relative roles of individual and school resources in accounting for variation in academic and behavioral outcomes.

In a similar way, we analyze the effects of individual- and settlement-level variation in racial epithets – as measures of individual and collective racial intent – on genocidal victimization. As summarized in Figure 7.1, we see racial epithets as forming the spark that transforms the specific forms of racial intent emphasized in international law into the "type 3" collective racial intent, or collective targeted fury and frenzy, that so often characterizes genocide. The government officials and militia leaders discussed in this chapter and earlier chapters are the agents who use their social skills and efficacy in igniting and directing this racial spark, whereas the racial epithets constitute their intentionally directed vocabularies of motive. This transformative action mediates supremacist and dehumanizing ideologies in the social formation – from the states of mind and actions of individuals – of the collective violence of the genocidal state.

## The Genocidal State in Action

In the Appendix, we present the details of the multilevel models we analyzed using the ADS data, and we summarize the results here. We present the most important aspects of this analysis descriptively, with the aid of a map and figures below. We also present one numerical table that summarizes specific findings about sexual violence at the end of this chapter.

We begin by describing the distribution of the racial epithets heard during attacks on the ADS survivors. First, we consider the distribution of racial epithets in terms of the characteristics of the *individuals* who heard them – that is, we answer the question, *Who* heard these epithets most often? Second, we consider how the reporting of these epithets varies across the *settlements* – that is, we answer the question, *Where* were these epithets heard most often?

At the individual level, men reported they heard racial epithets more often than women. This is probably because women are less likely than men to know the Arabic words of the shouted epithets. Respondents living in settlements in which there was rebel activity indicated they heard racial epithets less often than those in settlements without rebels. This finding strongly suggests that the scorched-earth tactics of the attacks actually focus on civilians, rather than on suspected rebels. Three of the four Black African groupings – the Fur, Masalit, and Jebal – heard racial epithets more often than did the Zaghawa. This is likely because Sudanese planes bombed the Zaghawa more than the other groups, and respondents could hear the epithets better during ground attacks. Respondents reported hearing epithets less often during the first wave of attacks than at other times, which suggests that the racialization of the attacks increased over the duration of the conflict.

Map 7.1, introduced earlier, portrays the variation in reported racial epithets across the settlements. It indicates variation in the proportion of respondents reporting epithets with circles of increasing sizes (calibrated in quartiles) in each settlement. About half of the respondents in the top quartile heard racial epithets during the attacks. Thus, 45 percent of the respondents heard racial epithets in Kebkabiya, where Musa Hilal began his early attacks, and from 43 to 50 percent of respondents heard these epithets in settlements in southwestern Darfur – in Al Geneina, Masteri, Habilah, Garsila, Foro Burunga, and Bendesi – the sites of attacks led by the other three Janjaweed militia leaders. Recall that the latter sites are in the more fertile and densely settled areas of Darfur.

Respondents also heard the racial epithets more often when the GoS forces joined with the Janjaweed in attacks and in areas of high settlement density. This finding – which reflects effects of both state

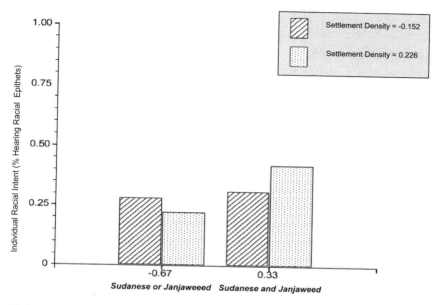

FIGURE 7.2. Cross-Level Interaction of Separate and/or Combined Forces with Settlement Density (mean centered) on Individual Racial Intent.

military organization and the opportunities and incentives provided by land-based resources – is summarized with a bar graph in Figure 7.2 that indicates the following: When Sudanese and Janjaweed forces attack together, elevated population density notably increases the hearing of racial epithets. When the Sudanese and Janjaweed forces attack separately, elevated population density slightly diminishes the hearing of these epithets. Recall that Sudanese and Janjaweed forces operate together in about two-thirds of the attacks. This *combination* of forces in the right-hand side of this figure – representing settlements with higher population densities – approximately *doubles* the hearing of racial epithets from about 20 to more than 40 percent. This constitutes compelling evidence that the Sudanese state intensified the expression of racial intent by joining with the Janjaweed in attacks on densely settled areas of Darfur.

We next summarize our individual-level findings using the total victimization scale to capture, in summary form, the sources of genocidal violence, including the role of racial epithets as the spark that elevates this violence to genocidal levels. First, we consider the patterning of the attacks at the individual level. For example, victimization decreases among adults with age, as is also the case in more conventional circumstances.[48] As with racial epithets, victimization also increases when the GoS forces and the Janjaweed attack together, and the Fur, Masalit, and Jebal are at higher risk than the Zaghawa. Again, this is evidence of the role of the Sudanese government forces in targeting and unleashing victimization when they attack in conjunction with the Janjaweed militias. As expected, victimization increases during the two peak attack periods. Finally, at the individual level, hearing racial epithets strongly and significantly predicts total victimization.

Recall our special interest in seeing whether, in addition to the individual-level effect of specific racial intent, we would find a settlement-level effect of collective racial intent. This collective effect would reflect the transformation of the racial spark into a genocidal fury and frenzy of racial violence.

We observed this genocidal impact of collective racial intent in two ways that summarize the findings from the multivariate and multilevel models discussed in greater detail in the Appendix. Map 7.1 provides the first illustration of a significant effect of collective racial intent. According to this map, racial epithets are heard more often in the Kebkabiya area, where Musa Hilal launched his attacks, and in the southwestern settlements in West Darfur, dominated by the other three leaders. Inside the circles on Map 7.1 reflecting these elevated reports of racial epithets, we also present the quartile ranks of victimization severity, as well as sexual victimization, which we discuss in greater detail later.

A clear pattern emerges in Map 7.1: The quartile ranking of the severity of victimization scores across settlements coincides with the quartile ranking of reported racial epithets. Thus, the top-quartile victimization scores are found in five of the six settlements that also feature elevated racial epithets in the southwestern part of West Darfur. Again, we note that this part of West Darfur is more fertile and densely settled. The models presented in the Appendix further show that the southwestern part is also the area where victimization is most severe, and this pattern is mediated by the pervasiveness of the racial epithets and their collective effect in increasing victimization. This part of the analysis supports Diamond's metaphor introduced earlier in this chapter, namely his expectation that collective racial intent is the transformative racial spark that ignites the powder keg of settlement density.

Map 7.1 also reveals another pattern: Higher victimization severity scores and racial epithet reports extend from Kebkabiya, through Adar, and northward to Karnoi. This pattern of scores reflects the northern line of attacks that Musa Hilal threatened during his remarks in the Kebkabiya market, described in Chapter 5. If the levels of settlement density were as high in North Darfur as they are in the affected areas of West Darfur, the scores observed in this part of the map would likely be even higher.

Another important finding summarized in Figure 7.3 involves the roles played by collective racial intent and bombing in the victimization models presented in the Appendix. At lower levels of collective racial intent, increased bombing is associated with decreasing levels of victimization, whereas at higher levels of collective racial intent, increased bombing elevates total victimization. We hypothesized that the Sudanese government enlisted the Janjaweed militias and channeled their hostility toward Black African groups. Given that the bombing by GoS planes is entirely under Sudanese state control, the combined use of the Janjaweed militias and the government bombing provides particularly striking evidence of the use of state power to divide and victimize subordinate groups. Figure 7.3 supplements the earlier findings in showing how, especially in densely settled areas, the concentration of bombing and collective racial hostility against African groups, such as the Fur and Masalit, produces elevated levels of genocidal victimization. The Sudanese government directed the bombing and enlisted the Janjaweed in racially

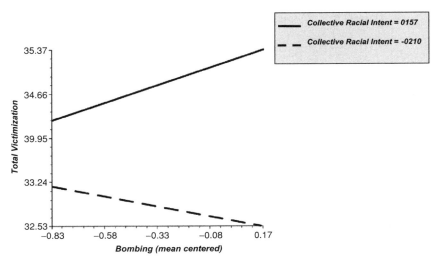

FIGURE 7.3. Cross-Level Interaction of Collective Racial Intent (mean centered) with Bombing on Total Victimization (standardized).

animated attacks that intensified victimization, thus enacting and accomplishing a joined, collective intent.

## A State-Supported Policy of Rape

There are few quantitative studies of sexual violence in international conflicts,[49] despite increasing attention to rape and sexual assault by human rights organizations[50] and in international humanitarian and criminal law.[51] The UN Inquiry on Darfur found that "various sources reported widespread rape" while warning that "many cases went unreported due to the sensitivity ... and stigma associated with rape."[52] Similar uncertainty prevailed in Rwanda, where "sexual violence was also widespread," but "the extent of this sexual violence is unclear and may never be fully revealed."[53]

The ADS interviews considered in earlier chapters documented the use of rape as an instrument of terror, and our victimization severity scale included rape. However, these interviews also offer an important opportunity to add a more specific quantitative grounding to the understanding of sexual violence in genocidal contexts.

Sexual violence has both severe medical and sociopolitical consequences. The damages range from physical and reproductive trauma, to pregnancy, shame, humiliation, and secondary consequences such as ostracism.[54] These consequences are further compounded in patriarchal Islamic cultures, such as Sudan, where a child's ethnicity derives from the father. The state can use rape as a uniquely powerful weapon of war against women.

The Trial Chamber in the Rwandan *Akayesu* case recognized this vulnerability of women and held that rape was part of the genocide and "one of the worst ways of inflicting...bodily and mental harm," as well as "an integral part of the process of destruction."[55] Several UN commissions have recognized rape as a powerful tactic for ethnic cleansing.[56] Article II of the Genocide Convention states that "measures intended to prevent births within the group" and more generally "deliberately inflicting on the group conditions of life calculated to bring about its physical destruction in whole or in part" constitute genocide. The court in *Akayesu* explicitly understood that these intentional measures and deliberate conditions included sexual violence.

We can reduce the impact of the societal taboos that hamper the quantitative study of rape with methods that focus on the *group* dynamics of sexual violence in armed conflicts. As we note throughout this chapter, an underemphasized aspect of research on genocide involves the *organizational* devices and *interactional* dynamics – for example, involving collective racial intent – that activate the perpetration and prosecution of war crimes.[57] This kind of focus shifts methodological attention from personal to collective experiences of victimization.

Respondents to surveys more comfortably answer questions about rape in relation to others than themselves. Moreover, when individuals report collective experiences, it is possible to cross-check responses by focusing on reporting by settings, rather than by individuals alone. The ADS interviews offer an important opportunity to use this approach to analyze sexual violence in an international armed conflict.

We also analyze here another aspect of the genocide in Darfur, namely a pattern of ethnic protection of Arab villages from GoS and Janjaweed militia attacks. Attacking forces spared Arab villages 6.3 percent of the time, according to the refugees. The UN Commission highlighted this kind of protective targeting by noting, "For instance, in an area of 50 km between Al Geneina and Masteri inhabited mostly by Arab tribes, no signs of destruction were recorded."[58] This selective protection further separates "us" from "them" in an organizational dynamics of genocide that includes sexual violence.[59]

We hypothesize that the Sudanese government joined with Janjaweed militias to create racial terror in a polarized "us" and "them" divide-and-conquer strategy leading to sexual violence, which in turn created its own terror. The ethnic protection of Arab villages is a counterpart to the racial intention already analyzed, separating "us" from "them" in further selectively targeting sexual violence as an instrument of racialized terror. Thus, we added the spared villages measure of ethnic protection to the earlier analysis of the hearing of racial epithets. Doing so revealed that hearing racial epithets is strongly associated with proximity to spared Arab villages. We then estimated four models of sexual violence.

The reports of sexual violence range continuously from one to ten or more and indicate whether respondents reported themselves or others as victims of sexual violence during attacks on their settlements. The analysis summarized in Table 7.1 parallels those described in the Appendix. The first model indicates that women and younger respondents reported more sexual victimization than men and older respondents and that hearing racial epithets also predicted sexual victimization.

The second model introduces the remaining individual-level variables. The results indicated that sexual violence increased when Sudanese government forces combined with Janjaweed attacking groups, in

TABLE 7.1. *Individual and Settlement Cluster Models of Rape and Sexual Assaults, Adjusted for Dispersion: Atrocities Documentation Survey, Darfur Refugees, Summer, 2004[a]*

| | Model 1 | Model 2 | Model 3 | Model 4 |
|---|---|---|---|---|
| *Individual-level respondent attributes* | B(se) | b(se) | b(se) | b(se) |
| Age | −.024** | −.024*** | −.024*** | −.024*** |
| | (.008) | (.001) | (.008) | (.008) |
| Gender | .080* | .032* | .016 | .016 |
| | (.194) | (.173) | (.174) | (.173) |
| *African group membership* | | | | |
| Fur | | 1.050* | .763 | .599 |
| | | (.504) | (.504) | (.505) |
| Masalit | | .408 | .209 | .0674 |
| | | (.320) | (.313) | (.290) |
| *Attacking groups* | | | | |
| Sudanese | | .520 | .564 | .524 |
| | | (.367) | (.373) | (.378) |
| Sudanese & Janjaweed | | .575* | .617* | .596* |
| | | (.250) | (.251) | (.252) |
| *Ethnic protection* | | | | |
| Arab villages spared | | .468 | .363 | .373 |
| | | (.301) | (.317) | (.321) |
| *Racial intention* | | | | |
| Racial epithets heard | .565* | .436+ | .432+ | .384 |
| | (.277) | (.257) | (.259) | (.260) |
| *Waves of attacks* | | | | |
| First peak | | .257 | .241 | .199 |
| | | (.221) | (.220) | (.230) |
| Second peak | | .564*** | .612*** | .618* |
| | | (.264) | (.265) | (.261) |
| *Settlement cluster level* | | | | |
| Ethnic protection | | | 2.992* | 2.185 |
| | | | (1.447) | (1.494) |
| Racial intention | | | | 1.850*** |
| | | | | (.922) |
| Intercept | 1.142* | 1.378 | 1.154 | 1.118 |

[a] N = 932 individuals (level-1) and 22 settlement clusters (level-2).
+ p < .10  *p < .05  **p < .01  ***p < .001

particular in attacks on Fur refugees, especially during the second peak in killings. We previously noted the particular targeting of the Fur in Darfur, but even more strikingly, we now observed the significant role of the combined government and Janjaweed forces and the elevation of this violence in association with the killings in the second government offensive.

The last two models in Table 7.1 extend the analysis of ethnic protection and racial intention to the settlement level. Model 3 introduces ethnic protection alone and indicated that the settlements where respondents reported sparing of neighboring Arab villages also reported higher levels of sexual violence. The introduction of the ethnic protection variable in this model reduced the effect of being Fur below statistical significance, probably because of the location of the Fur villages in West Darfur in close proximity to Arab villages.

The last model reveals further indication of protective and selective targeting through the introduction of the settlement-level measure of racial intent. This statistically significant effect of collective racial intent reduced the effect of ethnic protection to statistical nonsignificance. This effect indicates that ethnic protection of neighboring Arab villages operates through the impact of racial intention and terror in producing sexual violence at the settlement level against neighboring Black African villagers. The findings of Table 7.1 and the eyewitness reports noted earlier imply participation from residents of the spared Arab villages in attacks on Black African villages. Ethnic protection in this way likely plays an important role in the creation of the "us" and "them" pattern of racial intention and sexual violence in Darfur.

Meanwhile, consider the larger pattern of effects in the final model of sexual violence estimated in Table 7.1. These statistically significant effects indicate the causal role in sexual violence in Darfur not only of racial terror but also of combined Sudanese government and Janjaweed militia attacks and during the second government offensive. These findings indicate a salient role of the Sudanese government in the use of sexual violence as an instrument of genocidal violence, a role that continued at least five years after the current conflict began.[60]

## Killing, Rape, and the Crimes of Genocide

Sudan's President Omar al-Bashir recently denied his own and his government's involvement in genocide by conceding, "Yes, there have been villages burned. People have been killed because there is war." He then added, "It is not in the Sudanese culture or people of Darfur to rape. It doesn't exist. We don't have it."[61] Although the laws of war obviously do not allow the wholesale burning of villages or the indiscriminate killing of civilians either, al-Bashir's comments about sexual violence reflect some apprehension about the less equivocal (albeit woefully underenforced) legal standing of rape as a war crime. Killing is sometimes permissible in war. Rape is not.

The frequency with which rape is reported in Darfur and the evidence we present of its systematic association with state-perpetrated racism should reduce the uncertainty in characterizing Darfur as genocide. Yet, Gerard Prunier calls Darfur "the ambiguous genocide," and the UN Commission of Inquiry uses the terms "ethnic cleansing" and "crimes against humanity" while explicitly rejecting the charge of genocide.[62] It is much more difficult to escape the conclusion that the Darfur conflict constitutes genocide when the evidence of state- and race-linked rape is considered alongside the broader evidence of death and destruction. Our analysis supports Nicholas Kristof's assertions of a racially targeted Sudanese "policy of rape"[63] and Emily Wax's depictions of systematic rape in Darfur.[64]

We saw in our own descriptions of the militia leaders' activities how often killings and rapes occur alongside one another and in association with the shouting of racial epithets. Several additional quotes from the ADS interviews indicate the intertwined nature of the killings and rapes in these attacks:

- We will kill all the men and rape all the women. We want to change the color. Every woman will deliver red. Arabs are the husbands of those women.
- The government has killed... all the men, all the children, and raped the women.

• They said that they would kill as many Masalit as they could and that the rest would never lie there again. They also said, "We will take your women and make them ours. We will change the race."

The crimes of genocide in Darfur extend well beyond the usual emphasis on mortality and demonstrate that sexual violence occupies a central place in genocidal violence.

In this chapter, we analyzed killings and rapes along with theft and property destruction in a combined scale of the seriousness of genocidal victimization, and we also looked at rape and sexual violence separately. To reduce past reporting problems, our approach broadens the measurement of sexual violence by emphasizing the victimization of others in addition to the respondents and by aggregating these reports at the level of settlements to reveal policy-driven patterns. The evidence presented indicates that GoS forces and Janjaweed militia joined together in attacks with the intention of creating terror through the shouting of racial epithets and the perpetration of extremely violent crimes. The evidence presented further indicates that genocidal victimization and sexual violence intensified during the second government offensive and peak in killings in Darfur during the winter of 2003–2004. Evidence also indicates the intensification of this violence in Black African settlements near Arab villages protected from this violence. This evidence of ethnic protection and racial intention leading to sexual violence supports the charges by Kristof and Wax of an organized Sudanese policy of racially targeted rape in Darfur.

In addition to the use of sexual violence against Black Africans in Darfur, there is also evidence of a policy of harassment of researchers and aid workers who assisted victims of this policy of rape. In May 2005, Sudanese authorities arrested two aid workers from the Dutch Médecins Sans Frontières (MSF) after it published a report, based on medical evidence gathered from its hospitals in Darfur, of 500 rape cases over an eighteen-week period.[65] In September 2006, two MSF staffers were sexually assaulted in an area of Darfur under government control.[66] Thus, the policy of rape in Darfur may not only target the primary victims of this sexual violence but also those who study and assist them.

More generally, the findings of this chapter indicate that expressions of racial motivation and intent in the form of racial epithets are most commonly heard during the joint attacks of Sudanese government and Arab Janjaweed forces on African Fur, Masalit, and Jebal groups in Darfur. These racial expressions play an elevated role in areas densely settled by African groups, and individual and collective expressions of racial motivation and intent increase the severity of the victimization.

We found no evidence of an association between the presence of rebel groups and severity of victimization, but instead evidence that the Sudanese state participated and racially directed victimization of Black African groups in militarily unjustifiable ways. State-supported racial motivation and intent formed a collective crisis frame leading to genocidal violence in Darfur. Collective racial motivation and intent influenced the severity of victimization across settlements, above and beyond this influence at the individual level, and this collective frame mediated the concentration of attacks on densely settled areas and particular African groups; furthermore, this collective motivation and intent combined with GoS-directed aerial bombing to intensify the severity of victimization on the ground. This evidence documented the kinds of organized social processes increasingly emphasized in international criminal law and with special relevance to the determination of genocide in Darfur.

These findings support a collective action theory of what international law recognizes as "criminal organization," "common purpose," and "joint criminal enterprise." International criminal prosecutions increasingly emphasize ideas about collective action.[67] The prosecution of Slobodan Milosevic, albeit aborted because of his death, focused on his involvement in a "joint criminal enterprise" to commit genocide in the former Yugoslavia.[68]

A prominent legal scholar, Mark Osiel, emphasizes the need to better understand the "kind of influence...participants in such criminality actually exercise over one another, through what organizational devices and interactional dynamics."[69] Our analysis of the emergence of collective racial motivation and intent provides direct evidence of the "interactional dynamics" involved in Darfur. The backdrop to this state-organized criminal enterprise is the integration of legitimate government military and illegitimate paramilitary opportunity structures built around Arab Janjaweed militias in Darfur. The Sudanese government integrated the Janjaweed into its military strategy in the interests of maintaining its control over Darfur. The government could enlist the Arab Janjaweed because these landless nomadic groups needed grazing land for their herds. These circumstances formed the ecological context of a collective action and opportunity structure that used an "us" and "them" crisis framing of collective racial motivation and intent to direct the unfolding of genocidal victimization in Darfur. We found that racism operated as a collective instrument of organized terror that amplified the severity of this genocidal victimization in Darfur. In Coleman's terms, this socially organized and instigated terror constitutes a transformative "type 3" process with the features of a killing frenzy, or fanatical fury, which links targeted racial motivation and intent to genocidal violence.

There are, of course, limitations to the data from the ADS. The data were obtained from surviving refugees who lived close enough to the Chad border to allow their escape. Respondents reported attacks retrospectively and provided the evidence of both the racial epithets and victimization. Nonetheless, legally trained interviewers made special efforts to document the racial epithets in precisely reported phrases, and investigators recorded the violence and victimization in the ways police investigators take statements for later use in court. We also made a follow-up effort to obtain additional corroboration for our findings.

The follow-up effort consisted of three weeks of interviews and more than 100 hours of fieldwork conducted by the first author with the Darfur Investigation Team at the new International Criminal Court in The Hague. During that time, the first author learned that one of the investigators had interviewed a Janjaweed defector in London. Within weeks, the BBC released a parallel interview with an anonymous Janjaweed defector. Either the two interviews came from the same defector, or they corroborated one another's accounts. The interview[70] described much that we documented with the ADS data – for example, that Janjaweed fighters received instruction about racial epithets and orders such as "kill the Blacks," that the Janjaweed fought with direction from Sudanese forces, that Sudanese bombing characteristically preceded Janjaweed ground attacks, that attackers often abducted and raped women, and that attacks intentionally targeted civilians more than rebels. This interview also included an important assertion of repeated visits to the training camps run with the involvement of a Sudanese Minister of the Interior.

Such evidence about the conflict in Darfur might make its prosecution as genocide seem certain. Add to this our estimate of the deaths of 200,000 to 400,000 or more persons and the forcible displacement of from two to three million Darfurians. Yet, neither the European Union, the main funding source for the new International Criminal Court; nor the UN Commission of Inquiry in Darfur (2005), which recommended referral of the Darfur case to the ICC; nor the brief filed by the Office of the Prosecutor of the ICC in 2007 called this conflict genocide. They instead characterized Darfur as a lesser crime against humanity, and it was not until 2008 that Prosecutor Luis Moreno-Ocampo applied to the ICC judges for the arrest of Sudanese President al-Bashir for genocide.

It is possible that racism is a significant force not only in genocidal victimization but also in the language and naming of ethnic conflicts. Yet, as noted earlier, notwithstanding his own failure as the Secretary-General of the United Nations to stop the genocide in Rwanda, Boutros Boutros-Ghali cogently observed, "A genocide in Africa has not received the same attention that genocide in Europe or genocide in Turkey or genocide in other parts of the world."[71] This is despite demonstrated distinctive parallels between genocidal victimization in Europe and Africa.

The resistance to calling the Darfur conflict genocide may also stem from the requirement of evidence of *intent* that is *beyond a reasonable doubt* in its unequivocal linkage to the targeting of *protected groups*.

This, of course, is the kind of high standard designed in criminal law to make remote the possibility of conviction of innocent individuals.[72]

Criminal law and social science operate with different goals and standards of evidence. Edwin Sutherland confronted this problem in debates about his then-controversial use of the concept of white-collar crime. Sutherland famously insisted that designations of white-collar crime did not require the legal evidence necessary to find a specific *individual* guilty "beyond a reasonable doubt."[73] He instead argued that a civil law standard more consistent with social science and based on the "balance of probabilities" should apply. Today, he likely would add that our interest as social scientists should be more in collectivities than in individuals. The "specific intent" of greater importance for a criminology of genocide involves "collective racial intent." The kind of evidence presented in this chapter is highly relevant to a prima facie legal determination of genocide, but it is less relevant to the ultimate finding of the guilt or innocence of any specific accused individual.

Like the founding figure of genocide, Raphael Lemkin, Sutherland argued the importance of identifying white-collar crime as a crime, for the purposes of public discourse as well as scientific study. Yet, Sutherland also insisted that a social science of white-collar crime could not progress if it required the certainty of the criminal law. Social science is not bound, and cannot progress, with the same preoccupation about the guilt or innocence of specific individuals. Our attention focuses on more general social principles and processes, such as collective racial motivation and intent. More than fifty years after Edwin Sutherland added white-collar crime to the research agenda of criminology, it is time to do the same with Raphael Lemkin's concept of genocide.

# 8 Global Shadows

## The Global North and South

Should it be entirely surprising that the United States, a country with a history of importing African slaves and massively killing and displacing its indigenous people, would centuries later respond in ambivalent ways to Sudan, an African country that enslaved, killed, and displaced its own indigenous population? Perhaps these countries are not as entirely different as they at first seem. There may be lessons of broader relevance in the disconnected but in some ways similar and overlapping experiences of the United States and Sudan. Criminology can be one important source of these lessons.

We start with two jarringly different images of the consequences of Sudan's recent genocidal history. The first image involves the well-told story in Megan Mylan and Jon Shenk's documentary, the *Lost Boys of Sudan*, and in Dave Eggers's novel, *What Is the What*. These tell the true tale of the thousands of young boys who, when confronted with terrifying choices in the early 1990s between being child soldiers, becoming slaves, or being killed, chose to flee from southern Sudan to refugee camps in Ethiopia. When life proved desperate there too, many of these youth fled back through the still raging killing fields of southern Sudan, winding up in refugee camps in Kenya. Finally, in 2000, the U.S. government brought some of these youth to the United States, where they received help, often from church groups, in negotiating a challenging reintegration into more normal lives in the Global North.[1] This outcome was an enormously important accomplishment of restorative justice for the fortunate few who survived their early lives as child victims and soldiers in Sudan.

The second image presents a sobering reflection of the exclusionary stigma and punitiveness that more often confront refugees from Sudan's genocidal policies. It is a color photo appearing "above the fold" on the front page of the *New York Times* on New Year's Eve, 2005. It shows a Sudanese man crying out as another man tries to deliver his infant child to safety through a bus window as they are forcibly removed by Egyptian police from a protest in Cairo. That day, the police killed at least twenty-three people, including small children, when hundreds of Sudanese refugees refused to leave a public park they occupied to protest denials of their refugee claims by UN officials. Those officials denied sanctuary to thousands of Sudanese camped in the small park across from their offices because they said it was safe to return to their "homes" in Sudan. The article accompanying the photo reported the actions of the police this way:

> When the officers charged, women and children tried to huddle together, and to hide under blankets as some men grabbed for anything – tree limbs, metal bars – struggling to fight back, witnesses said. The police hesitated, then rushed in with full force, trampling over people and dragging the Sudanese off to waiting buses.

Police loaded the protesters onto buses and later released them on the streets of Cairo, with no possessions and nowhere to go.[2] They were yet again the victims of social exclusion.

We do not know what became of the latter group of refugee claimants and their children, but it is reasonable to assume they fared far worse on the streets of Cairo than the lost boys of Sudan who received refuge in the United States. Of course, the Global North also practices social exclusion, notably in the forms of homelessness and imprisonment, and the field of criminology examines the life-course outcomes of both young and older persons who are treated with analogously punitive (e.g., arrest and imprisonment) as opposed to reintegrative policies (e.g., shelters, alternative schools, and work programs) in North America. We can learn much from this criminological research in the Global North, and we argue in this chapter that this work can also increase our understanding of the Global South – not only because our fates are linked by the shrinking and interconnected dimensions of the joined worlds in which we live but also because even more fundamental aspects of our geographically separate lives are more intertwined than they ordinarily might seem.

In particular, we argue that there are lessons from the experiences of homeless youth and families in the Global North that can make the Global South, including the life prospects of the displaced and dispossessed in Darfur, more understandable. This chapter ultimately considers both similarities and differences in the state-based systems of selective exclusion found in the United States and Sudan. Readers may wish to jump ahead to Figure 8.1, presented later in this chapter, for a summary of where this discussion leads. Our discussion begins with a broader comparison of policies of social exclusion in the Global North and Global South.

## The Criminology of Two Hemispheres

Albeit in different ways and to different degrees, large numbers of homeless adults and children are denied the human right to secure shelter in the nations of both the Global North and the Global South. For some, this form of social exclusion leads to involvement in crime, whereas for others it is a form of criminal victimization in itself. For many, it is both. Homelessness and imprisonment are pervasive mechanisms of social exclusion in the late modern Global North; forced migration and mortality are persistent processes of social exclusion in the contemporary Global South. The shrinking dimensions of world history and worldwide population shifts connect these institutional trends, often resulting in conflict, as when the fear-driven exclusivity of the North pushes back against the successive waves of forced displacement and pleas for

sanctuary from the South. These hemispheric processes beg for comparative research and understanding, and criminological theory and research
can speak to this need.

Major contributions to late modern criminology address themes of
social exclusion and inclusion. Any accounting is highly selective, but
brief mention of some of the most notable contributions made by recent
recipients of the Stockholm Prize in Criminology can help make this
basic point. For example, John Braithwaite explains in his work with
Valerie Braithwaite how stigmatic social exclusion and more inclusive
and reintegrative shaming policies can characterize opposing regimes of
punishment and strongly influence the life paths of those who experience them.[3] Alfred Blumstein explains in his work with Richard Rosen-
feld and others how an exclusionary period of escalating imprisonment
and confinement of young Black males linked to a perceived drug epidemic in the United States prolonged the challenge of encouraging their
desistance from lifelong criminal careers.[4] Friedrich Lösel explains in
his work how social cognitive treatment programs in community settings can reduce persistent criminality.[5] Terrie Moffitt explains how adolescent, limited involvement in antisocial behavior followed by social
reintegration and inclusion can be distinguished from life-course persistence in antisocial behavior and its exclusionary developmental consequences.[6]

This contemporary criminology builds on the shoulders of giants.
For example, when we integrate the developmental concept of antisocial
behavior with Robert Merton's classic sociological typology that highlights "innovation" and "rebellion" as forms of criminalized deviance,[7]
we recognize the foundations of a late modern criminology that informs
us about the causes and consequences not only of the street crimes of the
Global North but also about crimes against humanity and the responses
they provoke in the Global South. The North can tell us much about the
South, whereas the lessons of the South are also consequential for the
North, if only partly as a result of the forces of displacement and immigration already noted.

We begin in the more familiar terrain of North American criminology before returning to the urgency of current lessons from the Darfur region of Sudan. We review research indicating that reintegrative and restorative justice policies providing shelter and assistance limit life-course persistence in delinquency and crime. Parallel research reveals that punitive and stigmatizing policies more often produce enduring criminal careers. Yet, leading late modern states in the Global North, such as the United States and Great Britain, currently are moving toward increasingly punitive and stigmatizing justice system policies,[8] which constitute policies of legalized social exclusion. We consider new evidence that the collateral intergenerational consequences of this kind of institutionalized legal exclusion of parents increase family disruption, homelessness, educational failure, delinquency, and crime. We find that underlying all these consequences are distinctive alternative collective framings of groups, such as the homeless and displaced, in exclusive as contrasted with inclusive terms. The difference is as distinctive as the alternative collective framings in the Global North of "*street youth* who can be *helped*" versus "*street criminals* who must be *punished.*"

Discouraging trends in the Global North foreshadow the more dire circumstances of the Global South. The challenge is to see the countertrends in what otherwise too often seems an accelerating downward descent. Out of this mixed story comes a rich research agenda for changing criminology, with the changes including a better understanding of some of the most desperate criminality of the Global South.

## Street Youth and Street Criminals in Three Cities

Two cities in the Canadian Global North, Toronto and Vancouver, adopted contrasting inclusive and exclusive policies in relation to homeless youth in the 1980s and 1990s. The results provided a research opportunity for the first author of this book and Bill McCarthy to consider how alternative policies of inclusion and exclusion affect homeless youth and street crime in the late modern urban settings of the Global North.[9]

Another study, undertaken at the turn of the millennium in Glasgow, Scotland, provided a subsequent opportunity to confirm and extend some of the findings of the Canadian research many thousands of miles away. We begin with Toronto and Vancouver.

Toronto implemented many features of an inclusive and restorative social welfare model that collectively framed youth living on the streets and away from home in the developmental vernacular of "street youth" or "street kids." In Toronto, provincial legislation allowed youth who lived apart from their families and without parental consent to receive emergency and longer-term public shelter and financial assistance. Thus, in the 1990s, Toronto reserved four hostels exclusively for youth aged 16 through 21. Some youth still preferred to live on the streets, but most clearly valued the shelter and other services provided by these youth-oriented settings.

The situation in Vancouver differed in significant ways. Vancouverites worried about the enticements of their city's mild climate and coastal location. They foresaw security threats in an unceasing onslaught of westward migration. In the 1990s, the province and city's welfare policies grew increasingly restrictive and exclusionary. Family and welfare legislation provided that youth living apart from their families in Vancouver could only receive publicly funded support in unusual circumstances. Care providers could offer shelter to youth only if parents first gave permission for them to be away from home – an unrealistic precondition for youth in violent conflict with their parents. In addition, authorities in Vancouver refused to implement a framing of "street youth" that was separate and apart from "street criminals." Thus, in the 1990s, Vancouver offered no hostels, shelters, or safe houses for the short-term housing of homeless youth. Very few settings provided support for these youth on the street. Vancouver stigmatized these youth as "ordinary street criminals," and they excluded them.

The situation in Vancouver made the police the first responders to homeless youth. The police responded either by returning youth to their families, who were liable to criminal prosecution if they refused to accept and promise to support their children; or by placing the youth in government care and sending them to a foster or group home; or by pre-emptively arresting and jailing these youth. These options did not offer promising solutions to the problems that caused these youth to leave their homes in the first place.

Our panel interviews with the youth in the two cities confirmed that the settings and alternative policy models made a difference. There was a strong tendency for the youth in Vancouver as contrasted with Toronto to be involved in crimes of theft, drugs, and prostitution. The results further highlighted another key difference in outcomes between these cities, one that further diminished involvement in street crimes in Toronto. Toronto's inclusive social welfare model of providing access to overnight shelters and social services reduced exposures to the criminal opportunities offered by street crime networks and subcultures, whereas Vancouver's exclusionary crime control model and absence of assistance made these exposures more common. Heightened exposure to the street and its criminal opportunities intensified a movement toward the ful-fillment of criminalized expectations, including embeddedness of these youth among criminal networks and away from legally employed peers.[10] Vancouver police more often charged these youth for their involvement in street crime, which is, of course, also consistent with an exclusionary crime control model and a collective framing of these youth as street criminals, and inconsistent with these young people getting and keeping jobs.

More generally, the direct and indirect effects of taking to the streets in Toronto's more inclusively and Vancouver's more exclusively framed policy settings illustrate the significant roles that macro-level policies play in determining life outcomes. Inclusive and exclusive framings and their connected policies can determine life paths leading away from or further into the criminally networked subcultures of the streets that per-vade cities of the Global North.

These findings were confirmed by a fascinating year-long intensive study of homeless youth on the streets of Glasgow, Scotland.[11] By year's end, this ethnographic field study confirmed that, among these youth, those who avoided the "homeless subcultures" of city centers and stayed in youth-specific ("street kid") shelters took advantage of social services and achieved better employment outcomes. These youth who participated in the specialized programs designed to reintegrate them into work and school programs and to reframe them as conventional adolescents avoided the "downward spiral" experienced by youth who remained outside this sphere in adult-dominated hostels. The latter youth spent much of their time hanging out on street corners with other homeless youth who were embedded in the world of street criminals.

## From North to South

What can the street experiences of homeless youth in the Global North tell us about the Global South? In the Global South, late modern economic policies imported from the Global North often combine with the strengths and weaknesses of local nation-states in ways that threaten family survival and intensify youth problems. Latin and South American cities are swollen with homeless children and adults, with corresponding problems of family disruption and heightened risky behavior among young people. As in the Global North, the latter problems peak in late adolescence and early adulthood.

Of course, some Latin and South American as well as African nations suffer from more direct forms of social exclusion, including state-led military and paramilitary regimes that organize massive "disappearances," as well as full-fledged massacres, resulting in even more extensive family displacement and destruction. Sub-Saharan Africa ranks as the current epicenter of one-sided, state-led violence against civilians and families. The Middle East and North Africa also are prominent sites of multi-sided violence against civilians. Rebellion against these circumstances predictably follows, and again the demography of age can shape the form of this rebellion. Darfur, of course, is our focus.

The remainder of this chapter provides new evidence from selected sites in Darfur to illustrate the range of consequences that assaults on the lives of African youth and their families create for current and future generations. There are, of course, differences of kind as well as degree between the experience of genocidal victimization in Darfur and the problems of the Global North. Yet, the U.S. National Academy of Sciences Panel notes in its report on "Lost Generations"[12] that life-course challenges exist for high-risk youth throughout the world.[13] Our argument is that these separate but related problems of youth constitute an urgent research agenda.

To introduce as well as stimulate this new research agenda, we present a comparative snapshot of both similarities and differences in the state-based systems of selective exclusion that we argue characterize the United States and Sudan. Other countries should be included in this comparison. For example, China probably occupies a place in Table 8.1 between the United States and Sudan, whereas Canada and many European countries likely fall to the left of the United States. We focus here only on the United States and Sudan.

Racial selectivity is a pervasive feature of both the U.S. and Sudan state-based systems of exclusion. Polarized racial images characterize both countries, resulting in practices of differentiation if not oppression. For example, the *New York Times* columnist Bob Herbert recently observed that, in the United States, "No one is paying much attention, but parts of New York City are like a police state for young men, women, and children who happen to be black or Hispanic. They are routinely stopped, searched, harassed, intimidated, humiliated and, in many cases, arrested for no good reason."[14] Of course, Herbert qualified his observation by noting a "likeness" and not "equivalence" between the United States and police states elsewhere.

Selective practices operate indirectly in the United States and directly in Darfur, which can be a crucial difference. Thus, in the United States, racial differentiation is customarily legalized through recourse to

TABLE 8.1. *State-Based Systems of Selective Exclusion (Institutionalized Forms of Removal and Relocation)*

| Example States | United States | Sudan |
| --- | --- | --- |
| Exclusionary method | Indirect | Direct |
| Selection mechanism | Racial differentiation | Racial oppression |
| Institutional authority | Legal/juridical procedure | Political/military and paramilitary chain of command |
| Operational mode | Individualized | Collectivized |
| Putative rights and protections | Domestic constitutional, civil, and criminal law | International humanitarian and criminal law |
| Forms of exclusion | Police harassment, arrest, and conviction Incarceration Homelessness Disenfranchisement Death penalty | Mass killings and rapes Displacement Deportation Property loss Refugee status |
| Theoretical metaphors | Crime as war ("war on drugs") | War as crime (genocide) |
| Predictable consequences | Criminal innovation, recidivism, and mass incarceration (street crimes) | Organized attacks, armed rebellion, and counterinsurgency (war crimes) |

juridical procedures, which may or may not prove to be discriminatory in themselves. The Sudanese state organizes racial oppression more visibly and directly in Darfur through the unchecked command chains of the polity and military and paramilitary forces. This difference implies individualized punishment in the United States and collective punishment in Darfur. We say more about collective punishment in Darfur later.

Ideally, there are checks on practices of racial differentiation. Of course, these due process checks and procedures depend on the enforcement of domestic constitutional, civil, and criminal law protections in the United States, whereas Darfur suffers from (a thus far) ineffective reliance on international humanitarian and criminal law. Organizations like the American Civil Liberties Union and Human Rights Watch report only limited success in delivering protection in both places, but especially via the International Criminal Court in Darfur.

Weaknesses in legal and other protective measures in both the United States and Darfur result in extensive racial disparities. In the United States, these disparities follow from discriminatory practices of police harassment and arrests, the massively disproportionate incarceration of young Black men, and misapplications of the death penalty. Increased homelessness and disenfranchisement also result. Meanwhile, the racial oppression in Darfur remains catastrophic. The racial consequences of the use of the political, military, and paramilitary command structures of the Sudanese state to organize militia attacks on Black African groups in Darfur continue to mount in scale. The results include hundreds of thousands of killings and rapes, displacement, deportation, property loss, and the confinement of millions of homeless Africans in internal displacement and refugee camps.

These similarities and differences between the United States and Darfur are reflected in their parallel descriptive policy terminologies of "crime as war" and "war as crime." In the United States, a crime metaphor is used intermittently but often explicitly, as in such policies as the "war on drugs," which began in the 1964 presidential campaign of Barry Goldwater and was implemented in the Nixon administration in the 1970s. The Bush administration more ambivalently used the language of war crimes when it labeled the armed conflict in Darfur as genocide and abstained on the UN's referral of the Darfur case to the International Criminal Court.

These wars of exclusion in both the United States and Darfur imposed enormous harm, and with predictable consequences. In the United States, Blumstein explains how the massive reliance on incarceration in a "war on drugs" against the crack epidemic in the 1980s resulted in the exclusionary imprisonment of older gang leaders and the creation of vacancy chains for new recruits to meet the continuing demands for drugs.[15] New but younger and therefore more violence-prone recruits filled the vacancies and set off spiraling increases in gun deaths and subsequent surges in imprisonment in the United States. The "war on drugs" produced the worst of several possibilities: an age-based and network-fed process in which mass incarceration led to more violent forms of crime through the 1980s and into the early 1990s.

A parallel exclusionary process is underway in Darfur – in this case involving state-led and supported violent attacks on African groups. In the same manner that mass incarceration aggravated a surge in violent crime in the United States, in Darfur military and paramilitary attacks intensified an armed rebellion among newer and younger recruits. It had the same result – an age-based and network-fed process in which exclusion led to more violence, in this case armed rebellion. This increasingly youth-driven rebellion spawns war crimes in its own right. The discipline of criminology enumerates and explains such processes of racial differentiation and violence.

## Desperation and Defiance in Darfur

Should it be entirely surprising that Darfur, a country in a region like sub-Saharan Africa, where scorched-earth tactics of ethnic cleansing against African groups persist, would produce a violent and defiant rebel movement that attracts youth whose families continue to experience vicious victimization? This violent response is predicted by a tradition of labeling and conflict theory in criminology, including, for example, Laurence Sherman's late modern version of defiance theory.[16] The more uplifting alternative prospect, of course, imagines the resilience of the youth depicted in *Lost Boys of Sudan*, with whom we started this chapter.

Yet, the true tale of the *Lost Boys of Sudan* features a restorative theme of inclusive turning points that are even less likely for the boys of Darfur than are the parallel probabilities of ghetto youth on the urban playing fields of America becoming successful professional athletes. As we demonstrate in this section, age-related patterns of death and displacement remain the more likely outcomes in Darfur. The lesson of defiance theory is that rebellion becomes the more plausible alternative for disadvantaged youth when they are confronted with sobering life choices in the killing fields of nations as different as the United States and Sudan. The larger lesson of defiance theory involves the unanticipated and self-perpetuating rage and rebellion produced by repressive policies in many social settings, especially settings that provide too few peaceful pathways to success or even survival. Merton classically predicted acts of innovation and rebellion in such circumstances.

Criminological theory and research address the age-connected forms of this innovation and rebellion. Again, there may be lessons of broader relevance in the disconnected but similar experiences of the United States and Sudan, and criminology offers an important source of these lessons.

Our starting point involves a third image, part myth and part reality, to consider in juxtaposition to the two considered earlier in this chapter. This image is of the adolescent and young adult males in Darfur referred to in the Sudanese conflict with the demonizing imagery of "Tora Bora." The Sudanese government simultaneously identified the Tora Bora with the history of the western frontier of the United States and the American pursuit of Osama Bin Laden into the same-named mountain range on the Afghanistan border with Pakistan. The Sudanese government worked to create the image of a scourge worthy of fighting by brutally repressive means.

In press releases disseminated by its embassies and through other news media, the Sudanese government described the Tora Bora as armed robbers and smugglers who preyed on the Arab groups in Darfur, drawing an analogy to the history of the settlers in the lawless American West:

> Historically, these groups have been existent in Darfur's extreme rural areas for many centuries conducting acts of highway robbery. The situation here is reminiscent of the eighteenth- and nineteenth-century American robber ... in the Wild West. The highway robbery is an ancient practice in nomadic societies which are not unique to Darfur. It is to be found in communities or similar circumstances in different parts of Africa. Groups such as the Tora Bora ... emerged as new fledglings conducting the old practice of highway robbery.[17]

The government cited threatening activities of the Tora Bora as provoking the self-defense–motivated actions of the Arab Janjaweed militias. Turning reality on its head, this propaganda effort argued that "the major function and the raison d'être for this militia are to protect herds of nomadic tribes in western Sudan from attacks of looters, highway robbery and particularly, attacks of rival nomadic tribes at times of conflict on pastures and water."[18]

The government news releases further linked the Tora Bora to Islamic extremism. "Any study of the conflict in Darfur," a government source reports, "can no longer ignore the clear involvement of Islamic extremists in fermenting rebellion in western Sudan." The evidence for this assertion again features the Tora Bora, noting that "amongst the rebels there is a self-styled 'Tora Bora' militia – named after the Afghan mountain range in which Osama bin Laden, al-Qaeda and the Taliban fought one of their last battles, and from which bin Laden escaped American capture."[19]

It is true that groups of young rebels who sometimes also describe themselves as Tora Bora form a small but growing part of the Darfur conflict. These youth constitute a small percentage of the large number of child, adolescent, and young adult soldiers in Africa. Although young males may always have been the majority of soldiers, members of this younger age group form an increasingly important and vicious part of African armed conflicts. The reasons for this involvement differ little from those in the Global North, where gangs recruit youth for their loyalty, fearlessness, willingness to take risks, and readily renewable availability.[20] In addition, like gang members in the Global North, these youth adopt media-driven symbols of rebellion. In Darfur and elsewhere in Africa, these menacing images include wraparound sunglasses, displays of weapons, and sometimes small leather pouches worn with string around their necks and containing good-luck pieces. Recruits often ride into conflict in rocket-equipped pickup trucks and gun-laden Land Cruisers.

It is important to emphasize the polarized racial identification of the Tora Bora in Darfur. Reports reveal a clear linkage to the increasing

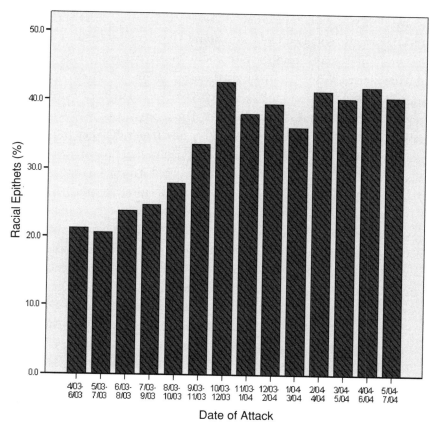

FIGURE 8.1. Moving Average Percentage of Refugees from Darfur Who Reported They Heard Racial Epithets during Attacks by Date of Departure, Atrocities Documentation Survey, Summer 2004.

racial polarization of life in Darfur, represented in our analyses of the racial epithets heard during Janjaweed militia attacks. Figure 8.1 summarizes the rise in this expression of racism in Darfur, using three-month moving averages of the reports of hearing racial epithets in the spring and summer of 2003 and of the same period in 2004. Killings rose and fell during this period, peaking in the early months of 2004 (see earlier Figure 6.1).

Figure 8.1 also shows a peak in reported racial epithets just before the first peak in killing, at the end of 2003. However, this figure further shows that, when attacks continued to occur in 2004, the level of reported racial epithets remained high, with about 40 percent of the respondents hearing these taunts, compared to about 20 percent at the beginning of the time series. When heard during the attacks, the Tora Bora references almost always featured racial epithets. The racial and Tora Bora taunts represent joined expressions of a racial demonology. In classical terms of labeling and subcultural crime theory, or Sherman's defiance theory, the youth who take on the Tora Bora role act as if to say, "We are everything you say we are, and worse." They adopt what Edwin Lemert calls the "symbolic appurtenances"[21] of the demonized cultural frame.

Thus, the question is less about the existence or size of these rebel groups than about the sources and sequences of their development in settings like Darfur. Rebel groups such as the Tora Bora clearly exist and pre-date the current conflict in Darfur. The most prominent of the organized rebel groups, the Sudan Liberation Army (SLA) and the Justice and Equality Movement (JEM), announced their existence in February and March 2003. The SLA and JEM rebels joined forces in a seven-hour attack on the el Fasher air base with thirty-three Land Cruisers in April 2003, destroying a number of Sudan air force bombers and gunships. The rebels killed more than seventy-five Sudanese soldiers and lost only nine of their own. Many accounts cite this attack as the beginning of the current conflict.[22]

Yet, the most exhaustive survey of reported attacks by both sides in Darfur reveals a very one-sided picture of this armed conflict, with relatively few but increasing rebel attacks over time.[23] Incorporating all known public sources, this survey uses 178 witness statements/accounts and reports of attacks involving 372 sites in Darfur from January 2001 to September 2005. It reveals at least eight significant attacks on African villages before the first major rebel attack on the el Fasher air base in the spring of 2003. In total, the survey reveals only thirteen attacks by rebel forces (3 percent of the total). Janjaweed militia groups conducted all of the remaining attacks (97 percent), either by themselves or with Sudanese government forces.[24] Furthermore, although three of the thirteen rebel attacks took place in 2003 and another three in 2004, the remaining seven attacks date from 2005. Six of these seven attacks occurred in South Darfur, with only one in North Darfur. The sequence and distribution of the rebel attacks is more likely a consequence than a cause of the government attacks. It is very doubtful that this survey includes all such attacks, but its findings may well be representative of the relative distribution and sequence of the attacks, with the rebel attacks increasing over time.

The number of rebels shows signs of increasing along with the frequency of rebel actions, both against Arab targets and between rebel factions. It thus becomes important to determine who the rebels are and from where they come. Our answer suggests that they are usually the victims and sometimes also the perpetrators of war crimes, as well as more common crimes of subsistence. They come from all the targeted African groups – most notably the Zaghawa, Fur, and Masalit. They are mostly young, and some are under 18. All of the rebel groups – the SLA, JEM, and the newer NMRD – include mostly males in their later teens and twenties.[25] In 2005, Sudan ratified the Optional Protocol to the Convention on the Rights of the Child that established 18 as the minimum age for forced recruitment and calls on states to assist with the rehabilitation of child soldiers.

Yet, hopes for rehabilitation or restorative justice ignore the reality that the Sudan government's strategy of counterinsurgency in Darfur features a policy of collective stigmatization and punishment concentrated on the families of the African farmers and villagers who are the targets of the joint government and Janjaweed militia attacks. An important Human Rights Watch report uses the term "collective punishment" to aptly describe the brutality in the southwestern part of West Darfur state:

These tactics – which were replicated throughout much of Darfur – were supplemented by other particularly brutal crimes in three Wadi Saleh, Mukjar, and Shattaya localities as a form of collective

punishment – and total subjugation – of the civilian population for its
perceived support of the rebel movement.[26]

Understanding the nature and dimensions of this collective punishment
requires a further look at the pattern of victimization associated with the
rebellion in Darfur. A key to understanding the consequences of collective punishment as a counterinsurgency strategy involves seeing its
impact on families.

### The Collective Punishment of Families in West Darfur

One important way to understand the impact of the counterinsurgency
policy of the Sudanese government in Darfur is to reconstruct the numerical changes in family composition resulting from attacks on farms and
villages. Table 8.2 provides a before-and-after picture of the average
family in twenty-two Darfur settlements from which the refugees in Chad
fled, in terms of the mean size, loss of life, and experiences of rape during
the eighteen months before the 2004 survey.

Across the twenty-two settlements, the average family before the
attacks included more than ten persons (10.44). By the time these families reached the refugee camps in Chad, however, they consisted of just
over six persons (6.25), having lost on average more than four family members (4.19). Males constituted nearly 70 percent of these lost
family members, whereas nearly 30 percent of the respondents (29.1%)
reported that rapes occurred during the attacks. These numbers reflect a
pervasive pattern of killing men and raping women. Especially high numbers of family members were lost in several settlements, most notably
Abu Gumra, Beida, and Karnoi.

The patterns of death, disappearances, and destruction in Darfur are
documented most accurately in the southwestern areas of West Darfur
known as Wadi Salih and Mukjar. These constitute the most fertile land
areas of Darfur, and the Mukjar area includes the strategically important
Sindu Hills where rebel forces hid. Table 8.2 highlights four settlements

TABLE 8.2. *Darfur Families Before and After Attacks, Atrocities Documentation Survey, Chad, 2004*

| Settlement | Average Family Size Before Attacks | Average Number of Family Killed | Percent Males Killed | Percent Reporting Rapes | Average Family Size After Attacks |
|---|---|---|---|---|---|
| Abu Gumra | 25.66 | 19.94 | .56 | .20 | 5.71 |
| Al Geneina | 9.29 | 2.43 | .87 | .45 | 6.86 |
| Beida | 22.62 | 16.31 | .55 | .14 | 6.31 |
| Bendesi | 6.75 | 2.19 | .92 | .38 | 4.56 |
| Foro Burunga | 6.68 | 1.44 | .78 | .41 | 5.24 |
| Garsila | 6.81 | 1.44 | .96 | .38 | 5.38 |
| Habilah | 8.63 | 2.15 | .90 | .41 | 6.48 |
| Kebkabiya | 8.63 | 2.18 | .95 | .33 | 6.45 |
| Karnoi | 17.88 | 11.68 | .64 | .31 | 6.21 |
| Koulbous | 8.39 | 1.23 | .94 | .00 | 7.15 |
| Kutum | 7.51 | 2.44 | .79 | .26 | 5.07 |
| Masteri | 9.59 | 2.33 | .76 | .47 | 7.22 |
| Seleya | 7.79 | 1.37 | .87 | .27 | 6.43 |
| Sirba | 7.23 | 1.13 | .89 | .29 | 6.10 |
| Tine | 7.13 | 1.13 | .97 | .22 | 6.00 |
| Umm Bourou | 8.66 | 2.69 | .77 | .27 | 5.96 |
| Near Karnoi | 8.56 | 2.44 | .87 | .23 | 6.13 |
| Adar | 10.06 | 3.88 | .76 | .35 | 6.18 |
| Tandubayah | 6.59 | .65 | .72 | .06 | 5.94 |
| Near Tine | 9.33 | 1.87 | .86 | .00 | 7.47 |
| Girgira | 8.44 | 1.06 | .53 | .00 | 7.38 |
| Near Abu Gumra | 7.76 | 2.12 | .91 | .12 | 5.64 |
| Total | 10.44 | 4.19 | .69 | .29 | 6.25 |

in this region: Bendesi, Foro Burunga, Garsila, and Habilah. Although the numbers of lost family members are somewhat lower in this area than elsewhere in Darfur, the overall destruction of African group life was overwhelming. We suggest that this destruction led to increased rebel recruitment and activity. This area thus provides an important illustration of genocidal victimization and its consequences in Darfur.

The damage to family life across the four settlements in the shaded part of Table 8.2 shows a consistent pattern. On average, family size varied between six and more than eight members (6.68 to 8.63) before the attacks. Families on average lost from about one to two members (1.44 to 2.19), so that after the attacks the average family ranged in size from about four to six members (4.56 to 6.48). About 40 percent of the respondents from these families reported that rapes occurred during the attacks on their settlements (38 to 41 percent). Three of the four settlements reported that more than 90 percent of the lost family members were male, whereas the fourth settlement reported that 78 percent of those killed were male. These reports reveal pervasive loss of family members and direct or indirect experience of rape. However, the narrative accounts and the numerical data we consider next make it clear how devastatingly comprehensive the destruction of group life was in this southwestern area of West Darfur.

### Death, Survival, and Rebellion

The killing, abductions, and the enslavement of children are longstanding parts of the conflict in southern Sudan, as noted in the *Lost Boys of Sudan*. Abductions form a smaller but still significant part of the Darfur conflict in western Sudan.[27] To measure the magnitude of the direct impact of these crimes, we developed a data file with the age and gender of every nuclear family member identified as killed or missing in the Chad refugee sample. We then constructed the population pyramids presented in Figure 8.2.

   This figure makes it clear who died and suffered most in the refugee families: the "fighting-age" population of Black African males between 15 and 29 years of age, and younger pubescent females between 5 and 14 years of age. About a third of both the young adult males and the pre-adolescent girls are represented among the dead or missing. This finding is consistent with a policy of killing the fighting-age males while raping and killing younger females. This is an exclusionary policy that is likely to intensify rebellion among victimized groups.

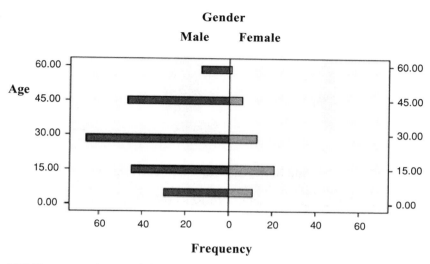

FIGURE 8.2. Age and Sex Distribution of Killed and Missing Household Members, Atrocities Documentation Survey, Darfur, 2004.

Note that the policy of killing fighting-age males parallels in demographic terms the earlier pattern we observed of incarcerating the young
adult leaders of drug gangs in the United States. Both create vacancy
chains for the recruitment of youthful replacements. The potential pool
of recruits emerges in the population pyramids presented in Figure 8.3
from three internal displacement camps in West Darfur. This figure displays the onset of what demographers call a "population bulge" of adolescent males.

The German demographer Gunnar Heinsohn indicates that sixty-
eight of the most populous nations of the world have an overrepre-
sentation in their populations of younger adolescents who will mature
into "fighting-age bulges"; of these nations, sixty-two report high levels of violent mortality.[28] As a result of its high birth rate, Sudan
already ranks high among these nations. The killing of fighting-age older
adolescent and young adult males intensifies this pattern in Darfur.
Criminologists, among all others, recognize the violent threat of these

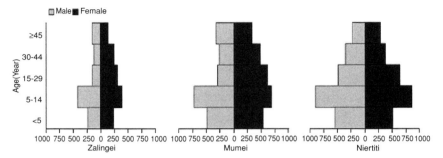

FIGURE 8.3. Age and Sex Distribution of Surviving Household Members. Figure from www.thelancet.com, published online October 1st, 2004. http://image.thelancet.com/extras/04art9087web.pdf

population dynamics. Both in the Global North and in the Global South, young adolescent males form the most violent and aggressive population group.

However, criminologists identify additional aggravating factors increasing the violence and aggressiveness of this group of young adolescent males – most notably, of course, the killing of parents and siblings, the raping of pubescent girls of approximately the same ages as the surviving males, and the general absence of legitimate opportunities for these youth to lead successful adult lives. Paul Collier, an economist of world development, adds, "Young men, who are the recruits for rebel armies, come pretty cheap in an environment of hopeless poverty. Life itself is cheap, and joining a rebel movement gives these young men a small chance of riches."[29] These factors combine to make an intensified rebellion predictable, with age-graded networks of recruitment and youthful resentments playing leading roles in focusing the group-based defiance.

The ICC prosecutor's brief also makes clear that the raping and killing reflected in these figures involve the demonization of the Tora Bora. This point is illustrated by the following witness report described in the brief:

DFR-023...witnessed a separate incident of rape in which Militia/Janjaweed and members of the Armed Forces selected and led away at least ten females between 15 and 18 years of age. She watched as the girls were raped in a field nearby.... While carrying out the rapes, the attackers were saying, "We have taken Tora Bora's wives, praise be to God."[30]

Despite the references to Tora Bora, the 2007 ICC brief explicitly indicates that "no defense was mounted by the residents, and there was no rebel presence in the town when it was attacked."[31] An exception was the nearby town of Kudun, whose residents killed fifteen attackers in late August.[32]

Some residents of Bendesi and Mukjar and other settlements stayed in the general area for months following, hoping that they could salvage some of their crops. Kushayb and Harun (see Chapter 6) stayed with their troops in the area as well. In the fall of 2003, the Arab nomadic groups brought huge herds of their camels and other livestock into the area to graze on the newly available farmlands, thereby further undermining the African groups' hopes to resettle and reclaim these lands.

The Arab militia leader, Ali Kushayb, also undertook a program to systematically eliminate the leadership of the African groups in this area in the fall of 2003 and winter of 2004. His forces took the "educated persons" and umdas and sheikhs of these groups into custody and executed them. A refugee in Chad explained, "They were told they were being taken to Garsila but we found them in a wadi about one half-hour between Mukjar and Garsila. The bodies were in long lines of twenty to fifty.... They had been shot – in the head, back, and waist."

The limited number of SLA rebel forces in the area hid in the nearby Sindu Hills. In February 2004, the SLA mounted some successful attacks on government troops and installations. The government struck back with an unprecedented show of force, as described in a Human Rights Watch report:

The SLA's presence and attacks prompted a massive response by
Sudanese government forces and militias that targeted civilians and
civilian villages. By mid-March, the government's scorched earth
campaign of ground and air attacks around the Sindu Hills had
removed almost all existing or perceived support base for the rebellion by forcibly displacing, looting, and burning almost every Fur village near the hills and then extending "mopping up operations" to
villages and towns farther away.[33]

The Black African groups fled to the refugee camps in Chad.

## Before and After the Government Offensives

A 2005 study of the Bendesi and surrounding area by Intersos, for the
UN High Commissioner for Refugees, provides some final insights on
the impact on families of the attacks.[34] In Bendesi and the surrounding
area, families lost on average one to two members, and these losses disproportionately involved young adult men and teenage girls. This loss
of life occurred in an intensely racial atmosphere that included both the
shouting of racial epithets during the attacks and claims about membership and support of the Tora Bora or rebels in the area.

In the offensive of August 2003, attackers struck about thirty villages
surrounding Bendesi. The surviving residents of these villages fled predominantly to Bendesi. When Bendesi came under attack, they moved
on east to Mukjar, and further south to Um Dukhum.

After remaining in these larger towns for a period, the displaced persons tended either to stay or move further away, including to the refugee
camps in Chad. Of the total number of 245 villages and towns considered in this research, about 100 were destroyed, with 8 more abandoned
but not destroyed. Furthermore, in most of the destroyed or abandoned
villages, nomad Arab groups moved onto the sites and started to put
the land to use for farming or grazing. This was especially true in areas
around Mukjar and Habilah.[35] Nearly 30,000 Chadian Arabs crossed the

border into Darfur with support from local Sudanese Arab sheikhs, such as Al Hadi Ahmed Shineibat, brother of the militia leader of the same last name discussed in Chapter 6.[36] Some Darfurians who escaped from Bendesi to Mukjar returned to Bendesi, but this is not to say that they returned to their former ways of life. They tended to settle in the more central part of town, probably for reasons of security.[37]

The families and children displaced by the government offensives live in very difficult conditions the ICC prosecutor calls "organized destitution." He reports that more than one of every three Darfurians lives in overcrowded IDP camps with no viable educational or livelihood opportunities.[38] Single parenthood remains the most common vulnerability, with most of these families headed by a female caring alone for her children. Before the recent conflict in Darfur, there existed a social norm known as "zaka" that fostered the reintegration of vulnerable children and families. This norm lost much of its force and protective capacity in the current circumstances. These are among the many and most disturbing collateral consequences of the armed conflict in Darfur.

## The Streets of the Global Village

The streets of Bendesi in West Darfur are distant and foreign, but they bear similarities and connections to the everyday world of the Global North. In revealing ways, they reside as close as the contrasting images of the *Lost Boys of Sudan* and the defiant rebels of Tora Bora. It is not a coincidence that the rebel youth hiding out in the Sindu Hills near Bendesi – with their wraparound sunglasses and menacing weapons – look very much like the indigenous and immigrant youth on the streets of the Global North. In the high-speed warp of late modern electronic technology, the mean streets of the global village overlap more closely than we often imagine.

The challenge is to see common themes as well as differences. The domestic policies of legal exclusion in the Global North – with their legal forms of arrest, due process, conviction, and incarceration – exist a world apart from the policies of criminal exclusion in the Global South, with their criminal forms of death squads, militias, disappearances, and displacements. In addition, the individualized punishments of the North are imposed with some protections. One important hope is that the institutions of international criminal law can narrow the distance between the troubled settings of the North and South. Yet, policies in both parts of the world are based on punishment more often than restoration. They share notable features in common: the impulses to exclude and repress. The alternative impulses, to include and support, are elusive in both the Global North and the Global South. Mass incarceration and genocidal death and displacement display an awkward symmetry along the mean streets of the global village.

The fragile and disrupted families of the North parallel the destroyed and displaced families of the South. They represent parallel faces of vulnerability. The mean streets of Vancouver and Bendesi are not the same, but their risks and vulnerabilities are joined by parallel and failed policies of punishment and exclusion. Their fates are joined by the shrinking distances between them.

# Epilogue: Collective R2P

Imagine you wake up in the early hours of the morning and hear the screams of a woman from the street outside your window. What would you do? About a dozen bystanders saw or heard Kitty Genovese sexually assaulted and stabbed to death in 1964 in New York City, but did nothing. The story became a national symbol of the loss of community in urban America and spawned a research literature on "bystander effects" and the "willingness to intervene." A body of jurisprudence evolved to support "Good Samaritan" laws encouraging help for fellow citizens in distress. The image of Kitty Genovese dying unaided on a New York City sidewalk haunted Americans.

For better or worse, idle bystanders are also members of communities. The criminologist Robert Sampson advanced our understanding of the collective propensities and capacities of communities to intervene by asking sampled respondents in Chicago neighborhoods in the 1990s about their willingness to watch out for the children of others and actively respond to neighborhood crimes. He found he could characterize whole neighborhoods in terms of their "collective efficacy" in monitoring and controlling crime victimization. The implication is that not just individuals vary in their willingness to intervene but that also neighborhoods, whole communities, entire societies, and even world bodies – such as the UN – are similarly enabled if not obliged.

At the beginning of the twenty-first century, the UN hosted a World Summit that mandated "collective action" in response to an emerging legal norm of "the responsibility to protect (R2P)." This collective responsibility evolved out of the language of the Genocide Convention and its requirement that ratifying nations act to stop ongoing mass murders. A late twentieth-century president of the United States, Bill Clinton, eventually apologized for his administration's failure in fulfilling its responsibility to protect Rwandan citizens from genocide. His successor, George Bush, promised not to let this happen on his "watch." This motivation led to Secretary of State Colin Powell's collection and presentation to the UN and U.S. Congress of survey evidence of genocide from the Atrocities Documentation Survey (ADS) of Darfurian refugees in Chad.

Powell informed Congress that genocide had occurred in Darfur – but then he insisted that our responsibility to protect the victims of this genocide consisted only of supporting the presence of African Union "monitors" in Darfur. Not fulfilling President Bush's pledge, these monitors did little but watch as the genocide continued to unfold. The Atrocities Documentation Survey of more than a thousand genocide victims, at a cost of nearly a million U.S. taxpayer dollars, was condensed into an eight-page report that received little attention in the State Department.

Condoleezza Rice succeeded Colin Powell as Secretary of State, and her deputy – current president of the World Bank, Robert Zoellick – shifted attention from the ADS data to new analyses of health and nutrition surveys that underestimated the genocidal violence in Darfur. Despite this lack of attention, the ADS is uniquely valuable as a criminological victimization survey. For the first time in history, surveys and narratives were collected during an ongoing genocide. This historically unprecedented data set is the source of essential evidence of the scale, composition, and consequences of the genocide in Darfur. This book argues that the emerging field of criminology shares in the responsibility, in a parallel way to that of the United States and the United Nations, to develop and advance knowledge and public awareness about genocide.

We must be knowledgeable and expand awareness of two different aspects of genocide. The first is the scale of the atrocities that constitute

genocide, and the second is the intent that directs genocide against protected groups. The issue of scale is inadequately addressed in the otherwise remarkable and important work done on "complex humanitarian
emergencies" by population and health researchers who emphasize illness and nutritional needs associated with genocide. The work of these
population health scientists often fails to measure the violence that led to
the displacement of survivors. In Darfur, the demands of the Sudanese
government and Ministry of Health compromised the collection of evidence of genocidal violence.

We argue that a crime victimization approach provides an essential supplement to health research about displaced persons by documenting and analyzing the deaths of community and family members.
This approach led us to estimate that hundreds of thousands, instead
of tens of thousands, of victims died in Darfur – correcting misleading
claims to the contrary by the U.S. State Department. Criminologists can
advance knowledge and public awareness of this kind of death and group
destruction.

The second salient contribution of a criminology of genocide is to
demonstrate and explain the role of state-led and organized intentions
in driving the fanatical fury and frenzy of genocidal killing and rape.
In Darfur, this collective intent developed along racial lines. Landless,
nomadic Arab groups became pawns in this vicious game. In a time of climate change and desertification, Arab nomadic herders encroached on
the lands and poached the livestock of African farmers and villagers. The
Sudanese government enabled the racial hatred exacerbated by these
environmental conditions and fostered a collective racial intent to kill,
rape, and destroy the necessary conditions for life among Black African
groups. The government did this by mobilizing, training, and collaborat-
ing with Arab Janjaweed militia in their attacks on the African Zaghawa,
Masalit, Fur, and other Black African groups in Darfur.

The Sudanese government is built on an Arab Islamic ideology that
dehumanized Black African groups and collectively punished their pur-
ported support for a rebel insurgency. To be sure, a rebel insurgency

developed over time in Darfur, but we demonstrated that the collective punishment of African villagers is dramatically disproportionate and collateral to this threat. The insurgency began as a small rebellion and grew, largely in defensive response to combined government and Janjaweed attacks. The Sudanese genocide constitutes a criminally organized collective enterprise with a common purpose. Although criminologists could and should have said more about this killing, and sooner, the field of criminology can still contribute much to our understanding of state-led policies involving war and crime. There are even disturbing parallels to explore between our own "wars on crime" in the American Global North and "wars of counterinsurgency" in the Global South, including Sudan's repressive and exclusionary policies in Darfur.

The instigation and motivation of collective racial intent form a socially framed and collectively driven force, as evidenced by the reports of racial epithets in the ADS data. The ADS data provide eyewitness accounts of the roles of named Arab Janjaweed militia leaders, acting under government direction in the organization of attacks on African groups. All of this evidence supports the legal charge of genocide and is abundant in the ADS interviews. Yet, this deadly evidence languished largely unanalyzed in U.S. State Department files.

The development of knowledge and awareness from such evidence is a responsibility of a science of criminology, and this knowledge and awareness in turn form the basis of a national and international responsibility to protect by recognizing and responding to events as genocide, "the crime of crimes." Classical and contemporary criminology neglected its responsibilities to develop the "collective efficacy" of a science of genocide. The future development of this "responsibility to protect" ultimately depends on a new generation of students of the nascent criminology of genocide. The next generation of criminologists need never again be bystanders to genocide.

# Appendix: Genocidal Statistics

The analyses summarized in Chapter 7 use hierarchical linear models (HLM) developed by Raudenbush and Bryk.[1] These models are well suited to the combination of settlement- and individual-level data we analyze from the ADS survey. HLM models can account for the nonindependence of observations within settlements and allow us to simultaneously estimate within- and between-settlement equations. Our particular theoretical interest is in the collective or settlement-level variance in such variables as racial epithets as our key indicator of collective racial motivation and intent, but our analytic approach also incorporates individual-level variation in this and other factors. Tables A.1 and A.2 summarize descriptive characteristics from the twenty-two settlements introduced in this book.

The HLM models that form the background for the analysis in Chapter 7 involve the estimation of within- and between-settlement equations. Using victimization severity as the example, the fundamental within-settlement model is

$$\text{Victimization Severity}_{ij} = \beta_{0j} + \Sigma \sum_{q=1} \beta_q X_{qij} + \varepsilon_{ij},$$

where $\beta_{0j}$ is the intercept; $X_{qij}$ is the value of covariate $q$ associated with respondent $i$ in settlement-level $j$; and $\beta_q$ are the partial effects on severity of victimization of the respondent's age; gender; rebels in town; missing rebel data; attacking Janjaweed, Sudanese, or combined Sudanese

223

TABLE A.1. *Rankings of Settlement Clusters on Selected Variables: Atrocities Documentation Survey, Darfur Refugees in Chad, Summer 2004*

| | Ranking of Mean of Month Fled | Ranking of Mean of Racial Epithets | Ranking of Mean for Rebel Activity | Ranking of Mean Standardized Victimization Severity | Ranking of Mean Total Killed | Ranking of Mean for Rape (Self) | Ranking of Mean for All Rapes and Sexual Assaults | Arab Villages Surrounding |
|---|---|---|---|---|---|---|---|---|
| Abu Gumra | 4 (32.23) | 8 (.40) | 10 (.03) | 11 (−.06) | 3 (25.51) | 6 (.03) | 15 (.20) | 10 (0.03) |
| Al Geneina | 15 (36.06) | 7 (.43) | 6 (.05) | 7 (.17) | 7 (14.51) | 4 (.06) | 2 (.45) | 3 (0.21) |
| Beida | 7 (33.48) | 12 (.31) | 13 (.00) | 16 (−.23) | 16 (6.79) | 8 (.00) | 16 (.14) | 7 (0.05) |
| Bendesi | 1 (31.56) | 1 (.50) | 13 (.00) | 6 (.21) | 17 (6.56) | 4 (.06) | 5 (.38) | 2 (0.25) |
| Foro Burunga | 13 (35.32) | 2 (.47) | 13 (.00) | 2 (.44) | 4 (22.41) | 6 (.03) | 4 (.41) | 12 (.00) |
| Garsila | 21 (37.50) | 5 (.44) | 3 (.13) | 20 (−.44) | 22 (3.13) | 4 (.06) | 5 (.38) | 1 (0.31) |
| Habilah | 11 (34.96) | 6 (.43) | 11 (.02) | 4 (.26) | 15 (7.50) | 2 (.09) | 3 (.41) | 5 (0.11) |
| Kebkabiya | 3 (32.04) | 4 (.45) | 5 (.06) | 9 (.13) | 9 (12.14) | 4 (.06) | 7 (.33) | 8 (0.04) |
| Karnoi | 17 (36.53) | 11 (.35) | 4 (.06) | 10 (−.05) | 10 (10.00) | 4 (.06) | 8 (.31) | 11 (0.01) |
| Koulbous (Chad) | 19 (36.62) | 20 (.08) | 13 (.00) | 15 (−.22) | 19 (6.23) | 8 (.00) | 19 (.00) | 12 (.00) |
| Kutum | 9 (34.51) | 9 (.40) | 13 (.00) | 8 (.15) | 13 (8.07) | 3 (.07) | 19 (.00) | 10 (0.02) |
| Masteri | 16 (36.35) | 3 (.47) | 13 (.00) | 3 (.26) | 11 (9.56) | 2 (.09) | 1 (.47) | 4 (0.13) |
| Seleya | 8 (33.82) | 17 (.25) | 9 (.03) | 5 (.23) | 5 (18.60) | 8 (.00) | 11 (.26) | 6 (0.1) |
| Sirba | 10 (34.84) | 18 (.19) | 13 (.00) | 18 (−.24) | 18 (6.35) | 1 (.10) | 9 (.29) | 12 (.00) |
| Tine | 6 (33.26) | 15 (.26) | 7 (.04) | 17 (−.23) | 21 (4.48) | 8 (.00) | 14 (.22) | 12 (.00) |
| Umm Bourou | 14 (35.80) | 13 (.31) | 12 (.02) | 14 (−.20) | 12 (8.24) | 3 (.07) | 10 (.27) | 12 (.00) |
| Near Karnoi | 14 (35.80) | 14 (.30) | 8 (.03) | 12 (−.12) | 8 (14.00) | 7 (.02) | 13 (.23) | 10 (0.02) |
| Adar | 2 (31.82) | 10 (.35) | 13 (.00) | 1 (.60) | 1 (37.47) | 8 (.00) | 6 (.35) | 12 (.00) |
| Tandubayah | 18 (36.59) | 22 (.00) | 13 (.00) | 13 (−.19) | 2 (35.71) | 8 (.00) | 18 (.06) | 12 (.00) |
| Near Tine | 12 (35.07) | 19 (.13) | 1 (.13) | 21 (−.49) | 20 (4.60) | 8 (.00) | 19 (.00) | 12 (.00) |
| Girgira | 20 (37.00) | 21 (.06) | 2 (.13) | 22 (−1.17) | 6 (15.50) | 8 (.00) | 19 (.00) | 12 (.00) |
| Near Abu Gumra | 5 (32.32) | 16 (.28) | 13 (.00) | 19 (−.40) | 14 (7.84) | 5 (.04) | 17 (.12) | 8 (0.04) |

TABLE A.2. *Individual and Settlement Cluster Statistics: Atrocities Documentation Survey, Darfur Refugees in Chad, Summer 2004[a]*

| Individual Level | x | s.d. |
|---|---|---|
| Respondents' attributes | | |
| Age | 37.100** | 14.634** |
| Gender (male = 1) | .400 | .491 |
| Zaghawa | .527 | .500 |
| Fur | .055 | .288 |
| Masalit | .275 | .447 |
| Jebal | .045 | .208 |
| Attacking groups | | |
| Janjaweed | .100 | .300 |
| Sudanese | .188 | .391 |
| Sudanese & Janjaweed | .672 | .470 |
| Rebel activity | | |
| Rebels in town | .017 | .130 |
| Missing rebel data | .562 | .496 |
| Particular targets | | |
| Women | .070 | .260 |
| Racial intent | | |
| Individual racial intent | .343 | .475 |
| Attacks | | |
| Bombing | .829 | .727 |
| First peak | .266 | .442 |
| Second peak | .499 | .500 |
| Victimization severity | 34.232** | 6.317* |
| *Settlement Cluster Level* | | |
| Settlement density | .182 | .151 |
| Collective racial intent | .312 | .144 |
| Bombing | .861 | .369 |
| Rebel news accounts | .318 | .497 |

[a] $N = 932$ individuals (level 1) and 22 settlement clusters (level 2).
* $p < .05$  ** $p < .01$  *** $p < .001$

and Janjaweed forces; victimized Zaghawa, Fur, Masalit, or Jebal groups; bombing; targeting of women; attacks during the first or second displacement peaks, and hearing racial epithets. The error term, $\varepsilon_{ij}$, is the unique contribution of each individual, which is assumed to be independently and normally distributed with constant variance $\sigma^2$.

The key between-settlement equation is:

$$\beta_{0j} = \theta_{00} + \theta_{01}(\text{collective racial intent}) + \cdots + U_{0j},$$

where $\theta_{00}$ is the overall average standardized victimization severity score, and $\theta_{01}$ is the regression coefficient of the effect of racial epithets measured as a settlement-level mean score on severity of victimization. Additional settlement-level covariates are incorporated as further controls, and we include significant cross-level interactions in elaborations of this kind of model later in the Appendix. Because the individual-level covariates at level 1 are centered about the sample means, $\beta_{0j}$ is the standardized mean severity of victimization in a settlement after covariates have been controlled. $U_{0j}$ is the settlement-level error term, assumed to be normally distributed with a variance of $\tau$.

A preliminary concern is the reliability of the outcome measure of severity of genocidal victimization, particularly the settlement-level reliability that results from the partitioning of the variance within and between settlements. This variance decomposition results in a settlement reliability of 0.733 for victimization severity, indicating that we can measure settlement differences in this outcome with a reasonable degree of precision. The intraclass correlation corresponding to this decomposition is 0.23 and is highly statistically significant, indicating that about one-quarter of the victimization severity scale's variance is between settlements, with the remainder resulting from individual-level variation and random error. The size of this between-setting variance is comparable to that found in analogous multilevel studies of organizations or schools.

## Multilevel Structural Models of Genocide Victimization

Before presenting models of victimization, we first consider several models of the mediating concept of racial motivation and intent that is at the center of our critical collective frame analysis. The racial epithets represent the framing of the conflict in Darfur in "us" and "them" motivational terms, with the intent to kill, rape, assault, steal, destroy, and displace. Because our measure of racial motivation and intent is a binary report of whether the respondent heard shouted racial epithets during the attack that preceded flight to the refugee camp, we estimate the models with the logistic regression equations presented in Table A.3.

The first of these equations yields several findings of interest. The most important finding is that these epithets are significantly more likely to be heard when Sudanese and Janjaweed forces are combined in the attack. This suggests a primary instrumental role of Sudanese forces in encouraging these epithets. The first equation also reveals that rebels are less likely to be in the villages in which racial epithets are heard. This negative finding strongly suggests the direct racial targeting of civilians, rather than of suspected rebels (i.e., in a more legally justifiable self-defense, counterinsurgency strategy). Table A.3 also indicates that the epithets are more likely to be heard by men than women. This is probably because women are less likely to know Arabic.

There are specific examples of the joint government-militia role in the survey accounts and in court documents. In anticipation of an August 2003 attack on the Darfur towns surrounding Kebkabiya, Musa Hilal, a widely recognized leader of Arab militia, announced the coming attacks in North Darfur. Hilal was identified (in a survey interview) as appearing with a government official (see Chapter 5) who introduced him in the marketplace of nearby Misteriha. Hilal there announced, "The government gave me the order to start killing the people here – all the Blacks from here to Karnoi and Tine and up" (see Map 1 in Chapter 5). He also indicated that he was told to "kill all the blacks in this area" and that his forces should "give the Arab people freedom" by "clear[ing] the land." A 2009 brief by the ICC prosecutor similarly reports a racist speech delivered by Hilal in a public setting where a government official was present. Fourteen respondents in the refugee surveys identified Hilal as leading attacks on villages. Hilal exemplifies the powerful role of the "ethnic entrepreneur" in mobilizing genocidal attacks.[2]

The second model in Table A.3 introduces the African groups that are potential targets of the racial epithets and the two peak periods of the

TABLE A.3. *Individual and Settlement Cluster Level Logistic Regression Models of Racial Intent Atrocities Documentation Survey, Darfur Refugees in Chad, Summer 2004*[a]

|                                         | Model 1 | | Model 2 | | Model 3 | |
|-----------------------------------------|---------|------|---------|-------|---------|-------|
|                                         | b(se)   | Odds | b(se)   | Odds  | b(se)   | Odds  |
| *Individual level* Respondents' attributes |       |      |         |       |         |       |
| Age                                     | −.005   | .994 | −.005   | .995  | −.005   | .995  |
|                                         | (.005)  |      | (.005)  |       | (.005)  |       |
| Gender                                  | .660*** | 1.934| .666*** | 1.947 | .685*** | 1.983 |
|                                         | (.178)  |      | (.169)  |       | (.170)  |       |
| Zaghawa                                 |         |      | .528    | 1.696 | .565    | 1.759 |
|                                         |         |      | (.296)  |       | (.344)  |       |
| Fur                                     |         |      | .890*   | 2.434 | .834*   | 2.302 |
|                                         |         |      | (.430)  |       | (.420)  |       |
| Masalit                                 |         |      | .733**  | 2.081 | .692**  | 1.996 |
|                                         |         |      | (.281)  |       | (.285)  |       |
| Jebal                                   |         |      | .819**  | 2.268 | .899**  | 2.445 |
|                                         |         |      | (.325)  |       | (.356)  |       |
| *Attacking groups*                      |         |      |         |       |         |       |
| Janjaweed                               | .194    | 1.214| .186    | 1.205 | .302    | 1.353 |
|                                         | (.331)  |      | (.338)  |       | (.328)  |       |
| Sudanese                                | −.316   | .729 | −.397   | .672  | −.348   | .706  |
|                                         | (.340)  |      | (.324)  |       | (.302)  |       |
| Sudanese & Janjaweed                    | .517**  | 1.677| .410*   | 1.508 | .467*   | 1.595 |
|                                         | (.197)  |      | (.209)  |       | (.229)  |       |
| *Rebel activity*                        |         |      |         |       |         |       |
| Rebels in settlement                    | −.977** | .376 | −.946   | .388  | −.941   | .390  |
|                                         | (.457)  |      | (.493)  |       | (.502)  |       |
| Missing rebel data                      | −.352   | .703 | −.289   | .749  | −.275   | .760  |
|                                         | (.225)  |      | (.251)  |       | (.250)  |       |
| *Particular targets*                    |         |      |         |       |         |       |
| Women                                   | .296    | 1.322| .243    | 1.275 | .239    | 1.269 |
|                                         | (.347)  |      | (.369)  |       | (.376)  |       |
| *Attacks*                               |         |      |         |       |         |       |
| First peak                              |         |      | −.628***| .534  | −.649***| .523  |
|                                         |         |      | (.186)  |       | (.186)  |       |
| Second peak                             |         |      | −.243   | 1.275 | −.232   | 1.261 |
|                                         |         |      | (.232)  |       | (.234)  |       |
| *Settlement cluster level*              |         |      |         |       |         |       |
| Settlement density                      |         |      |         |       | .603    | 1.828 |
|                                         |         |      |         |       | (.796)  |       |
| Rebel news                              |         |      |         |       | .138    | 1.142 |
|                                         |         |      |         |       | (.335)  |       |

*(continued)*

*Table A.3 (continued)*

|  | Model 1 | Model 2 | Model 3 |
|---|---|---|---|
| *Cross-level interaction* | | | |
| Sudanese & Janjaweed × Rebel news | | | .190 1.209 (.301) |
| Sudanese & Janjaweed × settlement density | | | 2.063** 7.873 (.845) |
| Intercept | −.725 | −.725* | −.736 |

[a] N = 932 individuals (level 1) and 22 settlement clusters (level 2).
* p < .05 **p < .01 ***p < .001

attacks. Three of the four African groups – the Fur, Masalit, and Jebal – are significantly more likely to have heard the racial epithets; only the Zaghawa are not. A separate analysis suggests that the Zaghawa are subjected to bombing more often than the other groups, and racial epithets are more likely to be heard in ground attacks. Meanwhile, controlling for the African group memberships in the second model reduces the effect of the combined Sudanese and Janjaweed attacks by about 20 percent, offering further evidence that these joined forces instrumentally directed their attacks with a socially constructed racial focus on these particular African groups. Finally, a significant negative effect of the first peak of attacks suggests that the racialization of the attacks increased over the period of conflict.

The third model estimated in Table A.3 adds both settlement-level and cross-level interactions to the analysis. There are neither significant main effects for settlement density nor rebel news (i.e., indicated by media reports). However, the bottom panel of Table A.3 indicates that there is a significant cross-level interaction effect of settlement density with the combined involvement of Sudanese and Janjaweed forces on the hearing of racial epithets. The meaning of this cross-level interaction is clarified with the graph presented in Figure 7.2 that averages estimates of combined Sudanese and Janjaweed attacks on racial epithets at the higher and lower quartile levels of settlement density.

We measured both of the interacting variables in Figure 7.2 in terms of variation from their sample means. This analysis indicates that increased population density makes racial epithets more likely when Sudanese and Janjaweed forces attack together. When the Sudanese or Janjaweed forces attack separately, increased population density diminishes the hearing of these epithets. The interaction of the combination of forces with the higher quartiles of population density approximately doubles the hearing of racial epithets from about 20 to more than 40 percent. This is compelling evidence of the instrumental role played by the Sudanese state in intensifying the expression of a socially constructed racial motivation and intent by joining with the Janjaweed in attacks on densely settled areas of Darfur.

Table A.4 explores the socially constructed influence of racial motivation and intent – measured at the individual and settlement levels by racial epithets – in increasing the severity of genocidal victimization. The ordinary least squares (OLS) regression equations estimated in this table take into account statistically the influence on severity of victimization of individual-level correlates previously included in Table A.3, as well as the influence of bombing. The first model estimated again reveals the instrumentally combined salience of Sudanese and Janjaweed forces in predicting victimization severity; Sudanese forces acting alone also significantly increase this victimization; Janjaweed forces acting alone do not significantly increase victimization severity. Nor does the presence of rebels in the settlement significantly increase victimization severity. This null finding undermines a self-defense, counterinsurgency justification for the attacks, yet is consistent with comments from respondents like the following: "My village was not defended and how could we defend? There was no equality in power. There were no rebels nearby."

The dummy variable representing the first two weeks of the survey when rebel presence questions were not asked (i.e., the missing rebel data variable) indicates this was apparently a period when less severe victimization was reported. This implies that asking these questions in the early weeks would likely not have resulted in the rebel presence

TABLE A.4. *Individual and Settlement Cluster Models of Victimization Severity: Atrocities Documentation Survey, Darfur Refugees in Chad, Summer 2004*[a]

| | Model 1 | Model 2 | Model 3 | Model 4 | Model 5 | Model 6 |
|---|---|---|---|---|---|---|
| *Individual level* | b(se) | b(se) | b(se) | b(se) | b(se) | b(se) |
| Respondents' attributes | | | | | | |
| Age | −.005** | −.004** | −.004** | −.004** | −.004** | −.004** |
| | (.002) | (.002) | (.002) | (.002) | (.002) | (.002) |
| Gender | −.057* | −.138*** | −.140** | −.132** | −.130** | −.136** |
| | (.056) | (.055) | (.056) | (.058) | (.059) | (.058) |
| Zaghawa | | −.023 | −.023 | | | |
| | | (.105) | (.104) | | | |
| Fur | | .321** | .257 | | | |
| | | (.125) | (.153) | | | |
| Masalit | | .265** | .012 | | | |
| | | (.099) | (.167) | | | |
| Jebal | | .224*** | .256*** | .174*** | .261*** | .214*** |
| | | (.050) | (.060) | (.031) | (.047) | (.056) |
| *Attacking groups* | | | | | | |
| Janjaweed | .157 | .162 | .144 | .145 | .143 | .137 |
| | (.178) | (.183) | (.184) | (.194) | (.189) | (.191) |
| Sudanese | .375** | .386** | .372** | .375** | .365** | .374** |
| | (.156) | (.150) | (.151) | (.151) | (.151) | (.152) |
| Sudanese & | .509*** | .432*** | .422*** | .428*** | .416*** | .425*** |
| Janjaweed | (.110) | (.116) | (.117) | (.121) | (.123) | (.125) |
| *Rebel activity* | | | | | | |
| Rebels in settlement | .138 | .228 | .229 | .215 | .204 | .210 |
| | (.239) | (.209) | (.211) | (.212) | (.217) | (.218) |
| Missing rebel data | −.330** | −.306*** | −.295*** | −.314*** | −.290*** | −.286*** |
| | (.111) | (.085) | (.085) | (.094) | (.089) | (.088) |
| *Particular targets* | | | | | | |
| Women | | .448*** | .442*** | .467*** | .462*** | .457*** |
| | | (.086) | (.087) | (.093) | (.095) | (.094) |
| *Attacks* | | | | | | |
| First peak | | .223*** | .216*** | .210*** | .189*** | .199*** |
| | | (.078) | (.079) | (.078) | (.075) | (.078) |
| Second peak | | .190*** | .189*** | .189*** | .211*** | .220*** |
| | | (.093) | (.091) | (.091) | (.090) | (.090) |
| Bombing | | .061 | .067 | .054 | .051 | .058 |
| | | (.045) | (.045) | (.043) | (.037) | (.041) |

(*continued*)

TABLE A.4 *(continued)*

|  | Model 1 | Model 2 | Model 3 | Model 4 | Model 5 | Model 6 |
|---|---|---|---|---|---|---|
| *Racial intent* | | | | | | |
| Individual racial | .387*** | .387*** | .394*** | | .365*** | .367*** |
| intent | (.067) | (.087) | (.085) | | (.083) | (.084) |
| *Settlement cluster level* | | | | | | |
| Settlement density | | | | .686*** | .449 | .243 |
| | | | | (.316) | (.299) | (.405) |
| Bombing | | | | | | .137 |
| | | | | | | (.288) |
| Rebel news | | | | | | −.032 |
| | | | | | | (.115) |
| Collective racial | | | 1.225*** | | 1.107*** | 1.066*** |
| intent | | | (.565) | | (.553) | (.518) |
| *Cross-level interaction* | | | | | | |
| Bombing × collective | | | | | .781** | .747** |
| racial intent | | | | | (.306) | (.341) |
| Bombing × | | | | | .131** | .133** |
| settlement density | | | | | (.156) | (.166) |
| Intercept | −.023* | −.011* | −.077* | −.013* | −.012* | −.014* |

[a] $N = 932$ individuals (level 1) and 22 settlement clusters (level 2).
* $p < .05$  ** $p < .01$  *** $p < .001$

variable being significant. Finally, the first model reveals among adults that severity of victimization decreases with age. This is also true of criminal victimization in more conventional circumstances.

The second model introduces the specific African groups as socially constructed targets, as well as these variables: the targeting of women, bombing, the peak attack measures, and the hearing of racial epithet measure of individual-level racial motivation and intent. Again, the Fur, Masalit, and Jebal are at significantly higher risk of more severe victimization, whereas the Zaghawa are not. The Fur respondents report extreme experiences of torture in the open-ended survey narratives – people were cut, their brains and skin removed, and their sexual organs cut off. Women are also a targeted group. Respondents report that the Janjaweed and Sudanese military troops targeted the women by raping and abducting them. Like the racial epithets, the words or phrases spoken by the perpetrators during the attack provide insight into their motivation and intent. One respondent reports hearing the perpetrators say, "We will take your women and make them ours. We will change the race." In another example, a respondent was raped, branded, and told, "You are now Arab wives." In these examples, the intention of targeting the women is to change the race of their offspring.

The effect of combined Sudanese and Janjaweed forces is reduced by about 15 percent in the second equation, whereas the Sudanese force effect is essentially unchanged. These findings again suggest the instrumental role of the Sudanese in targeting and unleashing victimization when they attack in conjunction with the Janjaweed. The two peak attack variables are predictably significant. Finally, the individual-level racial epithet measure of racial motivation and intent has a strong and highly significant effect on victimization severity.

The third model in Table A.4 adds the mean settlement-level racial epithet measure of collective racial motivation and intent, which is statistically significant. The addition of only this variable in the third model has the further effect of reducing the size and eliminating the significance of the African Fur and Masalit group measures. Consistent with the focus of our critical collective framing perspective, this means that settlement-level differences in collective racial motivation and intent account for the higher severity of victimization of the Fur and Masalit groups in Darfur. Further analysis at the settlement level can add clarity to this finding. To maintain the robustness of the significance tests, we remove the African group measures that are statistically insignificant with the inclusion of the racial motivation and intent variable in the model.

Models 4 and 5 in Table A.4 bring settlement density into the victimization analysis. When settlement density is introduced alone at the settlement level, it is statistically significant. This finding indicates that severity of victimization increases in densely settled areas of Darfur where the opportunities and incentives for attacks are greatest and resources are potentially the most strained. Nevertheless, recall also that we argued that collective racial motivation and intent is a crucial and socially constructed mediating mechanism through which settlement density would exercise its exogenous and Malthusian influence on population density.

Our data uniquely address the respective exogenous and endogenous roles of population density and racial motivation and intent. When the main effect of collective racial motivation and intent is added alone or in cross-level combination with bombing, the effect of settlement density is reduced by about one-third and becomes nonsignificant. The mediating effect of collective racial motivation and intent in removing the significance of the effect of settlement density on severity of victimization is striking evidence of the salience of race as the mediating mechanism that animates this conflict.

The cross-level interaction of collective racial intent with bombing on victimization severity adds another dimension to these results. Because the bombing is entirely under Sudanese state control, and because we saw earlier that the instrumental joining of the Sudanese with the Janjaweed in the attacks drives the racial epithet measure of racial motivation and intent, this cross-level interaction further points to the instrumentally agentic role of the Sudanese state. The final model (6) estimated in Table A.4 demonstrates that including both individual- and settlement-level measures of rebel activity in the villages does not account for these effects.

The cross-level interaction of Sudanese bombing with collective racial motivation and intent (measured with settlement-level differences in racial epithets) is particularly striking evidence of the instrumental use of state power to divide and victimize the socially constructed identification of subordinate target groups. A further way of clarifying the impact of this cross-level interaction again makes use of the graphical capacity of HLM in Figure 7.3.

As in Figure 7.2 discussed earlier, we measure both of the interacting variables in Figure 7.3 in terms of variation from their sample means, now with the following results. At the lower quartiles of collective racial motivation and intent, increased bombing is associated with decreasing levels of victimization severity, whereas in the higher quartiles of collective racial intent, the effect of increased bombing is to elevate the severity of victimization. It previously has been argued that the Sudanese government instrumentally directed the Janjaweed forces and channeled their socially constructed racial hostility toward African groups. Figure 7.3 therefore supplements Table A.4 in showing how, in densely settled areas, the concentration of bombing and collective racial hostility against specific African groups, such as the Fur and Masalit, produces elevated severity of genocidal victimization. The fact that the Sudanese government directed the bombing and enlisted the Janjaweed in racially animated attacks that intensified the severity of victimization indicates that the state intentionally joined in the collective enactment and accomplishment of genocide.

It may be significant to recall that our severity measure of genocidal victimization combines killings, rapes, and other forms of assault and destruction. Reported frequencies of killings and rapes for the settlement attacks are less reliable than the severity scale, but we also estimated equations with these outcome measures. The substantive pattern of results is similar to that for the severity scale. However, one interesting divergence is apparent. On the one hand, the cross-level interaction effect of collective racial motivation and intent and bombing is stronger and more significant when the variable, number of killings, is substituted for the severity scale as the outcome. On the other hand, this cross-level interaction is weaker and nonsignificant for number of rapes (both killings and rapes are estimated from one to ten or more). For rape, the main effect of collective racial motivation and intent remains salient. This divergence with regard to bombing is highly plausible, because although bombs obviously can kill, only persons can rape.

# Notes

**PROLOGUE**

1. Julian Borger, "Darfur by Numbers," *The Guardian*, 4 September 2007, http://www.guardian.co.uk/world/2007/sep/04/diplomaticdispatch.julianborger.
2. International Criminal Court, Office of the Prosecutor, Prosecutor's Application for Warrant of Arrest under Article 58 Against Oma Hassan Ahmad al-Bashir, July 14, 2008, The Hague, Netherlands.

**1. DARFUR CRIME SCENES**

1. The Darfurian survivors interviewed in the ADS survey analyzed in the book have been given pseudonyms and some identifying characteristics have been altered in order to protect anonymity.
2. Neil MacFraquhar, "Security Council Members Push to Condem Sudan," *New York Times*, June 6, 2008, p. A10.
3. See Marlise Simons, "Tribunal in Hague Finds a Bosnian Serb Guilty of Genocide," *New York Times*, August 3, 2001, p. A1, A8; and "Radislav Krstic becomes the first person to be convicted of genocide at the ICTY and is sentenced to 46 years imprisonment," Press Release, The Hague, August 2, 2001, p. 11.
4. Human Rights Watch, "Darfur Destroyed: Ethnic Cleansing by Government and Militia Forces in Western Sudan," vol. 16 (New York City: May 2004), pp. 7–8.
5. Ibid., p. 8.
6. Ibid., p. 36
7. We have supplemented the accounts of ADS interviews in this section with information found in the Human Rights Watch Report, ibid., pp. 20–21.
8. Physicians for Human Rights, "Darfur: Assault on Survival," (Cambridge, MA: 2006), p. 22.

9. Human Rights Watch, op. cit., p. 26.

10. Helen Young, Abdul Osman, Yacob Aklilu, Rebecca Dale, Babiker Badri, Abdul Jabbar, and Abdullah Fuddle, *Darfur: Livelihoods Under Siege* (Medford, MA: Feinstein International Famine Center, Tufts University, June 2005).

11. See Coalition for International Justice, "Soil and Oil: Dirty Business in Sudan," Washington, DC: CIJ, 2006, p. 63.

12. Young, op. cit., p. 43.

13. Ibid., p. 43.

14. Ibid., p. 80.

15. Coalition for International Justice, op. cit.

16. Ibid., p. 84.

17. With specific reference to Masteri, see, for example, UN News Centre, "Rape, Fighting Continue in Sudan's Darfur Region Despite Accords – UN," December 3, 2004.

18. See also Physicians for Human Rights, op. cit., Chapter 6.

19. Seventh Annual Report of the Prosecutor of the International Criminal Court to the UN Security Council Pursuant to UNSCR 1593 (2005) at 93, International Criminal Court, Office of the Prosecutor, June 5, 2008.

20. Human Rights Watch, op. cit., p. 36.

21. See Steve Bloomfield, "Arabs Pile into Darfur to Take Land 'Cleansed' by Janjaweed," *The Independent*, July 14, 2007.

22. See John Hagan, *Justice in the Balkans: Prosecuting War Crimes in The Hague Tribunal* (Chicago: University of Chicago Press, 2003), Chapters 3–4.

## 2. THE CRIME OF CRIMES

1. For a discussion of Louise Arbour and her role as the chief prosecutor who indicted Slobodan Milosevic for crimes against humanity at the International Criminal Court for the former Yugoslavia, see John Hagan, *Justice in the Balkans: Prosecuting War Crimes in The Hague Tribunal* (Chicago: University of Chicago Press, 2003).

2. The crime of genocide is defined by Article II of the Genocide Convention, as discussed later.

3. The UN Security Council voted 10–0, with four abstentions that included the United States, to refer a list of fifty-one people accused of crimes against humanity in Darfur to the ICC, after final wrangling over exemptions for U.S. citizens. The referral occurred late on Thursday, March 31, 2005. Earlier on this same day, the Board of Directors of the World Bank confirmed the appointment of Paul Wolfowitz as its president. The *Wall Street Journal* (April 1, 2005, p. A8) reported that "in keeping with tradition, no formal vote was taken," whereas the *Financial Post* (April 1, 2005, p. 2) indicated that "directors from

developing countries, Europe and the US representative spoke of the need for a better selection procedure for the future."

4. For a discussion of this term and the broader context of race relations in Sudan, see Ayesha Kajee, "Darfur Stereotyping Fraught with Danger," Institute for War & Peace Reporting, AR, No. 81 (October 2006): 31.

5. Gerard Prunier, *Darfur: The Ambiguous Genocide* (Ithaca, NY: Cornell University Press, 2005).

6. Samantha Power, *"A Problem from Hell": America and the Age of Genocide* (New York: Basic Books, 2002).

7. Edwin Sutherland, "White Collar Criminality," *American Sociological Review* 5 (1940): 1–12; "Is 'White Collar Crime' Crime?" *American Sociological Review* 10 (1945): 132–139; *White Collar Crime* (New York: Holt, Rinehart and Winston, 1949).

8. Albert Cohen, *Delinquent Boys* (New York: Free Press, 1955).

9. Asking and answering a similar question, see Stanley Cohen, *States of Denial: Knowing about Atrocities and Suffering* (Cambridge: Polity Press, 2001).

10. Joachim J. Savelsberg, "Underused Potentials for Criminology: Applying the Sociology of Knowledge to Terrorism," *Crime, Law and Social Change* 46, no. 1–2 (2006): 35–50.

11. Elizabeth Kolbert, "Dead Reckoning: The Armenian Genocide and the Politics of Silence," *New Yorker* (November 6, 2006): 120–124.

12. Helen Fein, "Genocide: A Sociological Perspective," *Current Sociology* 38 (1990): 7 and Helen Fein, *Human Rights and Wrongs: Slavery, Terror, Genocide* (Boulder, Colorado: Paradigm Press, 2007).

13. Sheldon Glueck, "By What Tribunal Shall War Offenders Be Tried?" *Harvard Law Review* 56 (1943): 1059; *War Criminals: Their Prosecution and Punishment* (New York: Knopf, 1944); *The Nuremberg Trial and Aggressive War* (New York: Knopf, 1946); see John Hagan and Scott Greer, "Making War Criminal," *Criminology* 40 (2002): 231–264.

14. Sheldon Glueck and Eleanor Glueck, *Unraveling Juvenile Delinquency* (New York: Commonwealth Fund, 1950).

15. House Congressional Resolution 30, 79th Congress, 1st Session, February 19, 1945. See "Statement of Professor Sheldon Glueck, Harvard Law School, In Regard to House Resolution No. 93, "Concerning the Trial and Punishment of Axis War Criminals," March 20, 1945. Box 43, Folder 2, Glueck Papers, Harvard Law Library, Cambridge, MA.

16. Glueck relocated from Harvard to Washington during this period. See letter from his secretary, Mary Wallace, to Sheldon Glueck, June 12, 1945. Glueck Papers, Harvard Law Library, Cambridge, MA.

17. Memorandum of Meeting Held June 28, 1945, Regarding Preparation of Evidence, June 29, 1945. Glueck Papers, Harvard Law Library, Cambridge, MA.

18. Memorandum to Mr. Whitney, Dr. Glueck, Colonel Storey, and Lt. Donovan. Glueck Papers.

19. See Glueck, *The Nuremberg Trial and Aggressive War*, p. vii.

20. See George Gallup, *The Gallup Poll: Public Opinion 1935–1971* (New York: Random House, 1972), p. 339.

21. Sheldon Glueck, "Punishing the War Criminals," *New Republic* 109 (1943): 708.

22. A newspaper spread from January 30, 1945, contrasts personal statements by Glueck and Allport. See Box 45, Folder 2, Glueck Papers, Harvard Law Library, Cambridge, MA.

23. Glueck Papers, p. 24.

24. Glueck, "By What Tribunal Shall War Offenders Be Tried?" pp. 442–443.

25. Michael Marrus, "The Nuremberg Trial: Fifty Years Later," *American Scholar* 66 (1997): 565.

26. Glueck Papers, p. 19.

27. Glueck Papers, p. 30.

28. Glueck Papers, p. 36.

29. William Chambliss and Robert Seidman, *Law, Order and Power* (Reading, MA: Addison-Wesley, 1971).

30. Glueck Papers, p. 29.

31. Glueck Papers, p. 6.

32. Glueck Papers, p. 7.

33. Glueck Papers, p. 19.

34. Marrus, 1997, p. 567.

35. Jens Meierhenrich, "Conspiracy in International Law," *Annual Review of Law and Social Science* 2 (2006): 341–357.

36. Memorandum to Justice Jackson, Subject: Theory of the Prosecution, July 3, 1945, pp. 2–3. Glueck Papers, Harvard Law Library, Cambridge, MA.

37. Bernard Schlink, *The Reader*, Carol Brown Janeway, trans. (New York: Vintage Books, 1999).

38. Austin Turk, *Political Criminality* (Thousand Oaks, CA: Sage Publications, 1982), p. 21.

39. Ibid., p. 21.

40. This latter phase of Glueck's work is told in detail by John Laub and Robert Sampson, "The Sutherland-Glueck Debate: On the Sociology of Criminological Knowledge," *American Journal of Sociology* 96 (1991): 1402–1440.

41. Peter Novick, *The Holocaust in American Life* (New York: Houghton Mifflin, 1999).

42. Paul Jacobs, *Is Curly Jewish?* (New York: Atheneum, 1965) cited in Novick, pp. 40–41.

43. The Robert Houghwout Jackson Oral History, Interview conducted in February 1995 by Harlan Phillips, Oral History Research Office, Butler Library, Columbia University, p. 1206.

44. Laub and Sampson thus note, "Both Sheldon and Eleanor Glueck were Jewish. One can speculate that discrimination against Jews at Harvard University... may have also contributed to isolating the Gluecks from the mainstream academic community." See Laub and Sampson, "The Sutherland-Glueck Debate."

45. Novick, 1999, p. 92.

46. Raphael Lemkin, "Genocide," *American Scholar* 15 (1946): 227, cited in Novick, 1999, p. 100.

47. Novick, 1999, p. 101.

48. John Laub and Robert Sampson, "The Sutherland-Glueck Debate: On the Sociology of Criminological Knowledge," *American Journal of Sociology* 96 (1991): 1402–1440.

49. See Edwin Sutherland, "Critique of Sheldon's Varieties of Delinquent Behavior," *American Sociological Review* 16 (1951): 10–13.

50. Ibid., pp. 1427–1428.

51. Ibid., p. 1422.

52. Ibid., p. 1421.

53. Sutherland, 1949, p. vii.

54. See, for example, Christopher Hitchens, *The Trial of Henry Kissinger* (New York: Verso, 2001) and Henry Kissinger, "The Pitfalls of Universal Jurisdiction," *Foreign Affairs* 80 (2001): 86–96.

55. See Edwin Sutherland's essays about his own theoretical contributions in Karl Schuessler and Edwin H. Sutherland, eds., *On Analyzing Crime* (Chicago: University of Chicago Press, 1973).

56. Sutherland, *White Collar Crime*, p. 247.

57. Joseph Persico, *Nuremberg: Infamy on Trial* (New York: Penguin Books, 1994), p. 38.

58. Steven Bach, *Leni: The Life and Work of Leni Riefenstahl* (New York: Knopf, 2007), pp. 143–144.

## 3. WHILE CRIMINOLOGY SLEPT

1. See David Halberstam, *The Best and the Brightest* (New York: Ballantine, 1972, 1992); *The Children* (New York: Ballantine, 1998); and *The Breaks of the Game* (New York: Alfred A. Knopf, 1981).

2. Albert Cohen, *Delinquent Boys* (Glencoe, IL: Free Press, 1955).

3. Sheldon and Eleanor Glueck, *Unraveling Juvenile Delinquency* (New York: Commonwealth Fund, 1950) and *Predicting Delinquency and Crime* (Cambridge, MA: Harvard University Press, 1959).

4. Alfred Kinsey, Wardell Pomeroy, and Clyde Martin, *Sexual Behavior in the Human Male* (Philadelphia: W.B. Saunders, 1948).

5. F. Ivan Nye and James Short, "Scaling Delinquent Behavior," *American Sociological Review* 22 (1957): 326–332.

6. Albert Biderman, L. Johnson, J. McIntyre, and A. Weir, *Report of a Pilot Study in the District of Columbia on Victimization and Attitudes Toward Law Enforcement*, Field Surveys 1, President's Commission on Law Enforcement and Administration of Justice (Washington, DC: U.S. Government Printing Office, 1967).

7. U.S. Department of State, "Documenting Atrocities in Darfur" (Washington, DC: Bureau of Democracy, Human Rights and Labor and Bureau of Intelligence and Research, 2004).

8. Anne Frank, *The Diary of a Young Girl* (New York: Doubleday, 1952).

9. Hannah Arendt, *Eichmann in Jerusalem* (New York: Viking Press, 1963).

10. See Peter Novick, *The Holocaust in American Life* (New York: Houghton Mifflin, 1999), Chapter 6.

11. Halberstam, *The Best and the Brightest,* op. cit.

12. William Chambliss and Robert Seidman, *Law, Order, and Power* (Reading, MA: Addison Wesley Press, 1971).

13. See Yves Dezalay and Bryant Garth, "From the Cold War to Kosovo: The Rise and Renewal of the Field of International Human Rights," *Annual Review of Law and Social Science* 2 (2006): 231–255.

14. Cited in John Irving, "A Soldier Once," *New York Times Book Review*, July 8, 2007, p. 19.

15. Aryeh Neier, *Taking Liberties: Four Decades in the Struggle for Rights* (New York: Public Affairs, 2003).

16. Ibid.

17. Austin Turk, *Political Criminality* (Newbury Park, CA: Sage, 1982).

18. See, for example, John Hagan, *Justice in the Balkans: Prosecuting War Crimes in The Hague Tribunal* (Chicago: University of Chicago Press, 2003).

19. Nicholas Kristof, "Bandages and Bayonets," *New York Times*, November 12, 2006, pp. 4, 13.

20. Ronald Waldman and Gerard Martone, "Public Health and Complex Emergencies: New Issues, New Conditions," *American Journal of Public Health* 89 (1999): 1483–1485.

21. Charles B. Keely, Holly E. Reed, and Ronald J. Waldman, "Understanding Mortality Patterns in Complex Humanitarian Emergencies," in Holly E. Reed and Charles B. Keely, eds., *Forced Migration and Mortality* (Washington, DC: National Academy Press, 2001).

22. See also Human Security Centre, "Human Security Brief 2006" (Vancouver, BC: Liu Institute for Global Issues, University of British Columbia, 2006), Chapter 2.

23. Eric Noji and Michael Toole, "The Historical Development of Public Health Responses of Disasters," *Disasters* 21 (1997): 366–376.

24. Barry Levy and Victor Sidel, *War and Public Health* (New York: Oxford, 1997) and Eric Noji, *The Public Health Consequences of Disasters* (New York: Oxford University Press, 1997).

25. Andrew S. Natsios, *U.S. Foreign Policy and the Four Horsemen of the Apocalypse: Humanitarian Relief in Complex Emergencies* (Westport, CT: Praeger/ Centre for Strategies of International Studies, 1997).

26. C.B. Keely, H.E. Reed, and R.J. Waldman, "Understanding Mortality Patterns," op. cit.; R. Waldman and G. Martone, "Public Health and Complex Emergencies," op. cit.

27. Patrick Bracken and Celia Petty, *Rethinking the Trauma of War* (London: Free Association Books, 1998).

28. Michael Toole and Ronald Waldman, "Prevention of Excess Mortality in Refugee and Displaced Populations in Developing Countries," *Journal of the American Medical Association* 263 (1990): 3296–3302.

29. Ibid., p. 3300.

30. Ibid., p. 3301.

31. Ibid., p. 3301.

32. Michael Toole and Ronald Waldman, "Refugees and Displaced Persons: War, Hunger, and Public Health," *Journal of the American Medical Association* 270 (1993): 600–605.

33. Ibid., p. 605.

34. Brent T. Burkholder and Michael J. Toole, "Evolution of Complex Disasters," *Lancet* 346 (1995): 1012–1015.

35. Paul Spiegel and Peter Salama, "War and Mortality in Kosovo, 1998–1999: An Epidemiological Testimony," *Lancet* 355 (2000): 2204–2209.

36. Bureau of Refugee Programs, *Assessment Manual for Refugee Emergencies* (Washington, DC: U.S. Department of State, 1985).

37. Centers for Disease Control, "Famine Affected, Refugee and Displaced Populations: Recommendations for Public Health Issues," *MMWR Recommendations Report* 41 (RR-13) (1992): 1–76.

38. Ian Timaeus and Momodou Jasseh, "Adult Mortality in Sub-Saharan Africa: Evidence from Demographic and Health Surveys," *Demography* 41 (2004): 757–772.

39. International Rescue Committee, *Mortality in the Democratic Republic of the Congo: Results from a Nationwide Survey* (New York: International Rescue Committee, 2004).

40. Goma Epidemiological Group, "Public Health Impact of Rwandan Refugee Crisis: What Happened in Goma, Zaire in July 1994," *Lancet* 345 (1995): 339–344.

41. International Rescue Committee, op. cit.

42. F. Watson, I. Kulenovic, and J. Vespa, "Nutritional Status and Food Security: Winter Nutrition Monitoring in Sarajevo, 1993–1994," *European Journal of Clinical Nutrition* 49 (1995): S23–32.

43. David Rohde, *Endgame: The Betrayal and Fall of Srebrenica, Europe's Worst Massacre since World War II* (New York: Farrar, Straus and Giroux, 1997).

44. R. Rogers and E. Copeland, *Forced Migration: Policy Issues in the Post-Cold War World* (Medford, MA: Tufts University Press, 1993).

45. Willliam Chambliss and Robert Seidman, *Law, Order and Power,* op. cit.

46. Austin Turk, *Political Criminality,* op. cit.

47. See, for example, A. Brannigan and K.H. Hardwick, "Genocide and General Theory," in Chester Britt and Michael Gottfredson, eds., *Control Theories of Crime and Delinquency,* Vol. 12 (New Brunswick, NJ: Transaction, 2003), pp. 109–31 and Irving L. Horowitz, *Taking Lives: Genocide and State Power* (New Brunswick, NJ: Transaction, 2002). See also Adam Jones, *Genocide: A Comprehensive Introduction* (New York, Routledge/Taylor & Francis, 2006).

48. John Hagan, Wenona Rymond-Richmond, and Patricia Parker, "The Criminology of Genocide: The Death and Rape of Darfur," *Criminology* 43 (2005): 525–561.

49. See, for example, Stan Cohen, *States of Denial: Knowing about Atrocities and Suffering* (Cambridge: Polity Press, 2001); George Yacoubian, "The (In)significance of Genocidal Behavior to the Discipline of Criminology," *Crime, Law and Social Change* 34 (2000): 7–19; and John Hagan and Scott Greer, "Making War Criminal," *Criminology* 40 (2002): 231–264.

50. Keely, Reed and, Waldman, op. cit., at p. 12.

51. See, for example, World Health Organization, Retrospective Mortality Survey among the Internally Displaced Population, Greater Darfur, Sudan (Geneva: World Health Organization, 2004). See also footnote 48 above.

52. Alex de Waal, *Famine Crimes: Politics and the Disaster Relief Industry in Africa* (Oxford: Currey, 1997).

53. A backdrop to these arguments is set in Alex de Waal, *Famine That Kills: Darfur, Sudan 1984–1985* (London: Oxford University Press, 1989).

54. House of Commons International Development Committee, *Darfur, Sudan: The Responsibility to Protect,* Fifth Report of the Session 2004–2005, vol. II, Oral and Written Evidence (London, Station Office Limited, 2005).

55. Ibid., p. EV 50.

56. Ibid., p. EV 52.

57. Ibid., p. EV 50.

58. Ibid., p. EV 52.

59. Ibid., p. EV 50.

60. See J. Van Dijk, "Criminal Victimization and Victim Empowerment in an International Perspective," Address to the 9th International Symposium of the World Society of Victimology, The Netherlands, August 25–29, 1997.

61. Uwe Ewald and Constance von Oppeln, "War-Victimization-Security: The Case of the Former Yugoslavia," *European Journal of Crime, Criminal Law, and Criminal Justice* 10 (2002): 39–44.

62. Physicians for Human Rights, *War Crimes in Kosovo: A Population-Based Assessment of Human Rights Violations Against Kosovar Albanians* (Boston: Physicians for Human Rights, 1999).

63. Paul Spiegel and Peter Salama, "War and Mortality in Kosovo, 1998–1999," op. cit.

64. ABA-CEELI/AAAS, *Political Killings in Kosova/Kosovo, March–June 1999, 2000* (Washington, DC: American Bar Association Central and East European Law Initiative and American Association for the Advancement of Science), at p. 9. This estimate used a capture-recapture method and a jackknife estimator for the variance.

65. U.S. Department of State, *Ethnic Cleansing in Kosovo: An Accounting* (Washington, DC: U.S. Department of State, 1999).

66. ABA-CEELI op. cit. and Patrick Ball, *Policy or Panic? The Flight of Ethnic Albanians from Kosovo, March–May 1999, 2000* (Washington, DC: American Association for the Advancement of Science).

67. Ibid.

68. International Criminal Tribunal for the Former Yugoslavia, Milosevic (IT-0 2–54), Kosovo, Croatia and Bosnia Transcripts, 2002, www.un.org/icty, at p. 2226.

69. Ibid. p. 2252.

70. See John Hagan, *Justice in the Balkans,* op. cit. at p. 114.

71. Ibid., at p. 18.

72. ABA-CEELI, at p. 19.

73. Boutros Boutros-Ghali, "Frontline" interview, posted online April 2004; http://www.pbs.org/wgbh/pages/frontline/shows/ghosts/themes/lessons.html

## 4. FLIP-FLOPPING ON DARFUR

1. U.S. Department of State, *Documenting Atrocities in Darfur, Human Rights and Labor and Bureau of Intelligence and Research* (Washington, D.C.: Bureau of Democracy, 2004).

2. Ibid, at Chart 1, p. 3.

3. Office of the Press Secretary, President's Statement on Violence in Darfur, Sudan, September 9, 2004, http://www.whitehouse.gov/news/releases/2004/09/20040909–10.html.

4. American Association for the Advancement of Science, "Using Science to Gauge Sudan's Humanitarian Nightmare," *New Release*, 26 October 2004.

5. Mark Goldberg, "Khartoum Characters," *American Prospect Online*, 3 July 2005.

6. See Chapter Five of John Hagan, *Justice in the Balkans: Prosecuting War Crimes in The Hague Tribunal* (Chicago: University of Chicago Press, 2003).

7. David Nabarro. Media Briefing Notes, UN Palais Press Corps, Geneva, "Mortality Projections for Darfur, 15 October 2004." Presented by David Nabarro, Representative of the World Health Organization Director-General.

8. Donald McNeil, "At the U.N.: This Virus Has an Expert 'Quite Scared,'" *New York Times*, 28 March 2006, p. F1.

9. Evelyn Leopold, "U.N. Envoy Says Deaths in Darfur Underestimated," Reuters 10 March 2005.

10. Reuters, "Over 180,000 Darfur Deaths in 18 Months – U.N. Envoy," 15 March 2005.

11. Jan Coebergh, "Sudan: Genocide Has Killed More than Tsunami," *Parliamentary Brief* 9 (7)(February 2005): 5–6.

12. Eric Reeves. "Darfur Mortality Update: June 30, 2005," *Sudan Tribune*, 1 July 2005.

13. John Hagan, Wenona Rymond-Richmond, and Patricia Parker, "The Death and Rape and Darfur: The Criminology of Genocide," 43 (2005) *Criminology* 525–561.

14. Kofi Annan. "Billions of Promises to Keep," *New York Times*, 13 April 2005, p. A19.

15. Marc Lacey, "Nobody Danced. No Drums. Just Fear. Some Holiday!" *New York Times*, 22 April 2005, p. A4.

16. Joel Brinkley, "A Diplomatic Lone Ranger with 3 × 5 Cards," *New York Times*, 17 April 2005, p. 1.8.

17. U.S. Department of State, "Sudan: Death Toll in Darfur," Fact Sheet, Bureau of Intelligence and Research, Washington, DC, March 25, 2005, p. 1.

18. Warren Hoge. "International War-Crimes Prosecutor Gets List of 51 Sudan Suspects," *New York Times*, 6 April 2005, p. A6.

19. Mark Goldberg. "Zoellick's Appeasement Tour," *The American Prospect Online*, 29 April 2005.

20. Sue Pleming. "Aid Group Criticizes U.S. Policy on Sudan," Reuters, 26 April 2005.

21. Ken Silverstein. "Official Pariah Sudan Valuable to American War on Terror," *Los Angeles Times*, 29 April 2005, p. A1.

22. S. Shane. "C.I.A. Role in Visit of Sudan Intelligence Chief Causes Dispute Within Administration," *New York Times*, 18 June 2005, p. A7.

23. Ken Silverstein. "Sudanese Visitor Split U.S. Officials," *Los Angeles Times*, 17 June 2005, p. A.1.

24. Alex de Waal, "Tragedy in Darfur," *Boston Review:* "A Political and Literary Forum," http:///www.bostonreview.net/BR29.5/dewaal.html. See also Julie Flint and Alex de Waal, *Darfur: A Short History of a Long War* (London: Zed Books, 2005).

25. Marisa Katz and Michael Safdie, "A Very Long Engagement: Bush Channels Neville Chamberlain," *The New Republic*, 15 May 2006, p. 20.

26. Greg Miller and Josh Meyer, "U.S. Relies on Sudan Despite Condemning It," *Los Angeles Times*, 11 June 2007, p. A.1.

27. Nicholas Kristof, "Day 141 of Bush's Silence," *New York Times*, 31 May 2005, p. A17.

28. See Ken Silverstein, op. cit.

29. John Burton, "Development and Cultural Genocide in the Sudan," *Journal of Modern African Studies* 29 (1991): 511–520.

30. See CRS Issue Brief for Congress, "Sudan: Humanitarian Crisis, Peace Talks, Terrorists, and U.S. Policy," Congressional Research Service, Library of Congress, 12 April 2006, p. 11.

31. Peter Beaumont, "Darfur Terror Chief Slips into Britain," *The Observer*, 12 March 2006.

32. Warren Hoge, "U.N. Council Imposes Sanctions on 4 Men in Darfur War Crimes," *New York Times*, 26 April 2006, p. A10.

33. Katz, op. cit., p. 25.

34. Debarati Guha-Sapir and Olivier Degomme with Mark Phelan (U.S. Department of State), *Darfur: Counting the Deaths: Mortality Estimates from Multiple Survey Data* (University of Louvain, School of Public Health, Brussels: Centre for Research on the Epidemiology of Disasters, May 26, 2005). http://www.cred@esp.ucl.ac.be.

35. *Washington Post.* "Darfur's Real Death Toll," Editorial Page, 24 April 2005, p. B06. http://www.washingtonpost.com/ac2/wp-dyn/admin (Accessed April 24, 2005).

36. R. Zoellick. "On Darfur, A Call for the Wrong Action," *Washington Post*, Letter to Editor, 27 April 2005, p. A22.

37. U.S. Department of State. "Sudan: Death Toll in Darfur." Fact Sheet. Bureau of Intelligence and Research, 25 March 2005. http://www.state.gov/s/inr/rls/fs/2005/45105.htm (Accessed April 26, 2005).

38. Glenn Kessler, "State Department Defends Estimate of Deaths in Darfur Conflict," *Washington Post*, 27 April 2005, p. A17.

39. Debarati Guha-Sapir et al., op. cit., p. 7.

40. Department of State Publication 11182, op. cit., pp. 5–7.

41. See, for example, World Health Organization, *Darfur: One Year On, WHO's Work to Save Lives and Reduce Suffering* (Geneva: World Health Organization, 2005).

42. John Hagan and Scott Greer, "Making War Criminal," *Criminology* 40 (2002): 231–264.

43. John Hagan, Heather Schoenfeld, and Alberto Palloni, "The Science of Human Rights, War Crimes, and Humanitarian Emergencies," *Annual Review of Sociology* 32 (2006): 329–349.

44. On this point, see especially the testimony of Mukesh Kapila, the former United Nations Resident and Humanitarian Coordinator for Sudan, to the House of Commons International Development Committee. *Darfur, Sudan: The Responsibility to Protect.* Fifth Report of Session 2004–05. Vol. II: Oral and Written Evidence. London: Station. Off.Ltd. http://www.publications.parliament.uk/pa/cm200405/cmselect/cmintdev/67/6711.pdf.

45. W. Courtland Robinson, Myung Lee, Kenneth Hill, Gilbert Burnham. "Mortality in North Korean Migrant Households," *Lancet* 354 (1999): 291–295.

46. David Nabarro. Op. cit.

47. CNN. Report: "Up to 70,000 Sudanese Dead." Oct. 17 http://www.cnn.com/2004/WORLD/Africa/10/17/un.sudan/.

48. House of Commons International Development Committee, op. cit., p. Ev 65.

49. Ibid., p. Ev 70.

50. Op. cit., Vol. I, p. 11.

51. Debarati Guha-Sapir et al., op. cit., p. 9.

52. For a fascinating account of MSF and other French NGOs, see Johanna Simeant, "What Is Going Global? The Internationalization of French NGOs 'Without Borders,'" *Review of International Political Economy* 12 (2005): 851–883.

53. Evelyn Depoortere, France Broillet, Sibylle Gerstl, Francesco Checchi, et al. "Violence and Mortality in West Darfur, Sudan (2003–04): Epidemiological Evidence from Four Surveys," *Lancet* 364 (2004): 1315–1320.

54. On the other hand, there is a different source of survivor bias involved in underreporting for this age group. These reports are likely downwardly biased by missing children whose entire unrepresented families have died.

55. Violence was reincorporated into the life table estimate on the basis of the proportion of violence reported in the surveys.

56. Since the confidence intervals are reassuringly narrow, this part of the analysis makes little substantive difference in the results.

57. Reuters. "Aid Groups to Meet War Crimes Prosecutor on Darfur." 17 June 2005.

58. U.S. Government Accountability Office, "Darfur Crisis: Death Estimates Demonstrate Severity of Crisis, but their Accuracy and Credibility Could be Enhanced," November 2006, especially p. 3.

## 5. EYEWITNESSING GENOCIDE

1. Andrew S. Natsios, The President's Special Envoy to Sudan, House Committee on Foreign Affairs, February 8, 2007.
2. Elizabeth Rubin, "If Not Peace, Then Justice," *New York Times Magazine*, April 2, 2006, p. 42.
3. Office of the Prosecutor, International Criminal Court, Situation in Darfur, the Sudan, Prosecutor's Application under Article 58 (7), February 27, 2007.
4. Seventh Annual Report of the Prosecutor of the International Criminal Court to the UN Security Council Pursuant to UNSCR 1543 (2005) at 98, International Criminal Court, Office of the Prosecutor, June 5, 2008. (No pages. See Section 98).
5. Situation in Darfur, p. 43.
6. Ibid., p. 30.
7. Ibid., p. 30.
8. Office of the Prosecutor, International Criminal Court, The Situation in Darfur, Fact Sheet, February 27, 2007.
9. Office of the Prosecutor, International Criminal Court, Situation in Darfur, op. cit., p. 66, italics added.
10. Jens Meierhenrich, "Conspiracy in International Law," *Annual Review of Law and Social Science* 2 (2006): 341–357.
11. John Hagan, *Justice in the Balkans: Prosecuting War Crimes in The Hague Tribunal* (Chicago: University of Chicago Press, 2003).
12. Mark J. Osiel, "The Banality of Good: Aligning Incentives against Mass Atrocity," *Columbia Law Review* 105 (2005): 1751–1862.
13. Robert Sampson, "Neighborhood and Community: Collective Efficacy and Community Safety," *New Economy* 11 (2004): 106–113.
14. Ross Matsueda, "Differential Social Organization, Collective Action, and Crime," *Crime, Law & Social Change* 46: 1–2 (2006): 3–33.
15. Daniel Chirot and Clark McCauley, *Why Not Kill Them All? The Logic and Prevention of Mass Murder* (Princeton: Princeton University Press), p. 89.
16. Nicholas Kristof, "The Face of Genocide," *New York Times*, November 19, 2006, p. 13.
17. For example, Jeffrey Gettleman, "In a Calm Corner of Darfur, Villagers Rebuild Fragile Ties with Former Enemies," *New York Times*, November 8, 2006, p. A14 and Somini Sengupta, "From Rare Glimpse inside Militia Camp, Clear Ties to Sudan," *New York Times*, October 21, 2004, p. A1.
18. Julie Flint and Alex de Waal, *Darfur: A Short History of a Long War* (London: Zed Books, 2005), p. 3.
19. R.S. O'Fahey, "A Complex Ethnic Reality with a Long History; Darfur," *International Herald Tribune*, May 15, 2004, p. 8.

20. Paul Doornbos, "On Becoming Sudanese," in Tony Barnett and Abbas Abdelkarim, eds., *Sudan: State, Capital and Transformation* (London: Croom Helm, 1988).

21. Ibid.

22. Karen Brodkin, *How Jews Became White Folks and What That Says About Race in America* (New Brunswick, NJ: Rutgers University Press, 1998).

23. Noel Ignatiev, *How the Irish Became White* (New York: Routledge, 1995).

24. John Comaroff and Jean Comaroff, *Of Revelation and Revolution: The Dialectics of Modernity on a South African Frontier*, Vol. 2 (Chicago: University of Chicago Press, 1997), p. 406.

25. Ibid., p. 406.

26. Roger Brubaker and David Laitin, "Ethnic and Nationalist Violence," *Annual Review of Sociology* 24 (1998).

27. Scott Straus, *The Order of Genocide: Race, Power, and War in Rwanda* (Ithaca, NY: Cornell University Press, 2006).

28. Anthony Oberschall, "The Manipulation of Ethnicity: From Ethnic Cooperation to Violence and War in Yugoslavia," *Ethnic and Racial Studies* 23 (2000): 982–1001.

29. Atta El-Battahani, "Towards a Typology and Periodization Schema of Conflicts in Darfur Region of Sudan," in Abdel Ghaffar M. Ahmed and Leif Manger, eds., *Understanding the Crisis in Darfur: Listening to Sudanese Voices* (Bergen: BRIC, 2006); see also Mohamed Suliman, *Sudan: Resources, Identity and War* (Cambridge: Cambridge University Press, 2006).

30. Atta El-Battahani, op. cit., p. 37.

31. R.S. O'Fahey, *State and Society in Dar Fur* (London: Hurst, 1980).

32. Joseph Winter, "Probe of Darfur 'Slavery' Starts," BBC News, March 21, 2007.

33. R.S. O'Fahey, op. cit., p. 39.

34. Joseph Winter, op. cit.

35. Kwame Anthony Appiah, "A Slow Emancipation," *New York Times Magazine*, March 18, 2007, p. 17; see also David Davis, *Inhuman Bondage: The Rise and Fall of Slavery in the New World* (London: Oxford University Press, 2006).

36. Samantha Power, "Dying in Darfur," *New Yorker*, August 30, 2004, pp. 1–18.

37. Nicholas Kristof, "Genocide in Slow Motion," *New York Review of Books* 53 (2006), p. 2.

38. Sebastian Mallaby, "Darfur: Origins of a Catastrophe," *Washington Post*, February 19, 2006, p. BW04.

39. Gérard Prunier, *Darfur: The Ambiguous Genocide* (Ithaca, NY: Cornell University Press, 2005), p. 162.

40. See Samantha Power, op. cit.

41. Julie Flint and Alex de Waal, op. cit., p. 101.

42. Julie Flint, Testimony to United States Committee on Foreign Relations Hearing, "Sudan: Peace, But at What Price?" (Washington, DC: June 15, 2004), p. 3.

43. Ralph Lemkin, "Genocide," *American Scholar* 15 (April 1946): 227–230.
44. Alexander Laban Hinton, "Why Did You Kill? The Cambodian Genocide and the Dark Side of Face and Honor," *Journal of Asian Studies* 57 (1998): 117.
45. Nancy Scheper-Hughes and Philippe Bourgois, *Violence in War and Peace: An Anthology* (London: Basil Blackwell, 2004), p. 14.
46. Augustine Brannigan and Kelly Hardwick, "Genocide and General Theory," in Chester Britt and Michael Gottfredson, eds., *Control Theories of Crime and Delinquency*, Vol. 12 (New Brunswick, NJ: Transaction Books, 2003), p. 122.
47. Prunier, op. cit., p. 165.
48. Edwin Sutherland and Karl Schuessler, *On Analyzing Crime* (Chicago: University of Chicago Press, 1973).
49. Robert Sampson, Jeffrey Morenoff, and Felton Earls, "Beyond Social Capital: Spatial Dynamics of Collective Efficacy for Children," *American Sociological Review* 64 (1999): 633–660; Robert Sampson, Stephen Raudenbush, and Felton Earls, "Neighborhoods and Violent Crime: A Multilevel Study of Collective Efficacy," *Science* 277 (1997): 918–924.
50. Sampson, Raudenbush, and Earls, op. cit., p. 918.
51. Matsueda, op. cit., fn. 13.
52. Ibid.
53. Herbert Blumer, "Collective Behavior," in R.E. Park (ed.), *An Outline of The Principles of Sociology* (New York: Barnes and Noble, 1939); William Gamson, *Strategy of Social Protest* (Belmont, CA: Wadsworth Publishers, 1990).
54. Erving Goffman, *Frame Analysis* (New York: Harper & Row, 1974); David Snow and Pamela Oliver, "Social Movements and Collective Behavior: Social Psychological Dimensions and Considerations," in Karen Cook, Gary Fine, and James House, eds., *Sociological Perspectives on Social Psychology* (Boston: Allyn and Bacon, 1995), pp. 571–599.
55. This formulation borrows heavily from Gamson, op cit., p. 155.
56. Albert Cohen, *Delinquent Boys: The Culture of the Gang* (Glencoe, IL: Free Press, 1955); Richard Cloward and Lloyd Ohlin, *Delinquency and Opportunity: A Theory of Juvenile Gangs* (New York: Free Press, 1960).
57. Scheper-Hughes and Bourgois, op. cit., p. 14.
58. Cloward and Ohlin, op. cit.
59. Per-Olof Wikstrom and Robert Sampson, "Social Mechanisms of Community Influences on Crime and Pathways in Criminality," in Benjamin Lahey, Terrie E. Moffitt, and Avshalom Caspi, eds., *The Causes of Conduct Disorder and Juvenile Delinquency* (New York: Guilford Press, 2003).
60. Edwin Sutherland, "Wartime Crime," in Edwin Sutherland and Karl Schuessler, eds., *On Analyzing Crime* (Chicago: University of Chicago Press, 1973), pp. 120–128.

61. Gresham Sykes and David Matza, "Techniques of Neutralization: A Theory of Delinquency," *American Sociological Review* 22 (1957): 664–670.

62. C. Wright Mills, "Situated Actions and Vocabularies of Motive," *American Sociological Review* 5 (1940): 904–913.

63. Matsueda, op. cit., p. 8.

64. Matsueda, op. cit., p. 9.

65. Flint and de Waal, op. cit., p. 9.

66. Emily Wax, "In Sudan: 'A Big Sheik' Roams Free," *Washington Post*, July 18, 2004, p. A1.

67. Ibid., p. A1.

68. Human Rights Watch, "Video Transcript: Exclusive Video Interview with Alleged Janjaweed Leader, March 2, 2005.

69. Power, op cit., p. 58.

70. Cloward and Ohlin, op. cit.

71. Scott Anderson, "How Did Darfur Happen?" *New York Times Magazine*, October 17, 2004, p. 52.

72. Flint and de Waal, p. 98.

73. Scott Anderson, op. cit., p. 55.

74. Flint and Alex de Waal, op. cit., pp. 103–104.

75. Julie Flint, op. cit., p. 5.

76. Office of the Prosecutor, p. 32.

77. Ibid., pp. 37–38.

78. Ibid., p. 53.

79. Ibid., p. 53.

80. Ibid., pp. 53–60.

81. Ibid., pp. 60–61.

82. Ibid., p. 55.

83. Emily Wax, op. cit., p. A1.

84. Jeevan Vasagar, "Militia Chief Scorns Slaughter Charge," *Guardian*, July 16, 2004.

85. Samantha Power, op. cit., p. 9.

86. Flint and de Waal, op. cit., p. 106.

87. Samantha Power, op. cit., p. 8.

88. Human Rights Watch, "Entrenching Impunity: Government Responsibility for International Crimes in Darfur," December 2005, Vol. 17 (17), p. 18.

89. Ibid., p. 17.

90. Ibid., p. 19.

91. Lydia Polgreen, "Over Tea, Sheik Denies Stirring Darfur's Torment," *New York Times*, June 12, 2006, p. A1.

92. Samantha Power, op. cit., p. 18.

## 6. THE ROLLING GENOCIDE

1. CNN.com, "Protesters around the World Plead: Intervene in Darfur," September 17, 2006.
2. Andreas Höfer Petersen and Lise-Lotte Tullin, *The Scorched Earth of Darfur: Patterns in Death and Destruction Reported by the People of Darfur, January 2001–September 2005* (Copenhagen: Bloodhound).
3. International Criminal Court Office of the Prosecutor, Situation in Darfur, The Sudan: Prosecutor's Application under Article 58 (7), February 27, 2007, p. 61
4. Julie Flint and Alex de Waal, *Darfur: A Short History of a Long War* (London: Zed Books, 2005), p. 116.
5. Amnesty International, "Sudan: Too Many People Killed for No Reason," February 3, 2004, p. 14.
6. Julie Flint, Testimony at United States Senate Committee on Foreign Relations Hearing, "Sudan: Peace, but at What Price?" Washington, DC, June 15, 2004, p. 4.
7. Human Rights Watch, "Darfur Bleeds: Recent Cross-Border Violence in Chad," Number 2, February 2006, p. 12.
8. Ibid., see fn. 17, citing IRIN, "Sudan: Thousands Said Fleeing Renewed Fighting in Darfur," January 4, 2003.
9. Human Rights Watch, "Darfur Destroyed: Ethnic Cleansing by Government and Militia Forces in Western Sudan," Vol. 16 (6): May 2004, pp. 43–45.
10. Human Rights Watch, "Darfur Bleeds," op cit., p. 7 at fn. 19.
11. International Criminal Court Office of the Prosecutor, pp. 32–33.
12. Ibid., pp. 54, 56.
13. Ibid., p. 57.
14. Ibid., p. 59.
15. Ibid., pp. 73–74.
16. Ibid., p. 76.
17. Ibid., p. 80.
18. Ibid., p. 81.
19. Human Rights Watch, "Darfur Bleeds," op. cit., p. 11.
20. Physicians for Human Rights, "Darfur: Assault on Survival," (Cambridge, MA: PHR, February 2006), p. 24.
21. Alex de Waal, "Who Are the Darfurians? Arab and African Identities, Violence and External Engagement," *African Affairs* 104 (415) (2005): 181–205.
22. Physicians for Human Rights, op. cit., pp. 23–24.
23. Ibid., p. 24.
24. Human Rights Watch, "Targeting the Fur: Mass Killings in Darfur," January 24, 2005, p. 6.

25. International Criminal Court, Office of the Prosecutor, Situation in Darfur, op. cit.
26. Physicians for Human Rights, op. cit., p. 24.
27. International Criminal Court, Office of the Prosecutor, op. cit., p. 73.
28. Physicians for Human Rights, op. cit., p. 25.
29. International Criminal Court, Office of the Prosecutor, op. cit., p. 74.
30. Joseph Winter, "Probe of Darfur 'Slavery' Starts," BBC News, March 21, 2007.

## 7. The Racial Spark

1. John Hagan, *Justice in the Balkans: Prosecuting War Crimes in The Hague Tribunal* (Chicago: University of Chicago Press, 2003).
2. UN High Commission on Human Rights, "Report of the High-Level Mission on the Situation of Human Rights in Darfur Pursuant to Human Rights Council Decision S-4/101," Advance Unedited Version, March 7, 2007, p. 2.
3. Jens Meierhenrich, "A Question of Guilt," *Ratio Juris* 19 (2006): 3141–42.
4. Anne Richardson, "Interview – Sudan Must Be Told to Stop Darfur Crimes – Arbour," Reuters, March 13, 2007.
5. Atta El-Battahani, "Towards a Typology and Periodization Schema of Conflicts in the Darfur Region of Sudan," in Abdel Ghaffar Ahmed and Leif Manger, eds., *Understanding the Crisis in Darfur: Listening to Sudanese Voices* (Bergen, Norway: Centre for Development Studies, 2006), p. 35.
6. Sharif Harir, "'Arab Belt' versus 'African Belt': Ethno-Political Conflict in Darfur and the Regional Cultural Factors," in Sharif Harir and Terje Tvedt, eds., *Short-Cut to Decay: The Case of Sudan* (Uppsala, Norway: Nordiska Afrikainstitutet, 1994).
7. Posen, Barry. "The Security Dilemma and Ethnic Conflict." *Survival* 35 (1993): 27–47.
8. Kaplan, Robert. *Balkan Ghosts: A Journey Through History.* (New York: St. Martin's Press, 1993).
9. Diamond, Jared. *Collapse: How Societies Choose to Fail or Succeed.* (New York: Penguin, 2005). See also Tubiana, Jerome. "Darfur: A War for Land?" In Alex de Waal, (Ed). *War in Darfur and the Search for Peace.* (Cambridge: Harvard University, 2007).
10. Hardin, Russell. *One For All: The Logic of Group Conflict.* (Princeton: Princeton University Press, 1995). See also Valentino, Benjamin A. *Final Solutions: Mass Killing and Genocide in the 20th Century.* (New York: Cornell University Press, 2004).
11. Kaufman, Stuart. *Modern Hatreds: The Symbolic Politics of Ethnic War.* (Ithaca, New York: Cornell University Press, 2001).

12. Oberschall, Anthony. "The Manipulation of Ethnicity: From Ethnic Coopera-
    tion to Violence and War in Yugoslavia." *Ethnic and Racial Studies* 23 (2000):
    982–1001. See also Benford, Robert and David Snow. "Framing Processes and
    Social Movements: An Overview and Assessment." *Annual Review of Sociology*
    26 (2000): 611–639.
13. James Coleman, "Social Theory, Social Research, and a Theory of Action,"
    *American Journal of Sociology* 91: 6 (1986): 1301–35.
14. Robert Sampson, "How Does Community Context Matter? Social Mechanisms
    and the Explanation of Crime Rates," in Per-Olof H. Wikstrom and Robert
    Sampson, eds., *The Explanation of Crime: Context, Mechanisms, and Develop-
    ment* (London: Cambridge University Press, 2006), pp. 311–360.
15. James Coleman, op. cit., p. 1321.
16. See Lawrence Cohen and Marcus Felson, "Social Change and Crime Rate
    Trends: A Routine Activity Approach," *American Sociological Review* 44: 4
    (1979): 588–608; D.W. Osgoode et al., "Routine Activities and Individual Delin-
    quent Behavior," *American Sociological Review* 61: 4 (1996): 635–655.
17. Carl Schmitt, *The Concept of the Political* (Chicago: University of Chicago Press,
    1996), p. 28.
18. Daniel Chirot and Clark McCauley, *Why Not Kill Them All? The Logic and Pre-
    vention of Mass Political Murder* (Princeton: Princeton University Press, 2006),
    p. 39.
19. Jack Katz, *The Seductions of Crime* (New York: Basic Books, 1988), pp. 361–370.
20. Roger Brubaker and David Laitin, "Ethnic and Nationalist Violence," *Annual
    Review of Sociology* 24 (1998): 427.
21. Ted Robert Gurr and Barbara Harff, *Ethnic Conflict in World Politics* (Boulder,
    CO: Westview Press, 2004).
22. Brubaker and Laitin, op. cit., p. 427.
23. Alexander Hinton, *Annihilating Difference: The Anthropology of Genocide*
    (Berkeley, CA: University of California Press, 2002), p. 36.
24. Herbert Blumer, "Race Prejudice as a Sense of Group Position," *Pacific Socio-
    logical Review* 1 (1958): 31–37.
25. Anthony Oberschall, "The Manipulation of Ethnicity: From Ethnic Coopera-
    tion to Violence and War in Yugoslavia," *Ethnic and Racial Studies* 23 (2000):
    982–1001.
26. William Gamson, "Hiroshima, the Holocaust, and the Politics of Exclusion,"
    *American Sociological Review* 60 (1995): 11–20.
27. Oberschall, pp. 997–998.
28. Gerard Prunier, op. cit., p. 165.
29. Jonathan Howard, "Survey Methodology and the Darfur Genocide," in Samuel
    Totten and Eric Markusen, eds., *Genocide in Darfur: Investigating the Atrocities
    in Sudan* (New York: Routledge, 2006), p. 67.

30. Evelyn Depoortere et al., "Violence and Mortality in West Darfur, Sudan (20031–04): Epidemiological Evidence from Four Surveys," *The Lancet* 364 (2004): 1315–20.

31. This daily field coding allowed follow-up clarification with respondents about ambiguities. During the data entry process in the United States, analysts reviewed the interviews and independently assigned codes as a cross-check for accuracy and to ensure no codes were missed. A third check was performed by coders from an international public opinion research organization who created the final data set. At each of the three stages, one-fifth of the surveys were randomly selected and recoded by an additional analyst/coder to assess accuracy. Each survey was double-punched to verify correct data entry, with computer cross-checks for consistency.

32. Compare with Depoortere et al., op. cit., p. 1315.

33. To take into account the fact that half of the individuals were not asked this question and thus were coded zero, we included a variable in our analysis that was dichotomized to reflect missing data.

34. When we assigned a mean score to each of the settlements based on the proportion of respondents who reported rebel presence and correlated this with a binary variable reflecting media reports of rebel activity in the settlement area, the bivariate correlation was 0.4.

35. We multiplied this measure of settlement density per square kilometer by 10 to make its metric consistent with other measures in the analysis.

36. Lawrence Cohen and Marcus Felson, op. cit. and D. Osgoode et al., op. cit.

37. Jared Diamond, *Collapse: How Societies Choose to Fail or Succeed* (New York: Penguin, 2005).

38. Ibid., p. 313.

39. Ibid., p. 327.

40. Ibid., p. 326.

41. Julie Flint and Alex de Waal, op. cit., pp. 1011–106.

42. See especially Physicians for Human Rights, *Darfur: Assault on Survival* (Cambridge: PHR, 2006).

43. In addition to this discussion, see Samantha Power, *"A Problem from Hell": America and the Age of Genocide* (New York: Basic Books, 2002).

44. Cyrena Respini-Irwin, "Geointelligence Informs Darfur Policy," *Geointelligence*, September 1, 2005.

45. See Michael Hindelang, "Race and Involvement in Common Law Personal Crimes," *American Sociological Review* 43 (1978): 93–109.

46. To illustrate the coding of incidents for the severity scale, we present the example of a 35-year-old Masalit woman with a score of 52. This attack occurred in a village near Masteri. Sudanese government troops and Arab Janjaweed militia attacked her village on December 1, 2003. Her report included twenty incidents

during the attack that occurred that day. Her report includes herself, her family, and others in the village. During the attack, she was beaten (3) and raped (4). Her father was severely beaten (3) trying to protect her, and he was subsequently abducted (4). Some women from her village were abducted (4), and no one from the village has heard from them again. Other women were abducted (4) and held for two hours. They were beaten (3) and raped (4) before being released. Another group of women (ages ranging from 16 to 20) were raped (4), and she personally witnessed one of the rapes and heard about the rapes from other victims. Additional villagers, including her brother, were beaten (3), shot (3), and stabbed (3). She witnessed dead bodies (5), all male, some of whom had their throats cut, and others were shot in the head. Her village was completely destroyed (2), except for three huts that were on the far edge of the village. Theft (2) included livestock, food, and water pots. She claims that there was no rebel activity in or around her village. The only weapons the villagers had were a few spears, which were no match for the attackers' guns, knives, aircraft, and pickups with mounted guns. She entered Chad in February 2004, becoming one of the two to three million Darfurians displaced (1) from the genocide.

47. See Stephen Raudenbush and Anthony Bryk, *Hierarchical Linear Models: Applications and Data Analysis Methods* (Thousand Oaks, CA: Sage, 2002), especially Chapter 4.
48. Travis Hirschi and Michael Gottfredson, "Age and the Explanation of Crime," *American Journal of Sociology* 89: 3 (1983): 552–584.
49. A partial exception is the *Report of the United Nations High Commissioner for Human Rights, Access to Justice for Victims of Sexual Violence*, July 29, 2005, Geneva. However, this empirical analysis is based on the tracking of cases from Darfur in the Sudanese justice system done to assess selectivity and bias in treatment, rather than an analysis of sexual violence itself.
50. An important nonquantitative analysis of sexual violence in Darfur is provided by Amnesty International, "Sudan, Darfur: Rape as a Weapon of War: Sexual Violence and its Consequences" (London, AFR 54/076/04, 2004).
51. See the Report of the International Commission of Inquiry on Darfur to the United Nations Secretary-General, January 25, 2005, Geneva, pp. 941–96.
52. Ibid., p. 87.
53. Scott Straus, *The Order of Genocide: Race, Power, and War in Rwanda* (Ithaca, NY: Cornell University Press, 2006), p. 52.
54. Michael Peel, ed., *Rape as a Method of Torture: Medical Foundation for the Care of Victims of Torture* (London: MFCVT, 2004).
55. United Nations Judgment Report, *The Prosecutor v. Jean-Paul Akayesu*, Case No. ICTR-961-4-T, International Criminal Tribunal for Rwanda, Office of the Prosecutor at 7.8., 1998.

56. Ethnic cleansing refers to the use of force or intimidation, notably including sexual violence, to render an area ethnically homogeneous by removing persons of nonmajority groups. The term "ethnic cleansing" was extensively used in conjunction with descriptions of sexual violence and to describe the conflict in the former Yugoslavia. See Cherif Bassiouni, "Final Report of the United Nations Commission of Experts Established Pursuant to Security Council Resolution 780," May 27, 1994 and Kelly Askin, "Analysis: Foca's Monumental Jurisprudence," *Tribunal Update* 226, 181–23, June 2001.

57. Mark Osiel, "The Banality of Good: Aligning Incentives against Mass Atrocity," *Columbia Law Review* 105 (2005): 1751–1862.

58. UN Commission of Inquiry, op. cit., p. 82.

59. Nancy Scheper-Hughes and Philippe Bourgois, *Violence in War and Peace: An Anthology* (London: Basil Blackwell, 2004), p. 14.

60. Seventh Annual Report of the Prosecutor of the International Criminal Court to the UN Security Council Pursuant to UNSCR 1593 (2005) at 77, International Criminal Court, Office of the Prosecutor, June 5, 2008.

61. The Associated Press, "U.S. Criticizes Sudan's President for Denying Rape in Darfur," *International Herald Tribune*, March 20, 2007.

62. Prunier, *The Ambiguous Genocide*, op. cit.; UN Commission of Inquiry on Darfur, op cit.

63. Nicholas Kristof, "A Policy of Rape," *New York Times*, June 5, 2005, p. A14.

64. Emily Wax, "Sudanese Rape Victims Find Justice Blind to Plight," *Washington Post*, November 8, 2004, p. A1.

65. Reuters Alertnet, "Sudan Arrests Annan's Darfur Translator," May 31, 2005.

66. Rod Nordland, Africa: War on the Rescuers, *Newsweek World News*, January 29, 2007.

67. Jens Meierhenrich, "Conspiracy in International Law," *Annual Review of Law and Social Science* 2 (2006): 341–57.

68. John Hagan, op. cit.

69. Mark J. Osiel, op. cit.

70. The interview can be heard at http://news.bbc.co.uk/nolavconsole/ukfs_news/ and read at http://news.bbc.co.uk/2/hi/africa/6060856.stm.

71. Boutros Boutros-Ghali, "Frontline" interview, posted online April 1, 2004; www.pbs.org/wgbh/pages/frontline/shows/ghosts/themes/lessons.html

72. Translated into the realm of genocide, the ICTY judgment in the trial of Goran Jelisic, a self-proclaimed "Serb Adolf" in the former Yugoslavia, concluded that (the Trial Chamber must verify whether the accused had the "'special' intention which, beyond the discrimination of the crimes he commits, characterizes his intent to destroy the discriminated group as such, at least in part."

73. Edwin Sutherland, *White Collar Crime* (New York: Holt, Rinehart and Winston, 1949).

## 8. GLOBAL SHADOWS

1. For other accounts, see Deborah Scroggins, *Emma's War: A True Story* (New York: Vintage Books, 2004) and Don Cheadle and John Prendergast, *Not on Our Watch: The Mission to End Genocide in Darfur and Beyond* (New York: Hyperion, 2007), pp. 115–117.
2. Abheer Allam and Michael Slackman, "23 Sudanese Die in Raid in Egypt," *New York Times*, December 31, 2005, p. 1.
3. John Braithwaite, *Crime, Shame and Reintegration* (Cambridge: Cambridge University Press, 1989).
4. Alfred Blumstein and Jacqueline Cohen, "Characterizing Criminal Careers," *Science* 237 (1987): 985–91; Alfred Blumstein, "Making Rationality Relevant," *Criminology* 31 (1993): 1–16.
5. Friedrich Lösel, "The Efficacy of Correctional Treatment: A Review and Synthesis of Meta-Evaluations," in J. McGuire, ed., *What Works: Reducing Reoffending* (Chichester: John Wiley & Sons, 1995).
6. Terrie Moffitt, "Adolescence-Limited and Life Course Persistent Anti-Social Behavior: A Developmental Taxonomy," *Psychological Review* 100:4 (1993): 674–701.
7. Robert Merton, "Social Structure and Anomie," *American Sociological Review* 3 (1938): 672–82.
8. David Garland, *The Culture of Control* (Chicago: University of Chicago Press, 2001).
9. John Hagan and Bill McCarthy, *Mean Streets: Youth Crime and Homelessness* (New York: Cambridge University Press, 1997).
10. John Hagan, "The Social Embeddedness of Crime and Unemployment." *Criminology* 31 (1993): 465–91.
11. Suzanne Fitzpatrick, *Young Homeless People* (New York: St. Martins, 2000).
12. Joel Handler, *Losing Generations: Adolescents in High-Risk Settings. National Research Council, Panel on High-Risk Youth.* (with Gordon Berlin et al.) (Washington, DC: National Academy Press, 1993). See also Human Security Centre, *Human Security Brief 2006* (Vancouver, BC: Liu Institute for Global Issues, University of British Columbia), Chapter 2.
13. See also, "Homeless Youth and the Perilous Passage to Adulthood," in D. Wayne Osgoode, E. Michael Foster, Constance Flanagan, and Gretchen R. Ruth, eds., *On Your Own without A Net: The Transition to Adulthood for Vulnerable Populations* (Chicago: University of Chicago Press, 2005).

14. Bob Herbert, "Arrested while Grieving," *New York Times*, May 26, 2007, p. A13.

15. Alfred Blumstein, "The Crime Drop in America: An Exploration of Some Recent Crime Trends," *Journal of Scandinavian Studies in Criminology and Crime Prevention* 7: 2 (2006): 17–35.

16. Laurence Sherman, "Defiance, Deterrence, and Irrelevance: A Theory of the Criminal Sanction," *Journal of Research in Crime and Delinquency* 30 (1993): 445–73.

17. Hassan E. El Talib, "Definition and Historical Background of the Janjaweed," Sudan Embassy in South Africa, August 21, 2004.

18. Ibid.

19. Ali Ali-Dinar, "Darfur: The Next Afghanistan?" Darfur Information, European-Sudanese Public Affairs Council.

20. Jeffrey Gettleman, "The Perfect Weapon for the Meanest Wars," *New York Times*, April 29, 2007, p. 41.

21. Edwin Lemert, *Social Pathology* (New York: McGraw-Hill, 1951), p. 76.

22. Julie Flint and Alex de Waal, *Darfur: A Short History of a Long War* (London: Zed Books, 2005).

23. This paragraph synopsis is based on Andreas Petersen and Lise-Lotte Tullin, *The Scorched Earth of Darfur: Patterns in Death and Destruction Reported by the People of Darfur, January 2001–September 2005* (Copenhagen: Bloodhound, 2006).

24. Ibid., p. 12.

25. Human Rights Watch, "'If We Return, We Will Be Killed': Consolidation of Ethnic Cleansing in Darfur, Sudan," *HRW Report*, November 2004.

26. Human Rights Watch, "Targeting the Fur: Mass Killings in Darfur," A Human Rights Watch Briefing Paper, January 21, 2005, p. 11.

27. Waging Peace, "Trafficking and Forced Recruitment of Child Soldiers on the Chad/Sudan Boarder," Waging Peace, London, 6 June, 2008.

28. Gunnar Heinshon, *Sohne and Weltmacht* [*Sons and World Power*] (Zurich: Orell and Fussli, 2003), pp. 59–71.

29. Paul Collier, *The Bottom Billion: Why the Poorest Countries Are Failing and What Can Be Done about It* (New York: Oxford University Press, 2007), p. 20.

30. International Criminal Court, Office of the Prosecutor, op. cit., p. 76.

31. Ibid., p. 78.

32. Human Rights Watch, "Targeting the Fur: Mass Killings in Darfur," op. cit., p. 9.

33. Ibid., p. 11.

34. INTERSOS, "Return-Oriented Profiling in the Southern Part of West Darfur and Corresponding Chadian Border Area," United Nations High Commissioner for Refugees, July 2005.

35. Alfred de Montesquiou, "Darfur Graves Unearth Evidence of Atrocities," *Moscow Times*, May 28, 2007, Issue 3665.

36. Edmund Sanders, "Resettlement or Land Grab?: 'Arabization' Scheme Is Feared in Darfur as Chadians Move In," *Los Angeles Times*, August 12, 2007, p. A.1.

37. De Montesquiou, op. cit., pp. 11–22.

38. Seventh Annual Report of the Prosecutor of the International Criminal Court to the UN Security Council Pursuant to UNSCR 1593 (2005) at 86, International Criminal Court, Office of the Prosecutor, June 5, 2008.

## APPENDIX: GENOCIDAL STATISTICS

1. Stephen Raudenbush and Anthony Bryk, *Hierarchical Linear Models: Applications and Data Analysis Methods* (Thousand Oaks, CA: Sage, 2002).

2. Daniel Clinton and Jennifer Edwards, "Make Sense of the Senseless," *Context* 2 (2003):12–19.

# Index

*Continued from page iii*